Taking It Big

*Developing Sociological Consciousness
in Postmodern Times*

TITLES OF RELATED INTEREST FROM PINE FORGE PRESS

This Book Is Not Required, Revised Edition, by Inge Bell and Bernard McGrane

Sociology for a New Century, by York Bradshaw, Joseph Healey, and Rebecca Smith

Illuminating Social Life: Classical and Contemporary Theory Revisited, Second Edition, edited by Peter Kivisto

Key Ideas in Sociology, by Peter Kivisto

Multiculturalism in the United States: Current Issues, Contemporary Voices, by Peter Kivisto and Georganne Rundblad

The Riddles of Human Society, by Donald Kraybill and Conrad Kanagy

Sociology Through Active Learning: Student Exercises for Exploring the Discipline, by Kathleen McKinney, Frank D. Beck, Barbara S. Heyl

Sociology: Exploring the Architecture of Everyday Life, Third Edition, by David Newman

Sociology: Exploring the Architecture of Everyday Life, (Readings), Third Edition, by David Newman

Social Prisms: Reflections on Everyday Myths and Paradoxes, by Jodi O'Brien

The Social Worlds of Higher Education: Handbook for Teaching in a New Century, edited by Bernice Pescosolido and Ronald Aminzade

Enchanting a Disenchanted World: Revolutionizing the Means of Consumption, by George Ritzer

The McDonaldization of Society, New Century Edition, by George Ritzer

Making Societies: The Historical Construction of Our World, by William A. Roy

Second Thoughts: Seeing Conventional Wisdom Through the Sociological Eye, Second Edition, by Janet M. Ruane and Karen A. Cerulo

The Production of Reality: Essays and Readings on Social Interaction, Third Edition, by Jodi O'Brien and Peter Kollock

Sociology in Action: Cases for Critical and Sociological Thinking, by David Hachen

Taking It Big

Developing Sociological Consciousness
in Postmodern Times

STEVEN P. DANDANEAU

PINE FORGE PRESS
Thousand Oaks, California
London ◆ *New Delhi*

Copyright © 2001 by Pine Forge Press

All rights reserved. No part of this book may be reproduced or utilized in any form or by any means, electronic or mechanical, including photocopying, recording, or by any information storage and retrieval system, without permission in writing from the publisher.

For information:

 Pine Forge Press
2455 Teller Road
Thousand Oaks, California 91320
E-mail: order@sagepub.com

Sage Publications Ltd.
6 Bonhill Street
London EC2A 4PU
United Kingdom

Sage Publications India Pvt. Ltd.
M-32 Market
Greater Kailash I
New Delhi 110 048 India

Printed in the United States of America

Library of Congress Cataloging-in-Publication Data

Dandaneau, Steven P.
    Taking it big: Developing sociological consciousness in postmodern
times / Steven P. Dandaneau.
        p.   cm.
    Includes indexes.
    ISBN 0-7619-8703-7
    1. Sociology. 2. Social sciences. 3. Critical thinking. 4. Critical
theory. 5. Postmodernism—Social aspects. I. Title.
HM585 .D36 2000
301—dc21   00-010928

01   02   03   10   9   8   7   6   5   4   3   2   1

Publisher:	Stephen D. Rutter
Assistant to the Publisher:	Ann Makarias
Production Editor:	Diana E. Axelsen
Editorial Assistant:	Candice Crosetti
Typesetter/Designer:	Marion Warren
Indexer:	Jeanne Busemeyer
Cover Designer:	Ravi Balasuriya

About the Author

Steven P. Dandaneau is Associate Professor of Sociology and Director of the Honors and Scholars Programs at the University of Dayton. He received his B.A. in economics from Michigan State University (1986) and his M.A. (1990) and Ph.D. (1992) in sociology from Brandeis University. His two previous books are *A Town Abandoned: Flint, Michigan, Confronts Deindustrialization* (1996) and *A Wrong Life: Studies in Lifeworld-Grounded Critical Theory* (1998), of which he is coauthor with Maude Falcone. He is also a contributor to Peter Kivisto's Pine Forge Press volume, *Illuminating Social Life: Classical and Contemporary Theory Revisited* (revised and expanded edition, 2000).

About the Publisher

Pine Forge Press is an educational publisher dedicated to publishing innovative books and software throughout the social sciences. On this and any other of our publications, we welcome your comments and suggestions.

Please call or write us at:

Pine Forge Press
A Sage Publications Company
31 St. James Ave., Suite 510
Boston, MA 02116
617-753-7512
e-mail: info@pfp.sagepub.com

Visit our World Wide Web site, your direct link to a multitude of online resources:

www.pineforge.com

In memory of my colleague,
Dr. Stanley L. Saxton, Jr. (1939-1999)

Contents

Preface

This book is intended as an accessible, current, and uncompromised introduction to what C. Wright Mills called the "sociological imagination." It explains and demonstrates the value of the sociological imagination vis-à-vis the demands of today's postmodern society, critically addresses the chief forces working against its development, and invites students to adopt this form of self-consciousness as their own.

Sociological thinking and, in turn, sociological learning, cannot get off the ground until the minds of students are freed from the myriad constraints that thwart the workings of a live, empirically exact imagination. The chief initial problem for the teacher and student of sociology is finding the means to accomplish this liberation. With this challenge in mind, I have composed *Taking It Big* in an unusual way, as a series of interrelated essays intended to encourage beginning students of sociology to think through a wide variety of topics from ecological crises to panic disorder, from hyperreality to the sociology of disability, and from Generation X to Generation Next. My hope is that this style of presentation will be true to the elusive nature of postmodern experience and will transform the reader's consciousness of this experience. This book is not Mills-in-a-box, a replication of Mills's mid-century distillation of the form of mind underlying the classic tradition in sociology. It is alive to today's social problems, the issues and troubles that afflict the postmodern world that Mills glimpsed only at its inception.

Any book that sets for itself the goal of presenting and encouraging the adoption of a form of self-consciousness that grasps the interrelations between history, biography, and society, the never-ending interplay between levels of reality, and seeks to define the primary political challenges facing today's young adults sets for itself a difficult task. But such a book is needed for a number of reasons.

First and foremost, people in this world and at this time need to develop a quality of mind that allows them to conceptualize the mind- and soul-boggling crises that confront humanity worldwide. There is no value in sugarcoating the fact that modern social development has left strewn in its wake a series of unprecedented human catastrophes and that the mindless extrapolation of modern society portends only greater catastrophes. Postmodernity is, as Zygmunt Bauman has defined it, "modernity without illusions." Students today, I believe, must be presented a candid appraisal of our situation, an unflinching assessment of empirical realities.

Of equal and related significance is the politically strategic importance of the present generation. Fundamental social change is a certainty in the near future. How will so-called First World societies act toward the demands for change associated with global ecological problems such as global warming? How will Americans use their economic, political, military, and cultural power to affect the tragic human experiences that result from increasing global inequality? Will Americans come to see their current way of life as unsustainable? These are the types of practical questions that confront members of postmodern society. We can expect the current generation of educated young adults in societies such as the United States to play a crucial role in answering them one way or another. It is vital that members of these mass democracies have the ability to bring such issues into focus and meaningfully relate them one to the other and to what Mills called our "cherished values." There is no other way, I think, to sustain hope for a viable democratic future than through efforts to make actual the everyday realization of the sociological imagination.

We must also appreciate the situation faced by individuals fated to live in postmodern culture. Postmodern culture is a disillusioning way of life awash in antidepressants and submerged in a sea of television reality. Properly developed, the sociological imagination not only addresses the phenomenon of globalization but it also offers a defense against postmodern cultural excess. Indeed, it is a means for confronting the violence and harm inflicted by disillusionment itself. Such far-flung ambitions have always stood back of the promise of sociology.

Taking It Big is a book that invites the reader to adopt a new form of self-consciousness appropriate to the challenges of today's globalized world and disillusioning everyday life. The reader is asked to critically engage topics chosen to highlight the postmodern extremes of imaginative sociological thinking and to take issue with any and every substantive argument presented. I do not, in other words, mean in this book to flatly present *the* truth of all things, nor do I mean to convey the sense that sociology has all the answers to the problems that confront human society and individual lives. Any effort to develop the ability to think sociologically—to think critically, reflexively, and with empirical moorings—is an open-ended project. This book is thus intended as a catalyst for learning, as an invitation to try on for size what is arguably the most fruitful form of self-consciousness developed in modern times, and then from this perspective, to weigh its value with respect to the troubles and issues of our postmodern lives. The point is not so much to learn *the* truth but to learn how to think about essential issues and troubles as sociologists themselves try to do, to become a participant with others in facing down the challenges of our present epoch.

The book is divided into four parts. The Introduction, Chapter 1, is the only chapter that could be said to stand on its own. It presents the book in microcosm. Part I (Chapters 2 through 4) discusses current global and individual realities as a precursor to a detailed and original explication of the sociological imagination. In particular, I survey the chief global problems such as global warming that beg for urgent remedy and introduce panic and cynicism as the current defining polarities of what Mills called the experience of "trap." I argue that the sociological imagination is the best means available for conceptualizing today's global problems and liberating one's mind from entrapment in postmodern culture.

Part II (Chapters 5 through 7) presents three models of the sociological imagination in practice. Each model emphasizes the extreme forms of history, biography, and social structure under conditions of postmodernity. In particular, I discuss the experience of disability, the hyperreality of Generation X, and the dynamics of postmodern religion. Each topic is treated as a liminal aspect of today's social and cultural world, that is, as edges and undersides of reality well suited to spark critical sociological thinking.

Part III (Chapters 8 through 10) addresses the chief forces working against the widespread adoption of the sociological imagination. I discuss aspects of postmodernity that take direct aim at the very possibility of a sociological conceptualization of history, biography, and social structure. In particular, I attend to the collapse of public life into postmodern forms of propaganda, the much-discussed but dubious thesis of the end of history, and the tendency of sociology itself to suppress its connection with people living everyday lives. This last topic also encourages an understanding of sociology as inherently reflexive and self-critical.

Finally, Part IV formulates the sociological imagination as a form of dialectical thinking dedicated to the practical development of critical social theories. That is, by way of conclusion, I underscore the ultimately political nature of the sociological imagination in part through an account of my own education in sociology.

In private conversation, often with students, Mills would wave his hand in the air and advise, "take it big." By this he meant to encourage expansive critical thinking not for its own sake but because the world—New York City, say, or the advent of nuclear weapons—demanded that we as humans learn to think in ways appropriate to the extraordinary nature of postmodern society, which, like its modern precursor, is a new and revolutionary type of society of our own design and construction and which in some ways is aptly regarded as a grand hotel and in others, alas, a grand hotel abyss. It is my contention that in the forty or so years since Mills originally penned his vision of what makes sociological thinking the most needed form of self-consciousness in the emergent postmodern world, our collective and individual problems have only grown larger, more insidious, and potentially more overwhelming. We must therefore, I believe, continue to pursue the project of taking it big but with renewed energy and with a more sober attitude than even Mills was able to maintain. We must work to develop our sociological imagination for these postmodern times in the hope that soon opportunities will present themselves for its effective use in the making of a human world organized around the values of reason and freedom. Even if the chances for its realization are increasingly distant, there is still a promise of sociology. This is not, in other words, a happy book. Given the state of the world, however, this should come as no surprise.

Acknowledgments

Many of the ideas in this book were first developed jointly with Maude Falcone and published in our coauthored book, *A Wrong Life: Studies in Lifeworld-Grounded Critical Theory* (1998). I thank Maude for allowing me to reproduce parts of her reading of George Orwell's last and most famous novel and especially for allowing me to again discuss our experience with our son Patrick; both these topics are more fully developed in this previous book.

I also benefited from my experience in the 1999 University of Dayton Faculty Seminar in the Humanities and Social Sciences, directed by Fr. James L. Heft, and from my participation in the 1999 National Endowment for Humanities Seminar on Morality and Society, directed by Dr. Alan Wolfe. Both seminars provided stimulating environments in which to think through many of the ideas presented in this book. Both also provided research support, as did a University of Dayton sabbatical for the 1999 fall term.

Many people read all or parts of the manuscript and provided advice and research assistance. In this regard, I gratefully acknowledge Maude Falcone, Steve Rutter, Dan E. Miller, Peter Kivisto of Augustana College, Daniel Chambliss of Hamilton College, and three University of Dayton undergraduates: Brandon Olszewski, Todd Cikraji, and Robin Dodsworth. I also received helpful comments from members of the University of Dayton Sociology, Anthropology, and Social Work Student Organization.

My developmental editor, Kathy Field, deserves special acknowledgment. Kathy's incisive editing and restructuring transformed the manuscript into a much-improved text. She also offered sound advice on the presentation of numerous substantive issues. I thank Kathy most of all, however, for her unfailing support and generosity. If this book is what I intend it to be—an accessible introduction to the sociological imagination—then it is so largely due to Kathy Field's expertise and concern.

I would also like to acknowledge the good folks at Pine Forge Press. Paul O'Connell initially encouraged me to undertake this project and, after overcoming my natural resistance, finagled a free lunch for me with him and Steve Rutter. As has been noted by many Pine Forge authors, Steve Rutter is an unusually involved and insightful editor and an amazingly supportive publisher. Although I probably tried everyone's patience, Ann Makaris kept the wheels turning even when I was uncooperative. I also thank those at Sage—Diana Axelsen and Kelly Gunther—who ironed out the final kinks and who saw the book through the production process, and Jeanne Busemeyer, who prepared the index.

I am also especially grateful to Michael Bérubé for his permission to reprint material from his book *Life As We Know It: A Father, A Family, and an Exceptional Child* (1998/1996) and to Yaroslava Mills for her permission to use unpublished archival material from the C. Wright Mills Papers at the Center for American History, University of Texas at Austin. I thank both Dr. Bérubé and Mrs. Mills for their generosity, the staff at the Center for American History for their able assistance, and John Summers of Rochester University for directing my attention to key documents in the archive.

On the homefront, I thank Cheryl Felton for helping me take care of my children, Patrick and Maxwell, which is no small feat and which was essential to my having the time and energy to waste hours away at the computer. I also thank my brother Marcus Dandaneau for his willingness to visit often and make innumerable domestic improvements.

Finally, this book is dedicated to my dear colleague Dr. Stanley L. Saxton, Jr. Stan was a great teacher and an even greater human being. He would tell his students that they were nothing but a "spot on a gnat's ass" unless they were mindfully engaged with the world and their lives in this world. Stan passed away just as I was beginning work on this book. Although I imagine him vociferously disagreeing with much of what I contend, Stan would also understand my concern for today's world and share my abiding interest in its young people. In his own way—and there are many ways—Stan always took it big.

1

Sociology, or Imaginative Reflections from Empirically Damaged Life

> The splinter in your eye is the best magnifying-glass.
> —*Theodor W. Adorno*[1]

Do fish in the sea know anything about ocean currents or marine biology? Probably not. Fish are not attuned to their environment in the way that humans are attuned to theirs, nor are fish self-aware beings who might say to themselves, "Gee, the water seems to be getting warmer these days." Similarly, fish do not have "bad hair days." True, they have no hair, but more interesting is the fact that the terms *bad, hair,* and *days* do not exist for them in any language. Fish swimming about in the ocean simply do not possess what we call "minds," or at the very least, we humans see no evidence of their possessing minds in the way that we possess minds. Although humans conceive a fabulously diverse and complicated aquatic world in which fish live their lives and which, in part, passes through their very gills, for fish themselves, there is no such conceptualization, no "gills," no thought about "passing through," no such "world."

To modern people, this is all obvious. Indeed, to seriously ponder whether fish know anything about marine biology is ludicrous. We presume, probably correctly, that fish do not theorize about fish nor, for that matter, about anything else. Stated differently, we see no evidence that fish create abstract systematic knowledge about themselves and their world or relate the two.

What is not ludicrous, however, is the proposition that most humans are more like fish than we would like to admit. Humans live in the natural world, of course, but in addition, we live in an equally important second world, a social and cultural world. Even though we swim in this world, even though it pulses through our gills, and even though we humans do possess language and minds, just for the most part and most of the time, we are as ignorant of what is going on around us and through us as fish are with respect to their lived experience in vast bodies of water. Worse, we as individuals are ignorant of that of which we are, collectively at least, the author. We do not generally understand the societies and cultures that we ourselves have created. Worse still, since each and every individual is largely the product of some aspect of the human-created world, we are also ignorant of our particular origins and of how our prospects in life are shaped by the human-created world about us or, rather, we are ignorant of these things if we do not work to develop our minds to conceptualize our human version of ocean currents and marine biology.

What if it were the case that oceans themselves regularly worked in such a way as to prevent individual fish from detecting the presence of oceans? In other words, what if there were something about oceans that prevented fish, even if this were possible, from becoming aware of oceans, perhaps from becoming fully aware of what oceans and fish were all about, or perhaps from developing the ability to act toward oceans with a clear sense of how oceans and fish were interrelated? Societies and cultures do just this with respect to their individual members. They actively resist our efforts to know them and, by extension, to know ourselves in relation to them. To be blunt, just because people very early in life acquire language and learn to live, more or less successfully, in a complicated world of cars, streets, and traffic signals; go to school and read textbooks on history, society, and marine biology; and so on does not mean that they will acquire the ability to make sense of their social and cultural world or themselves in relation to these phenomena. In fact, the scientific study of today's human existence—sociology—suggests exactly the opposite: habitual life in our kind of society and culture is more likely to work against the development of what in this book I am going to call (following the American sociologist, C. Wright Mills) the sociological imagination.

What, after all, are most people in today's highly complex, industrial, technical, urban, mass democracies of the world—the world's postmodern societies and cultures—typically encouraged to develop an awareness of? Who won the Super Bowl or the Academy Award for Best Actress? Where is Brazil in relation to the United States? What does the U.S. Federal Reserve Board do? How does one become popular in one's high school? How does one earn good grades? How does one secure access to beer and other drugs? There is nothing inherently wrong with knowing these and so many similar things, but they are more analogous to a baby fish learning how to swim and school than knowing what truly underlies swimming and schooling in the first place. Just because we live in the ocean does not mean we know anything about it. Although the ocean is deep, we may be stuck swimming in shallow waters.

The sociological imagination is a means to see through what is presented to us as adequate everyday knowledge, to gain a critical distance from this type of knowing via a theoretical, systematic form of knowing. But unlike popular notions about the uselessness of "theory," this type of theoretical knowing is in fact essential to knowing anything worth knowing about our world and ourselves. Everyday knowledge is limited and distorted. What Mills called the "close-up worlds" of everyday life are illusory, their workings clouded in mystification, unless understood in terms of the social and cultural forces that underlie them and bring them into existence in the first place. People cannot think and act freely if they do not possess a critical understanding of the many dimensions of social and cultural experience; they cannot even make adequate sense of their own lives if their self-consciousness does not include such understandings. They need the ability to conceive how their individual lives intersect with the underlying process of social and cultural development so that they can think and act toward these abstract, although no less powerful and constraining, phenomena. This is what the sociological imagination is all about. It is perhaps the only critical means available to swim beyond the shallow waters of beer, grades, and an Oscar.

The United States, to take just one example, is not a natural thing. Its existence is not in any way analogous to that vast body of salt water we call the Pacific Ocean. From the perspective of a person standing on the earth's moon and looking back at this planet, there is, of course, no visible natural boundary that marks off this nation-state from Canada, no naturally occurring line in the earth's crust that sets off this territory with its particular laws and form of government, its economic system, its peculiar way of life, and so forth. Like all nation-states, the United States of America is a human-created phenomenon, dating in fact from what some human-created calendars would call 1776 A.D.

Despite this obvious fact, the people born into this political entity are indoctrinated (well before they can conduct a rational assessment of the situation) to think and feel as though the United States of America was a natural phenomenon, in fact, a sacred phenomenon worthy of pledging one's allegiance to, a thing perhaps even worth dying for. Although Americans are encouraged to view themselves as members of this one particular nation-state and, furthermore, regard this one particular nation-state as God's country and as the best, most free, most democratic, most praiseworthy, and so forth, the United States of America is merely an artificial or

human-made and largely symbolic phenomenon. Yet, typical of such human-created realities, it stands over and against its individual member with an array of forces
that work like a machine to thwart a critical, theoretical understanding of it or any nation-state. One can easily imagine, for example, an American solider lying on the
jungle floor in South Vietnam and wondering to himself how it was he came to be involved in the killing of perfect strangers a world away from home, and how it was
that he came to be dying there as a result.

Sociologists possessed of a sociological imagination see the United States of
America as one historically new and, for the most part, very interesting instance of
the modern nation-state. They know that, like all nation-states, it is made to exist by
humans, and it is meaningful to us only because we continuously make it so. Otherwise, we would be talking about a random area on the surface of one planet in the vast
universe of stars. To be able to critically think about citizenship rights and obligations, nationalism, territorial sovereignty, political indoctrination, war, and so forth
and, perhaps, make sense of a dying soldier's last thoughts, one needs the type of
theoretical mind that can create critical distance between oneself and what is in one's
face day in and day out and placed between our ears before we had much say about
what we learned. In other words, we need an imaginative space in our minds that corresponds in some way to the created social and cultural world that exists "out there."
The only option is to live as an ignorant fish in the "United States of Fish," perhaps
half-aware of the plain facts stated above but not much concerned about one's ocean.

All of this could be discounted as airy abstraction, but one's level of interest
might be piqued if one were suddenly drafted to serve in an organized effort to kill or
otherwise subdue people born into another nation-state. In this event, one's citizenship obligations with respect to the nation-state would perhaps appear worthy of
sustained attention. When seemingly abstract phenomena such as citizenship become part of everyday experience and directly affect us, they are easier to see, and
we are compelled to see them. Indeed, as a general principle, we might suppose that
people tend to think theoretically about their ocean only when it rubs them the wrong
way, when somehow they feel threatened by its workings.

We can suppose that a fish, our friend in the sea, might be alarmed by a fishhook
snagging its eye, and if it could, it would probably want to think systematically and
critically about this new and probably unanticipated feature of its environment.
However, if another fish were hooked a few nautical miles away, our lucky, as yet un-
encumbered, fish would probably swim along oblivious to the fact of this distant
happening. Humans, however, can do two important things differently than the
lucky, if also oblivious, fish. We can identify with other damaged or soon-to-be dead
humans even if we have so far avoided this particular fate ourselves, and we can abstract from any particular incident to generally analyze this damaging hooking phe-

nomenon in and of itself, perhaps to find its systematic causes and therefore antici-pate its threats to ourselves and others. We can bring into our minds the notion of "fishing," a practice, and more significant, the notion of a "fishing industry," an insti-tutionalized set of practices. We can also make sense of the widespread cultural ac-ceptance of the idea that species are ranked on an invisible scale from greater to lesser relative to human beings, which, among other things, leads humans to view fishing as something other than murder and the existence of a fishing industry as something fundamentally different than a fish version of Auschwitz.

As we shall see, it is vital to make indirect human experience part of one's socio-logical imagination. It is also essential to develop the ability to analyze institutions and cultures. But it is also probably true, as Adorno suggested (and blending meta-phors), that the splinters in our own individual eyes make for the best magnifying glass. The development of sociological thinking requires, in other words, a close ex-amination of one's own experience and an identification with one's own rubs against the grain of social and cultural experience. Some people already have hooks (or splinters) in their eyes. Some have large hooks, others small. Some have been merely scathed, and others have only read about this hooking phenomenon in books. Some of those who have been scathed in the past will be hooked in the future. The possibili-ties are many and apply generally. After all, we are all in this ocean together. It is cru-cial that we realize this and use this realization as a basis for thinking theoretically about oceans and fish.

I emphasize that sociological thinking is born of imaginative reflection on "damaged life." The sociological imagination is not primarily an abstract moral or political proposition. Although we must think about what is right and wrong, what is good and bad, and what should be done and how, the development and use of the so-ciological imagination is not to be understood as a process of acquiring a philoso-phical understanding of morality or politics. The reasons for its necessity are instead themselves sociological, that is, rooted in the observable social and cultural world that we have brought into existence, which leaves its marks on human bodies.

Humans as never before are integrated with one another through worldwide so-cial institutions, and we are more interdependent as a result. The process of increas-ing worldwide social interdependence is termed *globalization*. Globalization re-quires that we conceive far-flung interconnections between people that are real, not simply imagined. The clothes on our backs, for example, are probably made by peo-ple a world away, under conditions with which we ourselves have little direct experi-ence, but we are connected to them nonetheless. We also receive information through a worldwide system of mass communication. This shrinks the world and obliterates the space that separates us one from the other. Approximately 1 billion people, for example, view the Super Bowl on television every year. We are interconnected politically as well, through such institutions as the United Nations. The Persian Gulf War and U.S. intervention in Bosnia, for example, both took place under the auspices of the United Nations. Economically, culturally, and politically, we are increasingly members of a worldwide society. This is an empirical fact and a lived reality, not a philosophical speculation.

Given also that the human sciences, including sociology, have been around now for more than a hundred years, we are at least potentially more self-aware about one another's lives than any people before us. We have created systematic knowledge about ourselves that was unavailable to our premodern predecessors. For example, it may be surprising to learn that *The Manifesto of the Communist Party,* authored in 1848 by Karl Marx and Friedrich Engels, includes a detailed sociological analysis of globalization. In particular, Marx and Engels argue that the inherently expansionary nature of capitalism is the primary underlying cause of worldwide European economic, political, and cultural domination. Capitalism, they conclude, "creates a world after its own image."[2] Likewise, in his 2000 State of the Union Address, President Clinton asserted that globalization "is the central reality of our times," although, unlike Marx and Engels, he chose not to cast globalization in terms of capitalist or European domination, nor did he acknowledge that the phenomenon has been "a central reality" for at least 150 years![3] In both instances, however, theoretical knowledge of history and society are used to make sense of the human world. Such knowledge is therefore necessary to anyone wishing to join the implicit discussion between Marx, Engels, and Clinton, regardless of one's moral or political values. This type of knowledge is readily available. One does not have to be a revolutionary scholar or a president to gain access to it.

Finally, the advent of planetary ecological problems means that all people are increasingly and inescapably fated to live and/or die together. Such problems require unified resolution and universal human action. It does not matter to the earth, for example, where carbon emissions originate. If they originate more from the United States and much less so from Bangladesh or vice versa, the worldwide climatic results are the same. Similarly, if the earth's protective ozone layer is depleted, then increased ultraviolet radiation from the sun is a problem for everyone. As with global warming, certain regions are affected more than others, but due to the economic, political, and cultural interconnections that result from globalization, we are all eventually affected by such phenomena. If ozone depletion causes crop yields to decrease in Argentina, the resulting social and political problems of this country will affect life elsewhere. If Brazilians slash and burn *their* rainforest as a means for economic development, the resulting carbon released into the atmosphere, the destruction of oxygen-producing foliage, and the steep reduction in species diversity will affect everyone on the planet, not just the people and other living things for whom and for which this tropical rainforest is home.

Imagining our real, theoretically understandable and often pressing interrelations with one another is thus really more a matter of being a good human scientist than it is of being a good person or having a particular philosophy of life. The splinter in one's eye is therefore a metaphor for the various splinters in everyone's eyes, which in turn says that acquiring a sociological imagination today means developing a sensitivity to the totality of today's real human experience, including especially systematically produced and predictably damaging experience, especially one's own particular brushes with the many hooks in the sea. The key, then, is to eschew life as a patriotic fish, at home in the pond of one's birth, in favor of life as a cosmopolitan and political fish, a knowledgeable citizen of all the ponds and oceans and seas, and a self-aware participant in the making of waves.

What Is This Book About?

This book is not about fish, nor does it rely on silly metaphors. In fact, this book is about a deadly serious topic. In the pages that follow, my aim is to explain what the so-called sociological imagination is, what it entails, what it looks and feels like when used in the analysis of various phenomena, what sort of forces exist in our lives that work against its development, and what type of moral and political dilemmas result from its adoption as one's own self-consciousness. In the end, I invite the reader to adopt this form of mind, this sociological self-consciousness, as his or her own, as I did when I was an undergraduate student. This is a lot to do and a lot to ask.

What, then, is this book about? The short answer is that this book is about the sociological imagination. The American sociologist C. Wright Mills (1916-1962) is the person who first articulated the general idea of a sociological imagination.[4] In his 1959 book *The Sociological Imagination,* Mills argued that the best sociologists, both past and present, seemed to possess a special way of thinking that allowed them to grasp the interrelationships between individual lives and societies and how these relationships change in the overall process of history making. These people, among them Karl Marx (1818-1883), Emile Durkheim (1858-1917), Max Weber (1864-1920), and George Herbert Mead (1886-1931), were no oblivious fish in the sea. Through a survey of these thinkers and the dozens more who stood in what he called "the classic tradition" of sociology, Mills distilled the essential forms of thought that sociologists have used to produce various ideas, and sets of ideas, about modern society and culture. Mills dubbed this "the sociological imagination."

I stress that the sociological imagination means to be conversant with forms of thought; it does not mean to have all the answers. Mills never argued that people such as Marx, Durkheim, Weber, and Mead provided all or even necessarily any of the answers for today's problems. We do not study them so that we can simply adopt what they said as the truth. We are more interested in the conceptual tools they used to say anything at all. Developing a sociological imagination allows one to pose the right type of questions. This book, then, is less about answers and more about developing a type of mind necessary for the conceptualization of crucially important questions.

Furthermore, Mills believed that this type of thinking would become, as he wrote, the "common denominator" of the "post-modern period."[5] In other words, Mills thought that his way of thinking about society would become popular and used by most people, not just by sociologists. Mills thought this would happen not because he thought himself an incredibly compelling writer but because understanding our problems requires a sociological form of mind that can imaginatively and precisely envision the many complicated connections between self and society in an ongoing history in the making. What is compelling are our problems. Mills argued that we needed a sociological imagination not only to make sense of our problems but also to be able to act toward these problems in an effective, transforming manner. In the end, the point of having a sociological imagination is to be able to pose the right questions about the world and then act intelligently toward these problematic aspects of the world. Questions lead to actions. The point is to become politically self-conscious and engaged. This book is, therefore, ultimately about politics.

Admittedly, to say that Mills believed that the sociological imagination would become the common form of mind in our time shades the truth. It is more accurate to say that Mills worked very hard to convince others, including his readers, that the sociological imagination *needed* to become the common denominator, *should* become the way that most people saw themselves and their social and cultural world. But he knew that many social and cultural forces stood in the way of this much-needed radicalization of popular consciousness. This book is also about these forces as we experience them today, and it is written, not in an apparently value-neutral way, but in the form of essays. Essays argue specific points and are openly rooted in specific values and interests. For my own part, and following Mills, I do my best to argue in accordance with the values of reason and freedom and in the interest of humanity's survival as a democratically organized and peaceful species. This book is about crucial questions, political decisions, and, also, about culture, how we shall live and what type of people we shall become. Therefore, this book is informed by utopian aspirations.

There are no doubt many more ways to describe what this book is about since the sociological imagination draws into its net nearly everything imaginable in the sea. The book is about learning to think critically by learning how to pose crucial questions, by learning the political significance of these questions, and by learning how this all ties together with utopian values and interests. A more straightforward way to introduce what this book is about is to simply list various topics broached in the chapters that follow. At various levels of abstraction, these topics include the following: abortion propaganda, disabled children, fundamentalist religion, the assassination of President Kennedy, species extinction, the poorly understood significance of Dr. Martin Luther King, Jr., baby boomers, *Time* magazine, George Orwell, television, and Germantown Avenue in Philadelphia. In other words, this book will deal with just about everything but the kitchen sink. This apparent hodgepodge of topics reflects another vital characteristic of the sociological imagination: its skillful use requires that we conceive the relationships between all things that are in fact meaningfully, if not always obviously or straightforwardly, related.

Is This Book Depressing?

In addition to the assumption that the sociological imagination is the most needed form of critical self-consciousness in the world today, a second and equally important assumption that informs this book is that time is quickly running out for the popular adoption of sociological thinking. There are at least two reasons for this assumption. First, the nature of our problems has changed since Mills's day. As I aim to demonstrate (in Chapters 2 and 3, especially), our problems are worse than those that confronted Mills. Since Mills dealt with the facts of the Cold War, in which two nation-states threatened one another with nuclear weapons, this is saying something. Even if somehow the sociological imagination quickly became the common denominator of our public and personal lives, we would still continue to suffer the harsh consequences of our past collective ignorance of modern society and today's postmodern society well into the current century. The problems that we face today, such as global warming, have already been allowed to develop in ways that do not permit quick, easy, or painless fixes. While we could potentially destroy all existing nuclear weapons, we probably could not destroy the knowledge needed to reconstruct them. While we could greatly reduce the emission of so-called greenhouse gases, we could not control the natural world sufficiently to alter the effects of those gases already emitted into the atmosphere. Our problems today are simply too entrenched, too fundamental, too unprecedented, and too menacing for too many human lives to warrant optimism about their speedy, permanent, much less morally rectifying resolution.

Second, the sociological imagination is difficult to develop. The idea of a sociological imagination has been around for some time now, but we are no closer today to the realization of what Mills called "the promise" of sociology—that sociological thinking would become everyday thinking—than when Mills first proposed this promise some forty years ago.[6] If not before, then why now should sociological thinking suddenly take hold? Even sociologists themselves are divided about the value of a sociological imagination. Indeed, most sociologists, especially American sociologists, are skeptical of its value, so much so that few bother to study it in detail. (The reasons for this will be explored throughout this book, especially in Chapter 10.) Sociologists swim in the same waters as everyone else and are subject to the same forces that work against the development of a sociological imagination as those not possessing a doctorate in sociology. This seems to be the greatest barrier to its development: the very workings of today's society and culture militate against the widespread adoption of sociological self-consciousness.

Use the book in your hands as an example. It is a textbook. In all likelihood, you are reading it only because it was assigned to you to read as part of a course you are taking in sociology. In all likelihood, you are taking this course in sociology, perhaps because you are required to, as part of your larger project of earning a postsecondary educational degree. In all likelihood, you have chosen to spend a great deal of money and time and, what is more, forgo all the money you could be making if, instead of being a college student, you were working full-time because you believe (and for the most part rightly so) that obtaining such a credential will substantially enhance your future earning potential and assist you in securing a meaningful form of work from which you will be able to live contentedly in a style and manner that meets your expectations of what a good life should be.

All of this is determined by the institutional and cultural nature of the United States, where education is typically treated as a means not for education but for upward social mobility. In this sense, you are engaged in a type of capitalist activity, in this case, adding to your own "human capital." Indicators of the value of your capital, say, grades and letters of reference from your professors, are therefore much sought after, in part also because they are distributed in a competitive manner. Furthermore, your views on the value of education and what makes for a good life are not, strictly speaking, your own. You have adopted these from your culture. Therefore, you are probably not ashamed but, rather, proud to be a college student, nor do you loath the idea of competition for grades and good jobs or the idea that one should aspire to earn as much money and live as lavishly as possible. Native Americans might look at these values and norms of behavior differently, but most people in the United States accept them as unquestioned givens and, regardless, ratify them through their daily participation in education as a means for climbing the social ladder. Given this type of institutionalized social and cultural situation, how can a mere textbook that asks its reader to radicalize their consciousness make much headway?

It would seem more likely that such a book would complicate rather than facilitate one's education.

As I will argue and demonstrate, the sociological imagination is a thoroughly radical form of mind, radical in the sense that it aims to get at the roots of all things human as well as radical in the sense that it points the way toward fundamental or radical social change. Not surprisingly, people do not readily radicalize their self-consciousness. Mind-sets are typically just that: set. As a radical form of mind, the sociological imagination causes considerable friction with today's social and cultural reality. For most of us, our daily routines and experiences leave little time for radical reflection and self-transformation. Between work and sleep, there is little free time available, and most of the types of reflection and emotionally charged personal activities that we are typically offered—prayer, mediation, television, sports, drugs, sex, rock and roll—distract us from rather than focus us on the underlying workings of our society and culture. What is more, people resist, understandably, what is difficult and perhaps even threatening. Why choose to develop a sociological consciousness if this difficult process promises many terrible, disturbing lessons about the world and, indeed, about oneself? When it comes to thinking theoretically and critically about our social and cultural world, denial would seem to make a fair bit of psychological sense. In the short run, individual life would plainly be easier without an internalized sociological imagination. Who would want to have in their heads even an imagined relationship with the victims of rape, war, poverty, child abuse, disease, and famine, just to list a handful of unpleasant realities?

What may make psychological sense for an individual may also spell disaster for society. Sociologically speaking, if we collectively seek to protect ourselves from social and cultural realities, then we encourage the creation of a society that is adrift, that stumbles its way into the future with self-imposed blinders. Short of that, we may create a society that is undemocratic; one in which only various types of elites (e.g., politicians, scientists) are expected to think about and discern ways to resolve these problematic realities. By adopting a fatalistic attitude toward our own participation in the making of the future, we would render democratic history making moot and treat widespread social and political irresponsibility as a therapeutic necessity. This is a no less depressing possibility. We would suppress panic in the face of current realities through cynicism, two reactions that (as Chapter 4 discusses) are the chief psychological pathologies of our postmodern epoch. This book suggests the sociological imagination as an alternative to inward panic and outward cynicism.

It is important to be candid about this paradoxical situation: we must be sturdy enough, emotionally and psychologically, to face down the nature of social and cultural reality. But the study of this very same reality allows us to understand why emotional and psychological sturdiness is so difficult to acquire and maintain. Every time we hear about the rates of child abuse, rape, and murder or about deaths from cancer, suicide, and auto accidents; every time we learn of another natural disaster or another famine; every time anything harmful to humans occurs in the world, we must remember that actual human beings bear the brunt of these hardships and deaths, while others suffer the consequences of close proximity to them. Cold social statistics about divorce, income inequality, racial prejudice, or prejudice and discrimination directed toward people who are gay, lesbian, or bisexual barely scrape the surface of the human experience of these things. They all take their emotional and psychological toll. Splinters may make for good magnifying glasses, but when pushed too far, they are lethal.

With this in mind, there is a way in which this book is not depressing and certainly not discouraging. After all, if one is still standing despite it all, still with mind and body intact, then acquiring the sensibilities and conceptual tools needed to make sense of the world and oneself within this world can also be, as Mills himself put it, a "magnificent" lesson.[7] The sociological imagination is a means for many eye-opening experiences. The sociological imagination empowers people to think about themselves, others, and what life is and could be in new and liberating ways. Whoever said ignorance is bliss perhaps never tasted the fruits of truth. After all, who would want to labor under illusions, like children and their attachment to Santa Claus, when they are *not* children, but are instead adults fully capable of understanding the true meaning of Christmas? Postmodernity may be, as Zygmunt Bauman has defined it, "modernity without illusions," but this is not necessarily a bad thing.[8] Postmodern culture offers an opportunity to face squarely human reality, a magnificent prospect if there ever was one.

This book is written, not to depress or discourage, but to demonstrate the inexorable intermingling of terrible and magnificent aspects of the sociological imagination in practice. There is much that is disquieting, say, about disabled children, the phenomenon of Generation X, and religion, the primary subjects of Chapters 5, 6, and 7, but there is also much that is extraordinary and fascinating about them. The proof of this assertion, if anywhere, is definitely in the reading. To judge how the sociological imagination will strike you, it is simply necessary to try it on for size.

Max Weber and the Classical View of Modernity

Why raise the question of whether this book is depressing? No one ever asks if the study of mathematics or astronomy is depressing, but sociology is often depressing.

An example from Max Weber (1864-1920) demonstrates how challenging it is for sociologists to maintain hope about the modern world.

Today, Weber is still regarded as the single most influential founding sociologist. Educated originally in economic history, Weber (pronounced Vey-ber) developed an unparalleled expertise in a stunning variety of fields—from Roman law to classical music—and was considered among the foremost intellectual and political figures in the Germany of his day. Still widely studied in numerous academic disciplines from history and political science to business administration and religious studies, Weber's most enduring contribution is his all-encompassing vision of modern society and culture. In the last analysis, Weber was a sociologist *par excellence,* since it is seeing the whole of modern times that defines the central ambition of sociology. That Weber's highly pessimistic view of modern times was based on an extraordinary breadth of scholarship is, in itself, a disquieting realization.

Advanced industrial society in the twentieth century had become, in Weber's view, an iron cage from which it will be forever impossible to escape. Weber developed the concept of rationalization to denote what made modern society unique in comparison with all previous and competing societal types. Weber's empirical assessment of this process of rationalization then formed the basis of his uncompromisingly pessimistic iron cage metaphor.

Modern societies are distinct and ill-fated because they are on their way to being fully rationalized societies. By this Weber meant that social life in modern societies is progressively formed in accordance with technical principles neutral to any particular set of values or cultural orientations. In a sense, Weber meant that, for modern people, there was or would soon be a science for everything, from the making of complex urban landscapes to the efficient production of effective greeting cards. He foresaw that human values, much less mere habit and frail emotion, would be viewed as irrational sources for motivation in comparison with the steel-hard power of science and technology. A Weberian sociologist would observe that faith, for example, does not put people on the moon, heal the sick, or build skyscrapers. Skyscrapers and, say, artificial hearts are built in Jakarta exactly like skyscrapers and artificial hearts in New York City, in accordance with universally adopted technical principles. Due to the undeniable efficacy of the mind-set of modern Western science in achieving mastery over nature, Weber anticipated a time that this mind-set would become, as it has, essential to the workings of virtually all human societies.

This science-for-everything mentality is, for Weber, a peculiarly modern reliance on instrumental reason.[9] Whatever the end to be achieved (e.g., birthing children, finding happiness, feeding the multitudes or providing them with transportation), modern people systematically endeavor to find the best technical means for achieving it. We do not, as a rule, rely on tradition—the way things have always been done—nor do we readily acquiesce before the limitations imposed by nature. Modern people seek total control over nature and over their own lives. We use technology to create artificial, which is to say, human-made environments and, as much as possible, artificial humans as well.

In putting instrumental reason into practice, however, we create a paradoxical social world that is highly complex, efficient, and powerful but, also, as observed by Weber, artificial, often mechanical, and as a result, disenchanted. Modern society is, in a word, dehumanizing because the means that are employed in its construction are themselves instrumental and dehumanized. Even the results of this dehumanization, when they are identified as problematic, are dealt with in primarily dehumanized ways. Politicians, for example, conduct market research to find the most effective campaign slogan to catch the electorate's jaded attention; to do otherwise would be irrational. Psychologists use standardized therapeutic techniques and mass produced drugs to make functional again the emotionally scarred individual; to do otherwise would be unprofessional. Large corporations with deep pockets typically rely on the expert knowledge of industrial sociologists to help them make the impersonal experience of the for-profit office cubical or assembly line less alienating to the labor commodity known euphemistically as an associate or team member. Indeed, the popularity of Scott Adams's Dilbert™ cartoons may be explained, in part, by their pseudo-humanizing message vis-à-vis such otherwise disenchanted environments, over which, alas, individual "Dilberts" have no real or effective individual control.

Although analytical and reserved in most of his writings, Weber was, at times, unsparing in his judgment of modernity. "This nullity," Weber wrote of modern culture, "imagines that it has attained a level of civilization never before achieved."[10] This nothing, this standardized cultural wasteland is, in other words, greatly self-deluded or "embellished with a sort of convulsive self-importance."[11] Despite what we might believe about ourselves ("The West is best!"), the truth is, for Weber, that once our mechanically structured institutions are set in motion, modern society operates as a social system apart from human needs and desires, subordinating or vanquishing altogether any attempt to alter its course of development. For Weber, modern society would overcome all spiritual obstacles and all supposedly utopian alternatives, such as socialism or communism.[12] In fact, he predicted that socialism or communism would only further the dominance of impersonal bureaucracy while the spirit of Enlightenment, no less than ultimate religious beliefs, would acquire a ghostly and "irretrievably fading" presence in our lives.[13] Weber also speculated that charismatic leaders might arise and attempt to establish one or another utopia or past tradition—perhaps a reactionary world of blood and soil or socialism in one country.

But charismatic leaders, not to mention popular cartoonists, would be no match for an inhuman system.

After a tour of the United States in 1904, which was even then the most advanced of advanced industrial societies, Weber speculated that the bureaucratized world of complex, interrelated, and value-neutral institutions would continue "until the last ton of fossilized coal was burnt."[14] In the meantime, modern people would exist as cogs in this machine of their own making: anonymous numbers, faceless consumers, pseudo-citizens of mass democracies, if not, even worse, the unfortunate denizens of what would come to be known as totalitarian regimes.

Weber died in 1920, and so he did not live to see the consolidation of totalitarian power under Stalin or the rise of Hitler's Nazism much less the advent of television, McDonalds™, and Dilbert™. For his own part, though, he had already seen enough. Near the end of his relatively short life, Weber was asked what motivated him in his expansive studies that had produced many thousands of pages of social and cultural analysis. His answer was, simply, "I want to see how much I can stand."[15]

Knowing that sociology was born of thinkers such as Weber may help to convey the peculiar sensibilities of sociology in the classic tradition. It is not that such sociologists have a bad attitude but that once invested in the project of looking behind and underneath everyday realities, it is difficult not to come away with a sober and even melancholy sense of modern life's meaning and possibilities. It may also be true, however, that a person actually needs a sensitivity to psychological anxiety to be open to the underside of social and cultural experience. This was apparently true of Weber, who spent six years severely afflicted by a kind of clinical depression and only after which did he produce the majority of his best work as a sociologist. This sober, melancholy attitude is therefore perhaps both a cause and an effect of being a critical sociologist possessed of a sociological imagination. Shiny, happy people and sociology do not readily mix. This is another way of thinking about the paradox: can we possess a sociological imagination and maintain emotional sturdiness? Can we maintain emotional sturdiness without possessing a sociological imagination?

Sociology as Critical Theory

The last parts of this book explicitly address the political importance of the sociological imagination. Chapters 8, 9, and 10 identify three forces that work against the development of the sociological imagination: the impoverishment of public life, the failure of utopian thinking, and sociology's own tendency to wander from its wellspring: real people as they live their everyday lives. The fact that social and cultural forces exist that suppress the sociological imagination implies that the choice to develop this type of mind is itself a political choice. That this political choice occurs in the midst of an ongoing struggle between competing versions of our collective future (even whether there will be a "future") further underscores the deeper political involvement of this book. That the forces working against the sociological imagination, in part, emanate from within sociology itself again points to the political nature of this type of study and work. Acquiring a sociological imagination is an unavoidably messy political experience. It is better to know this up front, however, than walk blindly into the storm. In the concluding section of this book, I look ahead to the future and attempt to distill the main political and personal challenges implied in the use of the sociological imagination today. This includes a few words about my own personal experience.

Such discussions imply a vision of sociology that is at odds with the usual understanding of sociology as a kind of apolitical, natural science of society. This is, in fact, the case: the version of sociology that fits with the development and use of the sociological imagination is called *critical theory,* and critical theory diverges fundamentally from the idea that social science is (or could or should be) modeled after natural science.

There are many ways to explain why social or human sciences cannot and should not adopt the self-understanding of natural sciences such as physics and biology. Perhaps the most obvious problem is that in the social sciences, and in sociology especially, humans are simultaneously the subject and object of each and every inquiry. Sociology is the study of ourselves as mindful creatures who live in the natural world but also in a social and cultural world. This study even includes our own striving for systematic self-knowledge. Fish do not study fish; molecules do not study molecules. Sociologists, however, are people studying people, including sometimes sociologists themselves. For this basic reason, any attempt to treat our object of study as a thing is just that, treating people and their lives as though they were things. It follows that sociologists must take responsibility as people studying people and, therefore, take responsibility for their own imaginations and for the versions of society they write based on the use of these imaginations.

This is not to say that one cannot benefit from imagining the social and cultural world from a distant, so-called objective point of view, but we cannot forget that such a perspective is in fact just an imagined point of view. Even though we create methods of research designed explicitly to limit and contain the biases of subjective or particular viewpoints, no humanly created method of research about humans can ever completely erase the humanness from our inquiry. We still decide what needs studying. We still must choose among methods of research. We still must interpret the meaning of "data," and we still must communicate these meanings to other human beings, who, what is more, might be expected to think and act differently based on such learning. Another way of thinking about this is to say that all sociology must be reflexive, mindful of its own unavoidable participation in the making and remaking of society and culture, which includes also the making and remaking of sociology itself.

If, however, sociologists repress this reflexivity in favor of a clinical, scientific self-understanding, they run the risk, as the American sociologist Ben Agger has argued, of turning "social facts into social fate."[16] Ironically, the only justification for using dehumanized methods of research to study a dehumanized world of social facts is that, following Weber, this *is* the type of world we have created. Cold scientific data may, in other words, reflect considerable truth about cold, scientific lives, but even this point does not relieve us of the need to take responsibility for our participation in this world, nor does it foreclose the possibility of imagining a different world. These are political and not, strictly speaking, scientific problems. Sociology can either mindlessly adapt to the world as it has been constructed, as is the case in a would-be natural science of an unnatural social and cultural order, or use the critical distance that feeds the sociological imagination to conceive its own ongoing participation in an always already ongoing, humanly created, open-ended, potential disorder.

Sociology does, however, share with natural science the desire to pursue the truth of things. Although social and cultural realities are constantly changing, there is usually enough constancy in social and cultural life to make systematic and empirical research a meaningful activity. If all social and cultural life were completely in flux and therefore all actions and meanings completely random, it would make no sense to try to get a handle on what is happening or why. What would be the point of trying to fix an exact understanding of the world if it were different from one moment to the next? There would be no patterns to observe, no regularities, nothing predictable. But social institutions do in fact fix patterns in social life. We can observe and map these patterns and then look beneath them in search of what causes the patterns in the first place. This means that sociology is much about understanding the structure and workings of the institutions of society.

For example, the rate of poverty in the United States declined from 22.2 percent in 1960 to 12.6 percent in 1970.[17] This did not occur because poor people left the country in droves and it did not occur because millions of Jed Clampets went out shootin' for some 'coon and up came a bubbling crude. Instead, to explain a society-wide decrease in the rate of poverty, one must attend to the changing structure of society itself, not to individual actions or random experiences. In this case, sociologists look for explanations through the analysis of the American economy and changes in state policy designed to reshape the workings of this economy. The 1960s, after all, was an era of economic growth in the United States. What is more, this era also witnessed the effects of the Kennedy and Johnson Administrations'

"War on Poverty," a set of government programs explicitly designed to reduce poverty. Although some people's experience with poverty may be the result of their individual circumstances or personal qualities, taken as whole, the sociologist possessed of the sociological imagination knows that the rate of poverty fluctuates with respect to structural forces such as the prevailing distribution of jobs, income, and wealth. Political decisions often affect these distributions, as did the War on Poverty initiatives. Explanations at this level of reality require looking beyond particular individuals and particular circumstances to the general nature of society itself. This type of thinking is characteristic of the use of the sociological imagination.

How is social structure fixed in the first place? How does it change? The answers are not very complicated. We reproduce our society and culture daily, and this creates continuity in social structure and in cultural patterns. One obvious way that we reproduce culture is through the socialization of the young. We teach; they learn. We teach what one should and should not do in a given situation, and in this way, norms are learned and acted on with the result being predictable behavior in given situations. We teach values that, once acquired, are acted on with the result being predictable types of value orientations among people in any given culture. As adults, having been socialized ourselves, we also continuously reproduce the ongoing rules of behavior and value orientations inasmuch as we act habitually on the basis of our past learning. Simply put, we recreate social institutions and our way of life by teaching new members of society how to participate in them and by participating in them ourselves as they are presently structured.

This means that how Americans behave in a restaurant is the product of routine acceptance of the established informal rules as to how one is to behave at a restaurant. This means that the U.S. capitalist economy exists through time and across vast spaces because laws and informal rules regulate economic behavior and distribute the ownership of wealth in such as way as to systematically reproduce this profit-oriented type of economy. This means that poverty exists because we implicitly choose to structure our society in such a way as to recreate conditions for its existence, and this means that people do not normally come to a supermarket meat case and scream "Murder!" Normative behavior in a restaurant or supermarket and the existence of an income- and wealth-polarizing capitalist economy are examples of the structured nature of social and culture life.

The trick is to remember that, although social and cultural life is highly organized, regulated, and difficult to change, it is not inherently a thing, nor is it ever as fixed as we imagine rocks and the workings of solar systems to be. It is, in fact, only as fixed as we make it. It is only as thing-like as we treat it. It has a structure, but it is not really an "it," even if we speak about it this way because it is convenient to do so. We all know that people can deviate from culturally accepted behavior (an animal rights activist might be horrified at the sight of hamburger, steak, or live lobsters and, as a result, let out a scream). And we know that economic systems can work to create equality instead of inequality (hunting and gathering people, such as the members of most traditional Native American societies, tended to strive for economic equality in their lives). Even if we do not typically see much social change occurring, at low levels it is always occurring, and at high levels, it is always a possibility.

Sociology contributes to or retards social change. Sociology either participates in the making of a new social order or in the reproduction of the status quo. It cannot stand apart from the total social process, cannot avoid its own participation in history making. Since sociology cannot avoid participation, Mills argued that sociology should participate in history making in a self-conscious and open manner. It should not hide behind the trappings of natural science, don white lab coats, and say to its readers, "We are scientists like any other, bow down before the facts!" Instead, the sociological imagination incorporates within itself the inherent mutability of society as well as the inherent reflexivity of sociology. It understands that sociological understanding is part and parcel of society and culture itself and that sociology is therefore destined either to be transforming or conservative or something in between.

This type of philosophy of social science is called critical theory. Whereas natural scientists seek only to understand and explain the apparently objective laws of the natural world, critical social theorists seek knowledge that will guide humans in their own freely chosen and self-conscious participation in the making and remaking of the social and cultural world. Critical theories are in this way practical and bound-up with interests and values, particularly the values of reason and freedom and particularly the interest in emancipation from the irrationality and unfreedom of everyday knowing. However, since critical theories always exist in a situation clouded by competing interests and values, even competing versions of what social science should be, critical social theories must take responsibility for arguing for whatever version of society and culture they articulate. The political dimension of critical theory is openly acknowledged.

Typically, critical social theory takes the form of criticism of arguably false or distorting views of social and cultural realities. An example of such a false view is the notion that social institutions and human cultures are determined by natural laws beyond human control. The laws of supply and demand and the sociobiologist's claim that racial inequality has something meaningfully to do with genetics are both derivatives of such a view. The idea that a society's poverty rate is the result of poor people, perhaps their own personal failings, is another example. Critical theory opposes these types of claims as false and as serving to render social facts as social fate.

Although our chances for averting piling human catastrophe on top of human catastrophe are slim, sociology should be understood as critical theory. If we are to change the probabilities for the future, it is only through the critique of our typically myopic consciousness and its replacement with a sociological imagination. Only then can we have any chance of taking responsibility for our heretofore-assumed fate. The work of developing a sociological consciousness for these postmodern times is thus the work of critical social theory; indeed, a primary, urgent, and unavoidable task and a prerequisite for rational, democratic social change. Rosy outcomes, of course, cannot be guaranteed. Critical theory appeals to no other power than the power that lies within our own human potentials. Therefore, sociology as critical theory is not a form of faith unless we are speaking about having faith in ourselves.

Looking Ahead

Part 1 of this book is organized in an unusual way. Chapters 2 and 3 are meant as precursors to Chapter 4; all three chapters should be considered as a whole. The problem is that one cannot study the sociological imagination as a thing standing apart from the ongoing reality of societies and cultures today. The first two chapters, then, present crucial aspects of this reality. The emphasis here is on social facts. One can then look more deeply into the type of mind I am aiming to present and even begin to experience its development. The emphasis in Chapter 4 is on conceiving social facts not as fate but as aspects of contemporary social and cultural reality that demand our attention and, ultimately, our action.

Part 2 is more straightforward. In this section, I think through several topics and in so doing display what it looks and feels like to make sense of specific aspects of social and cultural reality in ways consistent with a developed sociological imagination. These chapters are object lessons. The topics, however, are not randomly selected. I chose them to highlight the extremes of individual experience, social institutions, and history making and how these interrelate with one another. It is at the extremes that we find what is most meaningful in the use of the sociological imagination, and extreme phenomena are those best suited to jump-starting one's sociological imagination.

Part 3 shifts perspectives. Here I suggest that forces lurk around us that threaten our minds and make very difficult the development of a sociological imagination. If there were no built-in forms of resistance to sociological thinking, then the aim of this book would be much easier to accomplish. Indeed, there might not be a need for such a book at all, but there are such forces. In choosing these topics, then, I was left little choice. I present the degradation of public life, the end of history, and the idea

of a sociology without society as the chief forces retarding the development of critical sociological thinking but also as a means for further reflection on the nature and
significance of social institutions, history making, and everyday individual life. The
idea is that the forces working against the development of the sociological imagination take direct aim at the three most significant features of that imagination: the
ability to relate what Mills called biography to social structure and vice versa, and
these within the context of a fateless and always open history.

Finally, in Part 4, I address the question of politics and morality. The reader has
already been warned that the mere possession of the sociological imagination does
not provide specific answers to our social problems, nor does it entail the adoption of
a specific values or a single brand of politics. This is a good thing, not a bad thing. It
would not make sense, after all, to suppose that the ability to think critically should
lead directly to just one set of logically or politically obvious actions. It would not
make sense for a form of mind to determine a single moral sensibility. Indeed, as I
hope to make clear in these last chapters, it would be inconsistent, false, and morally
wrong to proscribe what would be possible if the promise of sociology were realized, that is, if the sociological imagination were to become the everyday form of
self-consciousness for members of a democracy. We cannot know the answer to the
question, "What is to be done?" until we are participating together in creating these
answers. If nothing else, the history of the twentieth century should teach us the perils of letting elites, including sociologists and other intellectuals, answer this question for themselves and by themselves. That is partly how we got into this difficult
situation in the first place.

In conclusion, I offer a few autobiographical reflections. This seems appropriate because this book is a highly personal treatment of sociology. I do not mean to
suggest that everyone should be or think like me, at least not exactly! The sociological imagination can be realized in many forms, and we are no doubt better off for this
diversity in styles of reflection. But everyone must come from somewhere, begin
somewhere, and move on to some new place. I offer a brief story about my own experience of working to develop a sociological imagination as encouragement to the
reader to write their own experience for themselves. That, after all, is the end game:
to develop within oneself the ability to take issue with every single thing in this
book but to do so from within the unavoidable entanglements that comprise the
stuff of sociological thinking.

Notes

1. Theodor W. Adorno, *Minima Moralia: Reflections from Damaged Life* (1951; reprint, New
York: Verso, 1974), 50.

2. Karl Marx and Frederick Engels, *The Communist Manifesto* (1848; reprint, New York: International Publishers, 1987), 13.

3. President William Jefferson Clinton, "The State of the Union," delivered before a Joint Session of Congress, 27 Jan. 2000. This document can be viewed at www.whitehouse.gov/ WH/sotu00/sotu-text/html.

4. C. Wright Mills, *The Sociological Imagination* (Oxford, U.K.: Oxford University Press, 1959).

5. Ibid., 13 and 166.

6. Chapter 1 of *The Sociological Imagination* is titled "The Promise."

7. Mills, *The Sociological Imagination,* 5.

8. Zygmunt Bauman, *Postmodern Ethics* (Cambridge, M.A.: Blackwell, 1993), 32.

9. See Max Horkheimer, *Critique of Instrumental Reason* (New York: Continuum, 1974).

10. Max Weber, *The Protestant Ethic and the Spirit of Capitalism* (1904-1905; reprint, New York: Charles Scribner's Sons, 1958), 182.

11. Ibid.

12. Ibid., p. 26. See also Max Weber, "Politics as a Vocation," in *From Max Weber: Essays in Sociology,* eds. Hans H. Gerth and C. Wright Mills (New York: Oxford University Press, 1946), 77-128.

13. Weber, *The Protestant Ethic and the Spirit of Capitalism,* 182.

14. Ibid., 181.

15. Marianne Weber, *Max Weber: A Biography* (1950; reprint, New York: Wiley, 1975), 731.

16. Ben Agger, *Public Sociology: From Social Facts to Literary Acts* (Lanham, M.D.: Rowman & Littlefield, 2000), 9.

17. U.S. Census Bureau, *Statistical Abstract of the United States: 1999,* 119th ed. (Washington, D.C., 1999), 483.

I

DEVELOPING AN ORIENTATION TO SELF AND SOCIETY

2

The Big Picture, or a Brief Survey of Our Dying World

The sole way of assisting nature is to unshackle its seeming opposite, independent thought.

—Max Horkheimer[1]

"Humanity stands at a defining moment in history."[2] These are the first words agreed to by the delegates at the 1992 Earth Summit sponsored by the United Nations. The *Rio Declaration* goes on immediately to state the following: "We are confronted with a perpetuation of disparities between and within nations, a worsening of poverty, hunger, ill health and illiteracy, and the continuing deterioration of the ecosystems on which we depend for our well-being." "However," continues the report,

> integration of environment and development concerns and greater attention to them will lead to the fulfillment of basic needs, improved living standards for all, better protected and managed ecosystems and a safer, more prosperous future. No nation can achieve this on its own; but together we can—in a global partnership for sustainable development.[3]

These four sentences contain a world of meaning. To make sense of them, we must take it big.

At the outset, it helps to translate the official language of a U.N. declaration into a blunt statement. Taken together, these sentences intimate that our world is dying and that, if all of humanity does not soon act in concert to revolutionize human life on earth, we shall not survive. Because the Rio delegates were composing a preface to an unprecedented global action agenda, it was presumably incumbent on them to use optimistic language such as "but together we can." Unlike in politics, science cannot merely assume the possibility of a managed ecosystem and a prosperous future for all, much less project such notions for the sake of motivation or political expediency. We may in fact urgently need a global partnership for sustainable development, and it may be inspiring to say state this, but it is vital for the social scientist to soberly observe what is actually happening or, in this case, what is not happening. As the Australian political scientist Lorraine Elliott notes, "While there are now many, many thousands of words on paper—in conventions, protocols, declarations, statements of principle, management programmes, action plans, communiques—environmental degradation continues to worsen."[4] For the would-be possessor of the sociological imagination, precise understanding of empirical realities is essential. The worsening of environmental degradation is today a prime observable reality.

Natural and social scientists have labored arduously to provide the world with an accurate and reliable picture of this, our defining moment. While not every scientist agrees with every conclusion, there is a remarkable consensus about the greatest and most pressing natural and social problems. Indeed, natural and social problems are intimately related. Put simply, scientists agree that modern forms of society are the single most significant cause of today's worldwide natural crises.

By *modern society* we mean essentially industrial, urban, and scientifically oriented societies. In contrast, the term *postmodern* indicates, as I have noted, a set of cultural shifts dating from the mid-twentieth century, the results of disillusionment with the previously held modern faith in progress and science or, more specifically, progress *through* science. Humans today are simply less convinced that human mastery over nature is achievable or even something toward which to aspire. They worry also about related implications of scientific mastery over *human* nature. All postmodern cultures therefore reside within modern societies and are responses to modernity; therefore, they are intimately related not only to disenchantment with science and technology but also to urban life, industrialism, and other facets of modern living. While this book is very much interested in the significance of postmodern cultural experiences, for the moment we can dwell on the nature of societies organized by industrial (or even postindustrial) economies, giant cities, and scientific institutions. These include the United States, Canada, the countries of the European Union, Russia, Japan, Australia, New Zealand, and a handful of others.

We know that such societies consume vast natural resources and emit vast amounts of pollution and waste. The result of modern society's rapid and increasingly widespread development has been the radical devastation of nature, and ecological devastation causes devastation for human as well as other forms of life. The result of this helter-skelter development is that the world as we know it is dying. Stated differently, the reason we are at a defining moment in history is because the intensely rapid and ravaging development of modern society has reached its limit. Let us examine this situation.

More Life, More Death

Many of the symptoms of the world's dying may be familiar, but it is important to recollect them so that later we may use them to fix an exact interpretation of our life and times. As I write these words, for example, the world's human population is approaching 6 billion. By the time you read them, it will have far surpassed this milestone. In 1998 alone, the world's human population increased by 78 million, roughly the equivalent of adding another Germany to the world's total.[5]

To put these simple figures in perspective, it is crucial to recall a few facts about history and demography. From the time that humans first appeared on earth (roughly 250,000 years ago) until about 250 years ago, demographers estimate that worldwide human population never exceeded 500 million and was in fact probably a lot less than that for most of human existence. Since roughly 1700, however, when modern societies first began to emerge, the world human population has exploded, reaching 1 billion in 1800, 2 billion in 1930, 3 billion in 1962, 4 billion in 1974, 5 billion in 1987, and 6 billion, as noted, in 1999. Bear in mind, then, that while it took all of human history to reach 1 billion people in 1800, it took only an additional 130 years to double that total, and then another 44 years to double the 1930 total once again. The total human population increased fourfold in just the twentieth century.

There is also an important geographical dimension to human population growth. More than 90 percent of the new people being added to this total live in the world's poorest nations, the so-called Third World, which is already home to more than 80 percent of the world's population. The world is increasingly dividing into two very unequal camps: the relatively few who are extraordinarily rich by virtue of the fact that they live in the fully modern, industrialized nations and the vast majority of the world's people who live in relative poverty at the periphery of these dominant societies.

The problem is not the sheer fact of more human beings. The problem is that human beings in modern societies wreak havoc on nature and that the majority of humans bear the brunt of this development. Scientists agree that the absolute number of human beings will in fact reach a limit and level off, probably at around

9 billion people by the middle of this century.[6] The exponential rate of growth in the human population is already diminishing, but what is to become of the vast number of human beings born into Third World poverty? What will they eat? What sort of life will they have? In what sort of world will they live?[7] And no less significant, what is to become of the rich nations whose current way of life is ensuring the advent of an unprecedented human and ecological catastrophe? Perhaps as many as 11 million people perished in the Nazi's death camps, but according to 1998 estimates, 1.2 billion people in the world live in extreme poverty, which is measured by adjusted relative purchasing power across countries of less than $1 per day and indicates life on the brink of existence, under conditions that cannot adequately support human life (see Figure 2.1). An additional 1.6 billion people earn between $1 and $2 per day. Together, then, roughly 2.8 billion human beings exist in today's world on less than $2 per day.[8] Many in this desperate group work very hard to make a living for themselves and their children, but according to a 1999 International Labour Organization worldwide estimate, "there are a billion people . . . engaged in subsistence agriculture or informal sector activities which do not produce a living wage."[9] The idea of a living wage parallels the notion of extreme poverty: both indicate minimum requirements for the reproduction of human life.

It is easy to pass over such figures without giving them much thought. We live in a society that tends to overwhelm us with facts such as these. In postmodern cultures, often these facts are presented as images, such as a fly-covered child dying in the midst of a famine somewhere in Africa. In part through repetition and simplification, disturbing ecological factoids and gut-wrenching, if also clichéd, images leave many desensitized to the meaning of human population growth and global inequality. We know about these realities but have little thought about them, little feeling for their human consequences, and even less understanding of how and why they exist.

It is here that the sociological imagination is needed. We need a form of mind that will allow us to place such realities into a social and cultural context, which will help us to pose the right questions, meet the potentially overwhelming challenges of our self-made world, and prevent our own minds and emotions from being overwhelmed. Developing a sociological imagination entails the ability to look beyond individuals and daily events to bring into focus the big picture and to do this without losing touch with one's emotions, indeed, without losing touch with the myriad dimensions of human experience contained in this so-called big picture.

For example, although millions of individual humans die every year, and thus *their* world ceases to exist, this is not what a sociologist means by a "dying world." In probably each and every instance of a human death, there are others who experience a loss, perhaps a tragic loss. The mother of the fly-covered child cradles her daughter in her arms until the child finally expires. This experience is not to be merely

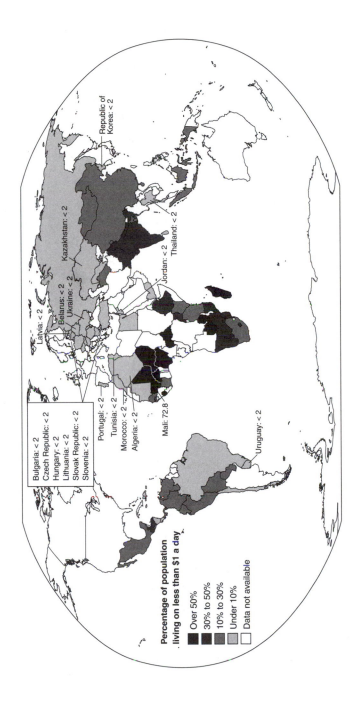

Figure 2.1. Incidence of Extreme Poverty: Population Earning Below $2 per Day

SOURCE: Organization for Economic Cooperation and Development. Online at www.oecd.org/dac/indicators/htm/map.1/htm

Republic of Korea: < 2

Kazakhstan: < 2

Latvia: < 2
Belarus: < 2
Ukraine: < 2

Jordan: < 2
Thailand: < 2

Bulgaria: < 2
Czech Republic: < 2
Hungary: < 2
Lithuania: < 2
Slovak Republic: < 2
Slovenia: < 2

Portugal: < 2
Tunisia: < 2
Morocco: < 2
Algeria: < 2

Mali: 72.8

Uruguay: < 2

Percentage of population living on less than $1 a day

- Over 50%
- 30% to 50%
- 10% to 30%
- Under 10%
- Data not available

subsumed in a larger picture. It stands on its own and demands to be understood in its tragic particularity. But what of the whole? One way to grasp the totality as opposed to the particularity of our experience—one way to begin this process of taking it big—is to recall that human beings are but one of millions of species of life on the planet we have named earth. When we take account of *all* life, we see that we live in systematically morbid times. When we take account of all life, we are driven to experience new forms of loss and new forms of mourning.

While it is terribly difficult to estimate the number of species that exist on the planet, either at present or in the earth's vast natural history, natural scientists generally agree that modern social and cultural development is the primary cause of a new and unprecedentedly high rate of extinction. A conservative figure is that 100 species of plants and animals are extinguished daily, which is a rate of extinction roughly 100 to 1,000 times what would be a natural or evolutionary rate of extinction.[10] We know that natural selection demands that some species survive and others perish. For the most part, we accept this fact without a sense of loss. But each and every day, 100 of our fellow species—whole species, not merely individual creatures—are put to death, and put to death forever, as a result of human social activity. When modern human society is working normally, it produces mass death. This suggests an entirely different level of reality and loss.

There are, as stated, millions of species in the world today, and most of these that are being extinguished, mostly insect species, are not terribly popular among human beings. Perhaps this explains in part why most people do not regard species extinction as a grave problem nor as a threat to their cherished values. It is also probably more significant to focus attention on the destruction of entire habitats, such as the Brazilian rainforest or the world's coral reefs, than it is to pine over the fate of any single species or class of species. In taking it big, it is important to develop an accurate sense of proportion. As in the case of habitats for animals, plants, and comparable social situations for humans, "environments" of various types tend to determine patterns in life and death. Such contexts are therefore accorded in theoretical thought the significance they have in practice; they are seen as shaping the fate of particular phenomena.

Still, the stark fact of human-led slaughter against the earth's living creatures is an extraordinary achievement of modern people. The long-term consequences of this devastation to the ecological "web of life" for humanity and the other remaining species are as yet unclear, although most scientists agree that they cannot be good. Indeed, some natural scientists are so disturbed by this development that they have begun to question the very idea of a disinterested, dispassionate, value-free science and have organized themselves as "conservation biologists" to save what is left of their object of study.

The Significance of Conservation Biology

Under the title, "An Emotional Call to Arms," conservation biologists Michael E. Soule and Bruce A. Wilcox write,

> The green mantle of Earth is now being ravaged and pillaged in a frenzy of exploitation by a mushrooming mass of humans and bulldozers. Never in the 500 million years of terrestrial evolution has this mantel we call the biosphere been under such a savage attack. . . . Perhaps the hardest thing to grasp is the geological and historical uniqueness of the next few decades. There is simply no precedent for what is happening to the biological fabric of this planet and there are no words to express the horror of those who love nature. . . . Perhaps even more shocking than the unprecedented wave of extinction is the cessation of significant evolution of new species of large plants and animals. Death is one thing—an end to birth is something else. . . . There is no escaping the conclusion that in our lifetimes, this planet will see a suspension, if not an end, to many ecological and evolutionary processes which have been uninterrupted since the beginnings of paleontological time. . . . For centuries to come, our descendants will damn us or eulogize us, depending on our integrity and the integrity of the green mantle they inherit.[11]

One does not usually expect natural scientists to issue "emotional calls to arms," but conservation biology is not a typical scientific discipline.[12] Established in the 1970s, conservation biology is a self-described "crisis discipline."[13] This means that scientists such as Michael Soule, who is considered the godfather of the discipline, see the political work of changing contemporary society as essential to the mission of biological science. In this, conservation biologists are at the forefront of an internal self-transformation of science, from a strictly value-free, unemotional, and politically detached enterprise to one that sees itself as a critical participant in the making of society.

Articles in the scholarly journal *Conservation Biology* suggest the extent of this crisis discipline mentality. Curt Meine, in his article "It's About Time: Conservation Biology and History," argues that the disciplines of history and conservation biology

> need the other to fulfill their potential in answering to current concerns; both liberate us by allowing us to understand more fully the forces that shape our lives and the lives around us; both allow us to step back, however momentarily, from the always confusing mire of current circumstances, not to escape them, but to comprehend them. Only then can we return to the present prepared to meet the future.[14]

In their article "The Persistence of Positivism in Conservation Biology," Paul Roebuck and Paul Phifer argue that

conservation biologists form a unique discipline as we combine ecological and ethical theories. . . . While positivism seeks to create a disjuncture between fact and
value, conservation biology creates its disciplinary territory by embodying a more
holistic and interdisciplinary view of science and the role of the scientist. . . . We do
not do valueless, neutral science and then turn over facts to public policy makers
who then make the moral decisions.[15]

In these statements, conservation biologists argue against the positivist self-understanding of science as an enterprise detached from the social processes of history
making and neutral with respect to human values. They are calling for a new form of
science appropriate to the demands of their subject matter and their historical epoch,
in effect, a natural science informed by a sociological imagination.

This is not to say, however, that conservation biologists are any less scientific
than their peers in other disciplines, or that they are beholden, for example, to fash-
ionable currents in social theory. As Michael Soule and Gary Lease make clear in
their edited book *Reinventing Nature? Responses to Postmodern Deconstruction,*
conservation biology is committed to the empirical analysis of a natural world conceived as existing "apart from humanity's perceptions and beliefs about it."[16] In
other words, conservation biologists focus their studies on the planet and its living
things and believe that "we can gain dependable, scientific knowledge about this independent, natural world, in spite of differences among us in class, culture, gender,
and historical perspective."[17]

This is not to say, either, that conservation biologists are generally optimistic
that their emotional call to arms and their attempt to reconceptualize the meaning of
science will, in the end, be successful. As Reed Noss, the 1999 president of the Society for Conservation Biology (SCB), contends, "As a discipline, conservation biology has had a marginal impact on policy decisions." Noss reflects, "Here I am, representing the most important, most needed professional society on earth and presiding
over the meltdown of industrial civilization. . . . Despite the best of intentions, SCB
has failed to live up to its promise."[18] Hundreds of journal articles and well-attended
scholarly conferences do not make a successful crisis discipline. Only an end to the
crisis can do that.

What the advent of conservation biology does reveal, however, is that many natural scientists are taking account of and beginning to act toward the fact of our dying
world. It is not difficult to see the broad connections between "the meltdown of industrial civilization" (i.e., modern society) on one hand and the threat to species diversity and, indeed, the whole of life on earth on the other. Conservation biologists
not only are working to document the specifics of this morbid process but also are
trying to change the social world that is the cause of the problem.

More Sun, Less Fun

The problems associated with human population growth, global inequality, and species extinction are only the tip of the iceberg. The "unsinkable" Titanic that is modern society faces a great many more and less easy to see obstacles in its path. Prominent among these is global warming. It was only thirty years ago that the primary environmental problems that concerned Americans and others in the First World were soil erosion (particularly on farm land), water pollution (chemically despoiled lakes, rivers, and groundwater), and air pollution (particularly the smog caused by auto emissions in major urban areas, such as Los Angeles). Rachel Carson warned of the hazards of DDT, people living close to highways and airports fretted about sound pollution, and I remember being gently cajoled by Woodsy Owl to "never be a dirty bird," to "give a hoot, don't pollute."[19]

Times have changed. These localized environmental problems have been eclipsed in significance by phenomena that strike at the vitality of the earth's ecosystem as a whole. As the popular environmentalist Bill McKibben writes,

> In the past ten or twenty or thirty years our impact has grown so much that we're changing even those places we don't inhabit—changing the way the weather works, changing the plants and animals that live at the poles or in the jungle. This is total. Of all the remarkable and unexpected things we've ever done as a species, this may be the biggest. Our new storms and new oceans and new glaciers and new springtimes—these are the eighth and ninth and tenth and eleventh wonders of the modern world, and we have lots more where those came from.[20]

Global warming is the force behind McKibben's new wonders of the modern world, and the modern world is the force behind global warming. First hypothesized in the 1970s, today global warming is an ongoing reality.

Although complex, global warming is primarily the result of carbon emissions produced by the burning of fossil fuels in industrial societies. When we power automobile factories with coal and manufactured automobiles with gasoline, carbon is emitted into the atmosphere. In 1998 alone, approximately 6.4 billion tons of carbon was released into the earth's atmosphere. The United States, the world's leading industrial nation, accounted for 23 percent of the world's total carbon emissions. Since 1950, about 200 billion tons of carbon has been released into the atmosphere as a result of human activity. The current rate of carbon emissions is, however, more than four times greater than it was in 1950. The overall result of this dramatic increase in the rate of carbon emissions is that atmospheric carbon concentrations are believed higher today than at any time in the past 160,000 years.[21]

Carbon in the atmosphere reacts with oxygen to form carbon dioxide, and carbon dioxide creates the greenhouse effect by trapping thermal radiation in the earth's atmosphere that would otherwise escape into space. The most obvious and immediate result of this process is elevated average global temperatures (see Figure 2.2). Historic record temperatures are already a common phenomenon. Current scientific models predict that the earth's average annual temperature will rise between 1 and 3.5 degrees Celsius, or roughly 2 to 8 degrees Fahrenheit, during the next 100 years. This will be the case regardless of any actions taken in the meantime to reduce carbon emissions.

While the simple warming effect of global warming is already being felt, the long-term related consequences of global warming are unprecedented and so potentially astounding as to defy reliable prediction. Already the earth's icecaps and glacier formations are showing rapid rates of melting, threatening higher ocean levels and difficult-to-predict climatic changes. Some islands have already been inundated. Many more island nations face imminent risk of being swallowed by the rising oceans, and the long term does not bode well for the world's heavily populated coastal regions. According to the 1999 *United Nations Chronicle* titled "Will We Survive the Next Century?" mountain glaciers require about 1,600 years to completely renew fresh water resources, whereas the polar ice caps require about 9,700 years, which is important since nearly one-half of the human population in the poorest countries of the world do not have access to safe drinking water.[22] Shifting worldwide climatic patterns, for their part, threaten the viability of the world's main agricultural regions and have already begun to alter the habitats for millions of species, including disease-carrying insect species. There is also the resulting increase in powerful storms and flooding, affecting, of course, tropical and subtropical regions especially.

While these are everyday realities and taken-for-granted scientific facts, many people, even a rare scientist, still doubt whether global warming is an ongoing reality. They regard it as a mere theory or as an outpouring of millennial anxiety. Of course, there are some people, even in societies otherwise fully committed to rational science, who reject Darwinian evolutionary theory and spurn the fruits of medical science. With regard specifically to global warming controversies, however, I shall have more to say in Chapter 8, in which I examine the degradation in the public sphere in terms of this perplexing controversy. For now, I recommend pretending that the above facts can speak for themselves.

Social Facts as Social Fate?

Modern society has only existed for 250 years or so. If all of human history were measured by a 24-hour clock, this span of time would represent only the last 30

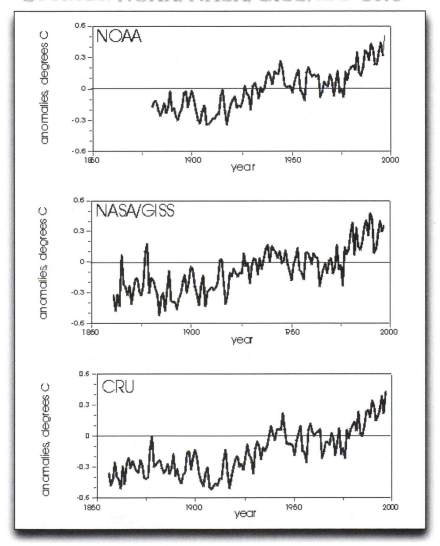

Figure 2.2. Global Temperature Anomalies
SOURCE: National Geophysical Data Center, A Paleo Perspective on Global Warming. Online
publication at www.ngdc.noaa.gov/paleo/globalwarming/images/anomalies.gif

seconds of the "human day."[23] In this snippet of time, from 11:59:30 to the witching hour, humans have built great cities and gone to the moon, but we have also changed the nature of nature.[24] Indeed, it has been argued that there is no "nature" anymore, no pristine land or untainted air or species of plant or animal unaffected by humanity and, particularly, by modern society's development.[25] One nonobvious result of this eclipse of nature is that natural and social science have become increasingly occupied with the same issues. In this situation, created by humans and never before faced by humans, all bets are off. It is not that global warming threatens the earth as a planet; the earth, per se, does not need saving. Rather, global warming threatens the modern way of life, billions of human beings, and all other species that currently reside on the earth's land and in its oceans. It is very much in doubt who or what will be "saved."

A rehearsal of facts about global warming, species extinction, and human population growth is essential, but we must not be lulled to sleep or driven to superstition by either their repetitious familiarity or their seemingly distant and eerie reality. We must not shut our minds down at the very moment they are most urgently needed. This is no time for defensive incredulity disguised as rational skepticism; this is no time for outright panic nor for blasé cynicism. We need natural science to supply us with facts, but we also need sociology to supply us with a means of making social and cultural sense of these facts. The natural and social sciences must in this way work together.

In this regard, it is useful to examine a few pertinent social facts that place into context the ignorance and complacency common in today's literate, rich, democratic, healthy, and thoroughly menacing First World societies. In this group, the most dangerous ignorance and complacency is arguably possessed by those 270 million people (less than 5 percent of the world population), who call the United States of America their home. Arguably, it is Americans, particularly average Americans, who are the most responsible for our dying world simply by virtue of their habitually living life as it has been constructed for them.

The United States accounts for about 25 percent of the yearly global total energy use, gives to the world's atmosphere (as previously noted) about 25 percent of its total carbon emissions, is the only nation to ever use nuclear weapons against another, and still today holds the largest, single usable arsenal of nuclear weapons with destructive capacity to forever destroy virtually all life on the planet many times over.[26] The last point may come as a surprise because most Americans seem to believe that, with the collapse of the Soviet Union, the threat of nuclear holocaust is forever abated. This view is short sighted. While it is certainly true that the threat of nuclear war has dramatically decreased since 1991, it is still worth pausing to fathom the significance of these still-abundant weapons of *total* destruction.[27]

The continental territory of the United States has not been seriously attacked by a foreign aggressor since the British did during the War of 1812. This is mostly the result of America's isolation between two vast oceans, but in the years following World War II, it is more aptly attributable to the overwhelming destructive capacity of U.S. military forces, the backbone of which is its nuclear arsenal. During the Cold War, the United States adopted a deterrence policy of mutually assured destruction (or MAD, as it was commonly known), which meant that a Soviet nuclear attack against U.S. vital interests would be deterred by the certainty of an American nuclear retaliation. This was a deterrence policy because neither side could expect to "win" a nuclear war. To work, this policy entailed full preparation for, and a staunch willingness to prosecute, world suicide. Therein was instituted a balance of terror. With this policy, the U.S. maintained a Pax Americana over a sizable portion of the world. The balance of terror provided an umbrella for the extension of U.S. power abroad, as it did also, but to a lesser extent, for the Soviet Union.

Yet, since the atomic bombing of Hiroshima and Nagasaki, Japan, the United States has chosen not to use its nuclear arsenal. The United States did not use its nuclear arsenal even when it was engaged in losing battles with overwhelming Chinese forces on the ground, Soviet pilots in the air over Korea, and with similarly formidable and ultimately victorious Soviet-backed national liberation forces in Vietnam. Nor has the United States used its nuclear weapons against any of the many lesser foreign powers that have run afoul of U.S. foreign policy over the years, such as Cuba under Fidel Castro, Panama under Manuel Noriega, or Iraq under Saddam Hussein. The United States has in fact withdrawn most of its nuclear arsenal from overseas, destroyed a large portion of its warheads, slated an even larger number for destruction, and sought international agreements to limit and eventually end all nuclear testing as well as to halt the proliferation of nuclear arms to nations that do not presently possess them. Presumably, this is all to the good.

Still, the U.S. nuclear arsenal exists alongside those of Russia, the United Kingdom, France, the People's Republic of China, India, Pakistan, North Korea, and Israel. Even at reduced levels, these weapons are capable of destroying all (or almost all) life on the planet. Although most of the nations of the world have demanded that they be eradicated, there is no genuine plan to eradicate these weapons. The product of human science and ingenuity, these weapons will threaten all living things with efficient and effective extinction indefinitely. This fact is so commonplace, this bequeathment of modern society so mundane, that most people, and certainly most Americans too young to have lived through the Cold War, are barely conscious of it. Yet a visitor to earth from another planet would surely regard the existence of, and readiness to use, weapons of total destruction as a primary characteristic of our way of life. Indeed, such a visitor, if "it" were possessed of a sociological imagination, would probably dwell a good while on the significance of this fact. Along with global warming, the possessor of the sociological imagination would place the world's nuclear arsenal as among the most remarkable achievements of modern society. And for both, the United States could be accorded pride of place.

That one species, on the basis of its investigation of the workings of natural forces, could bring under its control the power to exterminate all species, including itself, is a fact rivaled perhaps only by the somewhat slower, less dramatic suicidal tendencies that are part of the normal workings of modern society. These, too, are social facts. We have thus far avoided the fate of nuclear holocaust, but consider how industrialization, consumerism, and urbanization brought us to this precipice.

A predominately rural society in 1800, the United States became the world's leading industrial power at the turn of the last century, overtaking the world's first-ever industrial power, Great Britain.[28] By the end of World War II, the United States possessed nearly one-half of the world's industrial assets. Due to the efficiency, productivity, and perpetual innovation of its second-to-none economic system, the United States could, by the middle of the 1950s, boast that more than half its workforce had been freed from the drudgery of agricultural as well as industrial labor. During this time, the United States became the world's first postindustrial society because more than one-half of its workforce labored in so-called "service" occupations. Due to its commanding economic power worldwide, the United States also created the world's most lavish consumer lifestyle, where the American Dream of ever-expanding material prosperity became a reality for millions.[29] Correspondingly, the United States was the first society to have more than one-half of its population living in artificially built environments or what are commonly called "cities." These cities were and are designed primarily to accommodate automobiles, another American obsession. Today, roughly 80 percent of Americans live in urban areas and work in service sector occupations, and about 85 percent of Americans drive private automobiles to work, more than twice the rate of their rich Western European counterparts.[30]

Americans have more cars, phones, and computers than the people of any other society; indeed, Americans produce and consume more wealth of any kind than any other people in human history. An average American, for example, uses seventy times the energy per year as an average Bangladeshi. Among the richest tenth of Americans (which probably includes most who are reading this book), each person's annual consumption accounts for eleven tons of carbon emissions, whereas the average for First World societies as a whole is only 3.5 tons. In contrast, the average consumption for a member of the poor nations of the world results in only about one-tenth of a ton of carbon emission per year.[31] In the United States, as in Western

Europe, Japan, and the few other highly developed areas of the world, consumption is quite simply a way of life.[32]

While the creation of a mass consumer society, especially in the United States, has been good for many, its continuation is a disaster, not unlike nuclear holocaust, for the world. Soon, fully one-half of the world's human population will live as most Americans do, in urban areas. Yet their urban experience is not, nor will ever be, similar to the American experience. Every family in China, India, and Indonesia cannot have steak dinners and two cars in the garage; they cannot even have garages. As Molly O'Meara, a Worldwatch Institute researcher, notes,

> London . . . now requires roughly 58 times its land area just to supply its residents with food and timber. Meeting the needs of everyone in the world in the same way that the needs of Londoners are met would require at least three more Earths.[33]

O'Meara refers to the problem of inherently unavailable "ghost acreage," the distant resources nonetheless essential to the perpetuation of modern urban life. Ghost acreage is only "ghostly," however, for those who do not possess a sociological imagination.

Of course, life in most cities, especially the rapidly expanding cities of the Third World, is nothing like life in an American city. Cities in poor countries absorbed roughly 60 percent of the 1.3 billion people added to the world population between 1980 and 1995.[34] Choked by a dramatic increase in impoverished and densely packed dwellers, Third World urban centers are already lethal environments. China alone estimates that 3 million of its citizens died from unsafe levels of air pollution in just the period between 1994 and 1996. But unsafe air is a problem that afflicts all cities in the world, even those in the rich areas of Europe, Asia, and North America. In the United States, for example, 129 metropolitan areas in 1997 failed to meet the government-defined standard for safe air to breathe. Still, conditions are always much worse in the poor countries of the world. In Mexico City, Beijing, Shanghai, Tehran, and Calcutta, the five worst cities for children's lungs, a day's worth of "fresh air" is thought to be the equivalent to inhaling two packs of cigarettes.[35]

Much of the world may indeed admire and seek for itself a wealthy, industrial, urban society such as the one enjoyed for roughly 100 years in the United States, but clearly this is not possible. It is not even possible for the United States to continue as it is. Although it is the world's most powerful nation—a nation that could astonish all by going from the beaches of Kitty Hawk to the Moon's Sea of Tranquility in a mere 63 years and a nation poised to use nuclear power to destroy virtually all life on the planet—the United States of America is, as noted, less than 5 percent of the earth's human population positioned, mostly, in the middle of just one of its 7 continents, and it is heavily dependent on the rest of the world for its resources, its labor, and its atmosphere. The globalization of the world's various economies, political systems, and cultures, together with the lingering experience of the Cold War, have probably put an end to America's long-standing fascination with "isolationism," the sense that the United States is and should remain a world onto itself. But if these forces have not fully vanquished American isolationism, then global warming will.

Rich nations such as the United States may be able to better cope with the short-term effects of the dying global system than the poor, but in the end, even the United States cannot survive on its own apart from what the United Nations' Earth Summit document quoted at the outset of this chapter calls "a global partnership for sustainable development." A straight extrapolation of current structural tendencies cannot, in other words, be sustained into the future, much less can the American experience be replicated in other societies. Fundamental social change is therefore required, and it is not of the sort that nuclear weaponry can provide. That is what the United States agreed to, hesitantly, when it signed the Rio Declaration. Even the United States officially acknowledged that it is part of a dying world, that its military might is useless in the battle ahead, and that the continued fulfillment of what goes for the American Dream is a nightmare for the world.

Most average Americans, then, are living a life that is patently unsustainable, but most as yet apparently do not understand or care what the consequences of this life are or will be. Arguably, then, the half-aware, politically pivotal, American middle-classes stand between the present and a sustainable future like a camel stuffed into the eye of a needle. Until the world's most powerful, most "developed" nation, takes the lead, other nations and other people will be held hostage to American complacency. Needless to say, all it takes is a sociological imagination to conceive this defining moment in human history and replace complacency with some type of political orientation.[36] The resolve necessary to act toward the problems of the dying world, and the wisdom and power to do so effectively and in accordance with democratic values, is another matter entirely.

Notes

1. Max Horkheimer, *Eclipse of Reason* (New York: Continuum, 1947), 127.
2. *Rio Declaration on Environment and Development, Agenda 21: Programme of Action for Sustainable Development, Preamble* (New York: United Nations Department of Public Information, 1992), 15.
3. Ibid.
4. Lorraine Elliott, *The Global Politics of the Environment* (New York: New York University Press, 1998), 3.

5. Brian Halweil, "World Population Swells," in *Vital Signs 1999,* eds. Lester R. Brown, Michael Renner, and Brian Halweil (New York: Norton, 1999), 98-9.

6. Ibid.

7. See Lester R. Brown, "Feeding 9 Billion," in *State of the World 1999* (New York: Norton, 1999), 115-32.

8. Poverty estimates and a discussion of their measurement can be viewed at the World Bank's Web page at www.worldbank.org/poverty/.

9. These figures are reported in *United Nations Development Update,* no. 30 (Jan.-Feb. 2000), 8. This source can be viewed at www.un.org/news/devupdate.

10. On the difficulty of measuring rates of extinction, see John H. Lawton and Robert M. May, eds., *Extinction Rates* (Oxford. U.K.: Oxford University Press, 1995). See also E. O. Wilson, "Vanishing Before Our Eyes," *Time,* 155 (Apr.-May 2000): 29-34.

11. Michael E. Soule and Bruce A. Wilcox, eds., *Conservation Biology: An Evolutionary-Ecological Perspective* (Sunderland, M.A.: Sinauer, 1980), 7-8.

12. My understanding of conservation biology is informed by Erin M. Dougherty, "Conservation Biology and the Thesis of Reflexive Modernization: An Essay on Science and Society at the Fin de Siecle" (Honors thesis, University of Dayton, 1999).

13. Michael Soule, ed., *Conservation Biology: The Science of Scarcity and Diversity* (Sunderland, M.A.: Sinauer, 1986), 6-7.

14. Curt Meine, "It's About Time: Conservation Biology and History," *Conservation Biology* 13 (Feb. 1999): 3.

15. Paul Roebuck and Paul Phifer, "The Persistence of Positivism in Conservation Biology," *Conservation Biology* 12 (Apr. 1999): 446.

16. Michael Soule and Gary Lease, eds., *Reinventing Nature? Responses to Postmodern Deconstruction* (Washington, D.C.: Island Press, 1995), xv.

17. Ibid., xvi.

18. Reed Noss, "The President's Column: Dreams of a Millennial President," *Society for Conservation Biology Newsletter* (Aug. 1999), 1. This document can be viewed at conbio.rice.edu/scb/newsletter/aug99.

19. For a taste of this period and its retrospective interpretation, see Rachel Carson, *Silent Spring* (1962; reprint, Boston: Houghton Mifflin, 1994), with an introduction by Vice President Al Gore.

20. Bill McKibben, "A Special Moment in History," *The Atlantic Monthly,* May 1998, 71-2.

21. Seth Dunn, "Carbon Emissions Dip," in *Vital Signs 1999,* eds. Lester R. Brown, Michael Renner, and Brian Halweil (New York: Norton, 1999), 60-1.

22. See "Will We Survive the Next Century?" *United Nations Chronicle* 36 (1999): 35.

23. Anthony Giddens and Mitchell Duneier, *Introduction to Sociology,* 3d ed. (New York: Norton, 2000), 503.

24. On the ecological significance of the historically unprecedented modern society, see J. R. McNeill, *Something New Under the Sun: An Environmental History of the Twentieth Century World* (New York: Norton, 2000).

25. See Bill McKibben, *The End of Nature* (New York: Random House, 1989).

26. Mark Renner, "Nuclear Arsenals Shrink," in *Vital Signs 1999,* eds. Lester R. Brown, Michael Renner, and Brian Halweil (New York: Norton, 1999), 116-77.

27. See Mark Renner, "Ending Violent Conflict," in *The State of the World 1999* (New York: Norton, 1999), 151-68. See also Jonathan Schell, *The Fate of the Earth* (New York: Avon, 1982) and E. P. Thompson, *The Heavy Dancers: Writings on War, Past and Future* (New York: Pantheon, 1985).

28. See Paul Knox and John Agnew, *The Geography of the World Economy,* 2d ed. (London: Edward Arnold, 1994).

29. See, for example, Don Mayer, "Institutionalizing Overconsumption," in *The Business of Consumption: Environmental Ethics and the Global Economy,* eds. Laura Estra and Patricia H. Werhane (Lanham, M.D.: Rowman & Littlefield, 1998), 67-90.

30. Molly O'Meara, "Transportation Shapes Cities," in *Vital Signs 1999,* eds. Lester R. Brown, Michael Renner, and Brian Halweil (New York: Norton, 1999), 134-5.

31. See McKibben, "A Special Moment in History," 72.

32. See Roger Rosenblatt, ed., *Consuming Desires: Consumption, Culture and the Pursuit of Happiness* (Washington, D.C.: Island Press, 1999) and George Ritzer, *Enchanting a Disenchanted World: Revolutionizing the Means of Consumption* (Thousand Oaks, C.A.: Pine Forge Press, 1999).

33. O'Meara, "Transportation Shapes Cities," 134-5.

34. Molly O'Meara, "Urban Air Taking Lives," in *Vital Signs 1999,* eds. Lester R. Brown, Michael Renner, and Brian Halweil (New York: Norton, 1999), 128-9.

35. Ibid.

36. See Thomas Prugh, Robert Costanza, and Herman Daly, *The Local Politics of Global Sustainability* (Washington, D.C.: Island Press, 2000), which argues that "the rational process of figuring out how to achieve a sustainable world must begin with a nonrational act of imagination" (p. 41).

3

The Small Picture, or Yesterday's Dystopias as Today's Everyday Life

Things have gotten worse than George Orwell imagined.

—*Stjepan G. Mestrovic*[1]

Everyday life in highly developed, postmodern cultures corresponds surprisingly well to what thinkers in modern times regarded as *dystopia,* the very converse of uto-pia. Weber's vision of the "iron cage" was certainly dystopian, but when we think of such dark prognostications, usually works of literature come to mind. The central idea of Aldous Huxley's *Brave New World* (1932) is that individuals in the future (the year 632 of our [Henry] Ford) would be made unfree and their powers to reason rendered moot through the development of biomedical and social engineering.[2] The application of science to the human body would result in people manufactured—lit-erally, on assembly lines—to meet various social needs. Instead of training people to be janitors, for example, they would be *made* janitors in vitro. Huxley also intro-duced the idea of "soma," a pill that would quiet anxieties and produce political domination as a happy side effect. The most well-known alternative to Huxley's dystopia is George Orwell's *1984* (1949).[3] In Orwell's "Oceania," his imagined England in 1984, instead of "soma" there are "telescreens"; instead of engineered masses, the "proles" are distracted by "prole feed," which includes heavy doses of pornography and beer; instead of science being in charge, "the Party" rules through

"Newspeak," the ever-watchful eyes of "Big Brother," "doublethink," and, when necessary, the torture that takes place in the "Ministry of Love." [4]

There is, of course, much more to both Huxley's and Orwell's dystopian novels, and in this chapter I will provide additional details. But in a culture awash in medications—two-thirds of Americans take prescription medications[5]—and glued to television sets—21 percent of American 9-year-olds watch more than 5 hours of television per weekday—it pays to examine ourselves from the vantage of what intellectuals in previous generations regarded as dystopia.[6] Whereas Chapter 2 addressed the perils associated with the "big picture" (e.g., species extinction), this chapter addresses the perils associated with the "small picture," the extinction of free and reasoning individuals. In particular, I focus on people's experience of their emotions, bodies, and their power vis-à-vis the world.

I hasten to add that my goal is not to further diminish already diminished individuals by heaping dystopian descriptions of social and cultural life on the insult of having to live such lives. My point is certainly not to cast blame on individuals for their irrationality and unfreedom but quite the contrary. The point of this survey is to clarify what underlies even vague perceptions of individual crisis in the hope that individuals themselves, once conversant with theories of individual crisis, can revolutionize their typically fragmented worldviews and, working with others in similar situations, surmount the powerlessness embedded in their isolation. The goal, then, is the creation of a society and culture in which individuals can truly be individuals, in the classic sense of persons possessed of reason and freedom, and in which individuals can be self-knowledgeable agents in the making of history. As always, the means to achieve this goal is the popularization of the sociological imagination.

This discussion transpires, however, with an understanding of postmodern culture in which reason and freedom have largely become, as C. Wright Mills predicted they would, "moot."[7] Much of Huxley's and Orwell's respective dystopian visions are treated as having already been realized. Therefore, I aim to highlight theoretical ideas about current ways in which reason and freedom are rendered meaningless for individuals in postmodern culture and therein individuality itself liquidated.

I also provide empirical data that, indirectly at least, suggests the dimensions of the crisis of individuality in postmodern times. Given the nature of our object of analysis, indirect data is the only type of data available. For example, the U.S. Surgeon General estimates that between 28 percent to 30 percent of Americans—some 75 to 80 million people—suffer from a diagnosable mental or addictive disorder, but the experience of the many mental and addictive disorders cannot be understood through such gross numbers.[8] A more narrow focus does not help much. Roughly 33 percent of American adults report that they feel "really depressed" at least once per month, and roughly 12 percent take some form of antidepressant medication, but again, it is unclear what "depression" and the use of antidepressants means for each individual.[9] In fact, the only direct data is the bodily experience of each and every individual living life in postmodern society and culture, but a book can never truly get under a person's skin. To survey the small picture, I will have to work around the edges of individual experience. This means, first, the examination of the historical origin of so-called "big" and "small" pictures themselves.

The Making of the "Big Picture"

The lived experience of individuality and the cultural ideal of individualism are historical facts, not natural phenomena. Both are associated with the period in Western cultural history known as the Enlightenment. The dates for this period—also called "The Age of Reason"— vary, depending on what part of Europe one is talking about, but most Enlightenment ideas were spawned in the sixteenth and seventeenth centuries in Italy, France, Germany, and England. Painting in very broad strokes, these ideas included the revolutionary notions that individuals could possess reason and freedom; that the natural and the social world, so mysterious before, could be comprehended; and that humans could use scientific knowledge to make history in accordance with their newfound reason and freedom. The ultimate utopia would be a self-consciously created, self-edifying society in which reasoning individuals existed freely among other reasoning individuals. As the German Enlightenment philosopher Immanuel Kant (1724-1804) put it, "Enlightenment is escape from self-inflicted immaturity."[10] The result of this "escape" is not only modern society and culture but it is the making of the world itself.

The idea that humans live together on a single planet, the world, is, for example, a relatively new phenomenon, a result of the forces of modernization and the spread of Western culture over the face of the planet. When Christopher Columbus sailed the ocean in 1492 and discovered the new world, he meant new *world*. Even as late as 1818, there were still people living on what we now call Greenland who believed themselves to be the only people living on earth. In fact, for the vast majority of human history, this was the way that people understood themselves: their world included themselves, the earth beneath their feet, and the heavens shown above. It is easy to forget that earth, even for early modern Europeans, used to be in the center of the universe, only a few thousand years old, and flat. Likewise, Europeans did not treat discovered, non-Europeans as full-fledged human beings but instead cast them either as godless heathens who were members of inferior races or romanticized them as noble savages.[11] The escape from self-imposed immaturity has been a long and often violent process rooted in conceptual distortion. Although it frames our sense of human possibilities and undergirds what we regard as utopia and, likewise, dystopia, Enlightenment has not reached its conclusion.

Still, no one today thinks their own family, community, or nation define the boundaries of the world. We are all—rich and poor, northern hemisphere and southern hemisphere, East and West—self-conscious of our relative standing vis-à-vis other human beings spread geographically across the whole of the planet. Many people, perhaps most, have seen what earth looks like from the point of view of humans standing on the earth's single moon or from the point of view of a spacecraft orbiting the earth. Indeed, the forces of globalization—the spread of worldwide transportation and communication technology (including but hardly limited to today's fascination with the Internet and World Wide Web); the advent of a world economy that subsumes in its structure all national and local economies; the nation-state system and its many transnational institutions, such as the United Nations; the precise geographic mapping of the world and its division into standardized time zones; the worldwide migration of hundreds of millions of humans (forced and voluntary) from each and every continent to each and every continent (Antarctica excepted)—these forces mean that we are interconnected and interdependent as never before.

We know that we live in the world because this knowledge is grounded in everyday life. We also know that we are part of a common humanity. That is why we speak about "crimes against humanity" and have international laws prohibiting them, for such a thing exists for us. Indeed, modern society and culture, which originated in a relatively few small parts of Europe, lists among its many astounding historical achievements the social and cultural creation of humanity itself. Today, like so much else that is astounding about our lives, we take this achievement largely for granted.

The Making of the "Small Picture"

This chapter is a particular sort of survey of *our* world, the small picture, and modern society and culture is responsible for that as well. Modern society and culture created individuals.[12] The idea that each one of us stands apart from all groups, that each of us is a unique person distinct from every other person, and that our lives are to be self-directed or, ideally, as self-directed as possible are all modern ideas. Every time we unabashedly declare "I," we announce ourselves as modern people. Every time we reflect on our dreams, we underscore to ourselves the importance of our singular, wholly private experience. Every time we fear our own unavoidable, individual death, we experience what it means to be a reflective, isolated, modern individual, a being animated by a self-cultivated "inner world." This is the small picture.

The modern cultural ideal of individualism is supported and reinforced by modern social institutions in many ways. We are given a unique name, we are graded in school individually, we are employed, cast our ballots, and choose our religion as individuals. Identity, intelligence, economic well-being, citizenship rights, and questions of conscience are all individualized in our type of society. You are not your brother's keeper, and, for the most part, no one can make you be; your mental abilities are not measured in terms of your family average, nor are you guaranteed a livelihood by virtue of your skin color or gender. You cannot, in a single election, vote a million times even if you are a millionaire, but you can choose any religion you like or none at all and any moral code or none at all because there is no law against this.

However, it is against the law to engage in sexual intercourse at the back of a classroom, and most of us would be horrified at even the thought of it, although sexual relations, using the toilet, and most everything else we now deem as private were necessarily a family affair for most people living in the single room dwellings common only a few hundred years ago. Private places and privacy are indicative of an inner world seeking a protected space for expression. Likewise, romantic love, although seemingly a natural and invariant aspect of human nature, is a product of modern times. Shakespeare's "Romeo and Juliet" would be regarded as a play about a sickness in many cultures, whereas premodern Europeans would have never understood such feelings as the basis for anything so important as marriage or suicide. Similarly, if you consider yourself to be the member of one or another race, you are experiencing yourself as a modern person because the concept of race is an invention of early modern science.

From the vantage of postmodernity (i.e., modernity without illusions), we can see the many curious and false aspects of modern individuality. For example, although biologists today agree that there is no such thing as biologically distinct human races, the social construct of race lives on as a powerful myth disguised as a taken-for-granted natural reality. Patterns of gender identity, sexual orientation, and the meaning of able-bodiness, health, and the experience of time and space are also social constructions and have varied widely over time and among cultures. Understanding these phenomena for what they are entails acknowledging the radical discontinuities in the human construction of these phenomena, what Mills called appreciating "the human variety."[13]

In postmodern times, people are slowly becoming aware of what natural and social science have discovered about these categories of identity. More than ever before and more than in any other culture previously, average people in everyday postmodern life are more likely to transgress old boundaries or invent new ones. For example, the rate of intermarriage between blacks and whites in the United States has risen dramatically, creating the phenomenon of mixed-race couples and children. Although this hybrid still is rooted in the fiction of race, it represents a movement toward the truth of the nonexistence of biologically conceived race. The disjuncture between "sex," a biological attribute, and "gender," a set of psychological, social, and cultural characteristics, is also increasingly understood and, when acted on, produces new varieties of men and women. Likewise, the popular understanding of the disjuncture between sex and gender and "sexuality," an affective orientation, is also emerging. Like homosexuality, trans- and bisexuality are less often conceived, as they once were, as aberrations from some natural order. The inherent potential plasticity of our identities is slowly coming out of the closet.

Even in postmodern culture, the forces of modern society work to contain experimental self-development and impose the ideal of individuality. Whatever machinations people go through to extricate themselves from imposed identities (e.g., gender bending, tattooing and piercing, race mixing, body painting), basic institutional realities work to reproduce singular individuals in terms of established categories. People must still fill out forms that require self-identification in racial terms as though anyone were white. At a deeper level, despite how we choose to pose ourselves, the institutions of society will still not allow a transgendered couple to vote more than twice or receive a single bachelors degree; and in the end, most of us will have our earthly remains placed in a distinct plot of ground or designer urn with our name on it and our name alone. This is as true for transgender folks as it is for Ma and Pa Kettle. Mass graves are an affront because they negate the value of individuality. They are an affront to anyone and everyone, regardless of their particular form of identity. Although we all are, as the self-identified lesbian, feminist, mother, poet, and social critic Adrienne Rich once emphasized, "of women born," even this flesh-and-blood connection to others is in question.[14] Thanks to the development of modern reproductive technologies, females—and not only females—are less and less necessary to the practice of pregnancy and childbirth such that, in the future (the not-so-distant future), we may be born as individuals as well. Mass birth is taking its place alongside of mass death as a peculiarly modern accomplishment and fear.

At the Edges of the Small Picture

The simultaneous expansion and individuation of the/our world is one of the great paradoxes of modern social and cultural development. Indeed, postmodern culture is characterized by extreme development in both directions. On one hand, a planetary humanity is firmly established, whereas on the other, the singularity of the embodied individual is also entrenched. The universal confronts the particular and vice versa not as a philosophical problem but as a lived reality. Thus, it is impossible to survey our individual worlds for the obvious reason that only you, each individual reading these words, has access to your world, and each is separate from the other. There could be as many as 6 billion worlds now being experienced in the confines of the one big one. No one can know these inner lives unless their possessors communicate about them and share them with others. As a rule, however, we keep our private lives to ourselves.

This does not mean that sociologists have nothing to say about small worlds. It is possible to understand the historical origin of individuality, the contemporary social and cultural contexts in which individuals must live, and their powers vis-à-vis these constraining environments. It is also possible to assess the prospects for myriad individuals' efforts to understand, explain, and act in these environments. While a healthy respect for the power or agency of each and every person is advisable, productive and enlightening generalizations are possible and, in fact, much needed.

The utopian ideal of individuality has always been controversial and its fate very much in doubt. From its origins, sociology has been ambivalent in its assessment of the modern individual. On one hand, early sociologists deeply appreciated the ideals of the Enlightenment that supported the rise of individualism. Liberty, free inquiry, equal justice before the law, and so on were thought to be true advances over autocratic rule, religious dogma, and institutionalized inequalities of all sorts. On the other hand, early sociologists such as Max Weber also saw in individualism an ideal that could lead to new and dreadful forms of unfreedom, for example, the unfreedom of the faceless pawn trapped in massive bureaucracies or, just as harrowing, Karl Marx's concern for the unfreedom experienced by the worker treated as a mere factor of production in Blake's "Satanic Mills" of the industrial revolution. In other words, society would consist not of heroic individuals but of mere numbers, meaningless in themselves to the whole of society—at best cogs suited to its workings and at worst dysfunctional and costly components in need of being expunged or retooled.

For many sociologists, the Nazi Holocaust was the final straw. For decades, individuals had been habituated to regimentation in increasingly large-scale organizations (e.g., factories, prisons, schools, hospitals, nation-states, armies), and then the Holocaust demonstrated that it was possible for individuals to be subjected to methodical, efficient genocide, and this, not insignificantly, in the same land that was home to the Enlightenment's Immanuel Kant. Many critically minded sociologists agreed that the "banality of evil," which political scientist Hannah Arendt saw as evinced in the Holocaust, was not limited to Nazi Germany but, rather, was alive and well throughout the modern world in its mass democracies as much as in its dictatorships and emerging totalitarian regimes.[15]

In his famous and controversial study *Obedience to Authority,* social psychologist Stanley Milgram demonstrated that average Americans were capable of putting people to death based solely on orders from an "authority figure," which was represented in his experiment by a "scientist" wearing a white lab coat.[16] No one, of course, was actually put to death. Milgram and his coworkers tricked people into thinking that they were administering electric shocks to "learners" who failed to answer questions correctly. Some teachers shocked learners at increasingly high voltages until the learner's screams of pain fell silent. Milgram wanted to assess under what conditions and to what degree average Americans would behave as average Germans did when ordered to participate in prosecuting an impersonal genocide. He found that such obedience to authority was characteristic of two-thirds of his research subjects and thus inferred that many, perhaps most, people in modern society are amenable to being swayed by authority figures to act in ways that they would otherwise find repellent and strongly resist.

Indeed, Milgram's famous study was controversial and darkly ironic because Milgram's own attitude toward his unwitting experimental subjects—most of whom were just average people responding to an advertisement placed in a New Haven, Connecticut newspaper—mirrors the experimental subjects' attitude toward the people they were ordered to "teach." In both cases, a certain banality of evil was present because, in both cases, people were routinely treated as things to be experimented on with little regard for the violence or harm that might result. At the end of the experiments, Milgram's subjects were encouraged to feel good about their participation in his study—presumably, to feel good about their contribution to "science"—but it is doubtful whether this would be sufficient solace in the face of what their contribution demonstrated about themselves.[17]

For social scientists such as Arendt and Milgram, the Holocaust was seen not as an aberration of modern society and culture but, rather, as its epitome, revealing what was elemental to the whole of the modern way of life. That Milgram's experiment replicated this dehumanizing tendency underscores this point. Only the most naïve and sanguine sociologists of the first part of the twentieth century held out much hope for the realization of the original Enlightenment ideals of individualism, much less for the realization for the promise of sociology.

Emotions in Postmodern Times

Our immediate concern, however, is the individual at the beginning of the twenty-first century. First, what is happening to our emotions? As stated previously, such questions must be approached indirectly. You are, of course, capable of thinking about your own emotions yourself if you wish. Or are you?

Many of today's leading social theorists would be surprised if average readers could in fact skillfully and genuinely communicate with their feelings. If, for example, Stjepan G. Mestrovic, an American sociologist, is correct, we live in a "postemotional society," one in which individuals' emotions—indeed, individuals' capacity to have feelings at all—are severely degraded and otherwise largely detached from what they actually do in life. As a result, Mestrovic argues that we suffer from "emotion fatigue."[18] We aspire to be ignorant and nice, which is to say, emotionally flat. We shun indignation and are suspect of those with strong feelings about anything. We have no splinters in our eye, and if we do, we blithely ignore them. According to Mestrovic, most of the emotions we do experience are really pseudoemotions, commercially manufactured and managed by what he calls the "Authenticity Industry."

We are told, for example, that drinking the soda 7-Up, "the Un-Cola," makes you an "Un," that is, a unique and critically minded individual. The idea of being an "Un" is promoted with a healthy dose of irony; its silliness is openly acknowledged. We are also told that drinking Sprite, which is produced by Coca Cola, Inc. and is a leading competitor with 7-Up in the non-Cola youth soda market, should result from your "obeying your thirst," not from listening to their advertisement jingle that criticizes advertisement jingles, not from listening to their celebrity spokespersons who criticize advertising's use of celebrity spokespersons. In their economic competition with 7-Up for market share and, ultimately, greater profits, the advertisers hired by Coca Cola, Inc. are thus implying that Sprite drinkers, not 7-Up drinkers, are the truly authentic, savvy Gen Xer's because Sprite drinkers resist manipulation and obey their genuine thirst. Obey your thirst or be an Un, you decide.

These advertising strategies are no doubt based on considerable market research and are skillfully designed to resonate with the perceived cynicism of today's nonetheless authenticity-seeking young adults. After all, everyone wants to feel as though they are unique and authentic, not plain Jane and fake. Similarly, everyone knows that a commercial, even one that criticizes commercials, is inherently manipulative. No one wants to feel duped. The task for these advertisers is to subvert this common sense with marketing strategies that put common sense to work on behalf of a particular product. In these examples, the would-be young soda consumer is flattered inasmuch as the advertisers acknowledge the manipulative nature of their medium and engage in self-mockery. But this does not change the basic nature of the manipulation; it only drives the manipulation to new levels of sophistication.

People are also subject to manipulation of their emotions at work. As American sociologist Arlie Russell Hochschild demonstrates in her book *The Managed Heart: On the Commericalization of Human Feeling,* the demands of many of today's occupations, similar to the flight attendants and bill collectors she studied, involve the strict supervision and management of employee emotions.[19] "Emotion work," thinks Hochschild, is an ever-more common feature of the service economy, in which the product being sold is the capacity to give the customer a happy, satisfied feeling. One means of managing emotions at work is through the strict scripting of interactions. As a result, the fast-food counter employee is required to end each and every interaction with "Have a nice day," and the telemarketer is directed to use tried and true methods of manipulation to make it difficult for the would-be customer to refuse a sale or even hang up the telephone. Both consumers and producers have their emotions systematically manipulated in commercialized interactions. A robot-like quality comes to predominate in everyday life.

Mestrovic's and Hochschild's are but two studies that stand in a long line of sociological research that underscores the manipulation of emotions in modern society and culture. Whether we focus on mass sports, shopping malls, or planned residential communities, our emotions are entangled in managed and commercialized interrelationships, none of which is truly authentic. Shopping malls are designed with market-tested themes and constructed to funnel consumers into stores and prevent their easy exit from these "cathedral[s] of consumption."[20] Likewise, planned residential communities create a community atmosphere based on a formula for creating a community atmosphere. However, the exact effect or configuration of systematic emotional manipulation on doubt varies with each individual. It must be the case, for example, that some people watch no television advertisements, whereas others enjoy occupations that demand very little if any routine scripting of interactions. Emotional manipulation is ubiquitous. If one does not confront it at work, then one will confront it elsewhere. The examples of its effects are potentially endless.

When, for example, Princess Diana of the United Kingdom was killed along with her fiancé and driver in a Paris automobile accident, people all over the world paid unusual attention. There was an outpouring of grief and evident distress on the part of millions who, of course, did not personally know The Princess of Wales, but who ventured out of their homes to attend the funeral of the People's Princess. Millions more watched via their televisions, out of curiosity perhaps, for there was a great spectacle afoot. Much of the same occurred after the tragic death of John F. Kennedy, Jr., a magazine publisher and the son of a former U.S. President. People reacted emotionally to this event, as though the nation had lost its beloved crown prince. During the war in the Persian Gulf against the nation of Iraq, Americans watched the war unfold on their televisions. They hurriedly bought produced T-shirts with patriotic slogans on them, such as shirts depicting the American flag and the words, "these colors don't run." There was no mass outcry against being presented images of people slain by "smart bombs," which carry video cameras in their nose. Americans, like people in other societies, become deeply identified with professional sports teams. These are for-profit entertainment enterprises with a vested interest in cultivating a fan base, but they can nonetheless come to possess a sacred meaning in people's lives. When the owner of the National Football Leagues' Cleveland Browns moved his team to Baltimore, millions of Cleveland Browns fans (an abbreviation of "fanatics") were not only incensed but they were emotionally affected with a sense of loss. They grieved and they protested this perceived betrayal. A war between Uruguay and Paraguay was associated with a controversial soccer match; soccer fans in Liverpool are sometimes buried on the sacred "pitch" that is home to "Liverpool United."

In Orwell's *1984,* during "Hate Week," crowds jeer and spit with great emotional fervor at the enemy announced to them by their government, "The Party." They cannot help themselves. If the enemy suddenly changes, which it does in Orwell's novel, the crowds forget there ever was a previous enemy and begin to immediately feel and espouse hatred toward the new or, as they experience it, same old enemy. The book's main character, Winston Smith, is a middle-level ("Outer Party") intellectual who participates in Hate Week just like everyone else even though sometimes he deludes himself into thinking he can stand apart. Winston loathes "the proles," which represent about 85 percent of Oceania's population. He is contemptuous of their consumption of "prole feed," which his Outer Party brethren produce by order of the "Inner Party" elite. But, like the proles, Winston hordes scare razors, imbibes "Victory Gin" (the Outer Party variant of beer), and is convinced that the simple arithmetic problem $2 + 2 = 4$ is the key to the revolutionary liberation of his society. Different from the proles only in occupation and the content of his self-delusion, Winston Smith, whose ambition is to revolutionize the history that at his job in the "Ministry of Truth" he takes pleasure in daily falsifying in accordance with Party demands, is the true expert in the ways of "doublethink." For all his education and political sophistication, he jeers during Hate Week and deploys his expert history-falsification skills with manic dedication. He is a pseudoindividual who is, at best, half aware of his predicament. After his imprisonment and torture in the Ministry of Love, he is not even that, although he is no less a functional member of his society. Orwell concludes his novel with Winston sipping Victory Gin, loving Big Brother, and free to talk to whomever he chooses at the "Chestnut Tree Cafe."[21]

Orwell's literary Oceania had become the land whose masses mourned the People's Princess via their steady consumption of her image in the pages of its many tabloids, and whose middle-level intellectuals were busy writing commentaries on this mass phenomenon, which were then fed back into the system as expert analyses.[22] Similarly, in the United States, the images of JFK, Jr.'s sudden death raced around the television circuit and through the pages of mass-circulation magazines. Learned experts appeared on television, drew the somber parallels to his father's and uncle's assassinations, and posed the predictable questions. Thus, they filled the air time that needs filling if American postmodern culture is to continue whirling on. Although everyone knows it's trifling—that there is a real world that never receives this attention nor causes this emotive response—everyone, or so it seems, is drawn into this vortex of images and emotions. Some may sneer at those who consume supermarket tabloids, but who does not mourn the loss of JFK, Jr. or spit at the thought of Saddam Hussein (or insert the name/image of a more recent evil Third World dictator here) and lovingly support the troops?

Postmodern Bodies

Emotions are experienced in one's bodies, and our flesh and bones are also increasingly the object of manipulation. This manipulation is so multifaceted, taken for granted, and essential to our daily lives that it is barely perceived as manipulation at all.

Drugs, legal and illegal, play a role in engineering our emotions. Caffeine-filled coffee, tea, and soda give us a jolt; nicotine-filled tobacco products provide stimulus; and alcohol products (beer, wine, and liquors) bring us up and then, eventually, send us down. Indeed, in 2.7 million instances in 1996, police made alcohol-related arrests, another form of going down.[23] Nonprescription medications fill the shelves at the local market or, as it were, drug store, whereas prescription medications fill our medicine or, as it were, drug cabinets at home. In America, the pharmaceutical industry is the most profitable of all industries. The antidepressant medication Prozac alone has been prescribed for more than 17 million Americans, is the third most used drug in the United States, is available in more than 100 countries in the world, and nets its manufacturer, Eli Lilly, close to $3 billion in annual sales, which is about one-third of this giant corporation's gross annual revenue.[24] Likewise, Zoloft is another leading SSRI (or selective serotonin reuptake inhibitor) antidepressant medication, is the 7th most used drug in the United States, and nets its manufacturer, Pfizer, Inc., more than $2 billion in annual sales.[25] In both instances, more than two-thirds of these sales are made in the United States. Of course, illegal drugs of all kinds compete with the likes of Ritalin and Viagra for our affections. In its first year of availability, more than 5 million people tried Viagra, but marijuana remains the nation's leading cash crop.[26] Americans spend roughly $7 billion per year on marijuana, which is more than the money spent on Prozac and Zoloft combined, and roughly $57 billion per year total for illegal drugs of all kinds.[27]

Drugs are just one obvious means by which we manipulate our bodies. We also spend billions on health care to keep us alive, cure us of disease, replace dysfunctional organs with artificial organs or replacements from human donors, surgically improve our faces and our vision, replace lost hair, and in other ways augment our naturally occurring appearance and abilities. Birth control devices are used to temporally disable one ability in particular, whereas in vitro fertilization, artificial insemination, and other fertility technologies work to reinstate, augment, or replace it with man-made substitutes. Beyond the manipulation of our insides, many people also tan and sanitize their exteriors, and some people engage in superficial body mutilation such as tattooing and piercing. It is estimated, for example, that roughly 28 million Americans tan indoors each year and that more than a million of these people make daily visits to tanning parlors.[28]

In addition to the money and worry invested in preventing mouth, armpit, and crotch odor, billions more are spent on exercise and dieting initiatives because we are also obsessed with our weight and body shape. The eating disorders anorexia nervosa and bulimia—in which people, usually young women, starve themselves, sometimes to death—are strictly First World diseases; they are an ironic and tragic result of our abundance, not lack, of food.

Still less obvious is the discipline imposed on our bodies. In the process of acquiring our adult selves and learning to comport ourselves appropriately in school, work, and public places, we learn to sit still and be quiet for hours. We also learn to muffle (if not take steps to eliminate all together) the public expression of farts and burps, to flawlessly perform repetitive tasks, and to train our minds to endure a tidal wave of information and images all while we hold our bodies, for the most part, under control. Self-discipline is at work even when we put our bodies to play. We measure an athlete's speed over distance in tenths of seconds, the precise height of their vertical leap, their range, their power in terms of the length of their home runs, and their artistic display from 0 to a perfect 10. Whether on the field of sport, battle, or in the bedroom, the body is also often treated as a mechanism for conquest. We hone, control, and stimulate it as though it were a mechanism; our goal is superior performance, and we take pleasure and find happiness, or meet frustration and failure, in pursuit of this goal (see Figure 3.1).

The French historian and philosopher Michel Foucault (1926-1984) used archival research in the history of human social development to arrive at the conclusion that today's bodies are, for the most part, disciplined and docile. In his studies of prisons and penal codes, mental hospitals and medicine, sexual conduct and sexuality, Foucault documented the domination, mostly very subtle, that bodies subjected to in the discipline of modern institutions endure, day in and day out.[29] For example, the knowledge that we are nearly always being watched (by cameras in every store, police on the street, the boss at work, or the teacher at the front of the classroom)

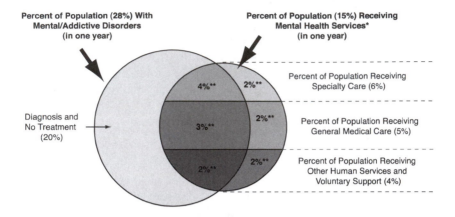

*   Due to rounding, it appears that 9 percent of the population has a diagnosis and receives treatment. The actual
    figure is closer to 8 percent, as stated in the text. It also appears that 6 percent of the population receives
    services but has no diagnosis, due to rounding. The actual total is 7 percent, as stated in the text.

** For those who use more than one sector of the service system, preferential assignment is to the most
    specialized level of mental health treatment in the system.

Figure 3.1. Annual Prevalence of Mental/Addictive Disorders and Services for
Adults
SOURCE: U.S. Department of Health and Human Services, *Mental Health: A Report of the Surgeon
General.* Rockville, MD: U.S. Department of Health and Human Services, Substance Abuse and Mental
Health Services Administration, Center for Mental Health Services, National Institutes of Health,
National Institute of Mental Health, 1999, p. 76.

makes us conform our bodies to what these sources of authority want of them.
Foucault called this phenomenon "surveillance." Even buildings and public places
are constructed to enhance surveillance, and in this way, authority is depersonalized
and made constant, literally built in. Individuals who slouch in their seats or smoke
cigarettes are engaged in mild forms of resistance to body discipline, but such random, individual acts are unlikely to alter body-discipline's entrenched place in
postmodern life.

Foucault also studied the human sciences, and found them, too, to be participants in the disciplining of modern bodies. The U.S. Census is an example of what
Foucault had in mind. It is a fully public exercise in surveillance. Every ten years,
government-employed social scientists and their minions gather data on the entire
population of the United States: how many people are there? Where do they live?
How do they live? As the public relations campaign for the year 2000 Census emphasized, this information is used to distribute public monies and plan public projects, and it is also used to apportion political districts. For many social scientists, it
is the bread in their bread and butter because without the census, they would have

no data to analyze and thus no reason for existence. Standardized information is the lifeblood of both social science and the governments that social science often serves. Refusing to have one's head counted is punishable by law.

Probably the most intrusive form of body manipulation is not, however, as yet fully realized. The Human Genome Project is expected to soon complete the mapping of human DNA. Many of the specific genes have already been sold and patented for later proprietary use in the development of "gene therapies." The cloning of plants and, to a much lesser extent, animals is already a common practice. Genetically engineered foods are a daily staple for millions of consumers. In addition, research on human "stem cells," the rudiments of all other cells, portends in vitro technologies that can produce replacement human organs and tissues. Indeed, advancements in microbiology are so rapid that it has been observed that scientists learned more about human biology in the last decade of the twentieth century than in all previous human history. However, although the *Brave New World*'s picture of an engineered population is a near technical possibility, it is not a social probability. For ethical reasons, it is unlikely that this revolutionary understanding of human genetics will produce Huxleyesque human cloning and inaugurate a society of "alphas," "betas," and "gammas," social classes bioengineered to function happily in a specific occupational strata.

Huxley's "soma" dependent society is, however, an everyday reality in rich nations such as the United States. In the United States, people are financially able to routinely consume expensive prescription medications as well as the nonprescriptions alternatives, such as herbals. Although such agents are ingested for specific purposes, conceived as a whole, they indicate the routine nature of today's bioengineered life. In *Brave New World,* the fruits of social science also stand in back of Huxley's picture of soma-like social distractions, such as his fictional complex games "Centrifugal Bumble Puppy," "Obstacle Golf," and, for the privileged classes, the possibility of worldwide travel in search of amusement. In our world, we have video games, enhanced television, and Club Med. In *Brave New World,* socially expected sexual promiscuity is also a factor contributing to popular contentment. In our world, the percentage of American girls between the ages of 15 and 19 who have had sexual intercourse rose from 29 percent in 1970 to 50 percent in 1995; among college freshman in 1998, 40 percent agreed that "if two people really like each other, it's all right for them to have sex even if they've known each other for a very short time."[30] Furthermore, it is estimated that Americans spend $9 billion per year on pornography, with the number of annual hard-core pornographic video rentals increasing from 75 million in 1985 to 686 million in 1998.[31] Like "soma," soma substitutes are taken-for-granted aspects of postmodern culture.

The situation elsewhere in the world is, of course, markedly different. Due to worldwide inequality, a large proportion of humanity is blocked from access to even inexpensive, basic, and life-saving medicines. Technology-based amusements, from Disney World to play stations, are also rare, and sexual activity takes on an entirely different meaning, for example, in AIDS-ravaged Africa. Of the 14 million people worldwide who have died of AIDS, 11 million have been Africans, and a quarter of these were children. In Botswana, for example, it is estimated that 64 percent of deaths occurring before the age of 5 are the result of AIDS; in South Africa and Zimbabwe, the rate is 50 percent.[32] But in postmodern culture, the materially well off live in a technological bubble of satisfying amusements, and when nonamusing experiences intrude, there is access to a panoply of biomedical quick fixes. We even have medications for Alzheimer's disease in our pets. The significance of our dependence on soma and soma-like social distractions can easily be imagined. As a sociological experiment, imagine removing from our culture all coffee, tea, tobacco, herbal and vitamin supplements, beer, wine, liquor, cocaine and cocaine derivatives (e.g., crack), and marijuana. Next, eliminate television, radio, amusement parks, movie theaters, home videos, and professional sports. Finally, institute and enforce a ban on pre- and extramarital sexual relations and eliminate the Internet as well as old-fashioned pornography. Would social order continue under such hypothesized conditions? How long would it take for the masses to rise up and reconstitute a society hooked on drugs and entertaining distractions? I must confess that this book would simply not exist without its author's steady consumption of nicotine delivery systems (i.e., cigarettes).

Power and Agency

Beyond our reactions through our emotions and bodies, our private worlds also involve actions toward the world. The ability to act toward the world is our agency. If we assume that everyone is born with and to some degree retains agency (i.e., the power to act and not just react; the power to slouch, as it were, when upright attention is implicitly demanded), how much power do individuals in this society have? No one is thoroughly powerless or completely omnipotent, but what are the personal ramifications of relative powerlessness and relative omnipotence? Moreover, do individuals have enough power to make possible the transformation of society?

The vast *asymmetrical relations* of power that characterize everyday life are in part the result of material inequalities. In the United States, the richest 1 percent of the population owns roughly 50 percent of the total financial wealth of the society, the top 5 percent own roughly 70 percent, and the richest 10 percent own about 90 percent of the wealth.[33] By "wealth" I mean society's capital or financial assets, measured primarily by the ownership of stocks, bonds, and real estate and leaving out equity in owner-occupied housing and in automobiles. As one observer notes, "it is exaggerating only slightly to say that the poor have no net assets, the middle class owns its homes and has modest retirement accounts, and the rich own everything else."[34] The single richest person in the United States, Bill Gates, owned in 1999 roughly 15 percent of the Microsoft Corporation, which gave him more wealth than the poorest 100 million Americans.[35] Most of these least-wealthy 100 million Americans themselves own very little if they own anything at all. Even among them, there exist important disparities. Research by the American sociologists Melvin Oliver and Thomas Shapiro documents the enormous disparities between whites' and blacks' ownership of wealth.[36] In 1988, white households had a median net worth of $43,800, but the figure for black households was only $3,700.[37] Disparities such as this exist between many groups.[38]

Income is also unequally distributed, although less so than is wealth. "Income" is money that people earn, not the value of what they own. In the United States, income is more unequally distributed than in any other of the world's rich societies.[39] In 1997, the top fifth of the population earned 47.2 percent of the total income while the bottom fifth earned just 4.2 percent of the total income. There are more than 30 million people who live below the meager and inadequately defined official standard for poverty, where, for example, a family of four in 1999 was impoverished if they earned less than $17,050 per year.[40] In the same year, an even larger number of American citizens, roughly 44 million, had no medical insurance.[41] Even in the richest society in human history, hunger and homelessness are not unknown.

Facts such as these are relatively familiar to most Americans. What is less well appreciated, perhaps, is how material inequality shapes the distribution of power and how this affects people's sense of themselves, their identity, and their personal well-being.[42] For example, sociologists have long identified relative powerlessness as a major cause of social and individual pathologies, such as criminal behavior, poor educational attainment, and ill health. People at the bottom of society's ladder live in a state of habitual low-intensity fear and anxiety because they are often denied access to secure, stable, respected, and well-paying jobs; denied the security that comes from ownership of assets that can cushion unexpected hard times; denied a socially acceptable, easy-to-use, publicly provided "safety net" when in dire need of assistance; denied the peace of mind that comes from safe neighborhoods and schools; and they are often unable to purchase quality education, entertainment, and leisure. These people are forced to surrender to leveled aspirations in life, are made to feel relatively inferior to others who never experience such conditions, and suffer the physical and psychological affects of cultural deprivation and social isolation.[43] They are, individually, relatively incapable, that is, relatively powerless, to change their distinct circumstances. It is no wonder that state-sanctioned lotteries, which are primarily in the business of selling false hope, prey on this segment of the U.S. population.[44]

One might imagine that this is a description of life in the most impoverished American "inner city" neighborhood: the stereotypical ghetto, barrio, or slum.[45] As countless sociological studies have documented, it is just that, but it is also a description of how many Americans feel about their lives, even if only vaguely perceived.[46] Indeed, it is perhaps a description of how most people in all the world feel about their lives, if they are lucky enough to have time for such reflection. The bottom of the ladder is, after all, a relative experience. It can and does include almost everyone because most people value the lives led by the world's materially very rich, and we measure ourselves by this ultimate and perpetually expanding standard. Just as people in the world's poorest countries wish to have their Big Mac and Coca Cola, middle-class Americans wish to have their children attend Harvard or Stanford and vacation on Martha's Vineyard or the French Rivera. Given that most American's have little wealth and income relative to those whose lifestyles they wish to emulate, it is not surprising that most people carry in them at least a vague sense of insecurity and relative deprivation that matches their credit card debits and college tuition bills. Given that most Americans exercise few of their political rights by voting, lobbying their representatives, or joining protests, it is not surprising that they should feel trapped at their particular "level" or that they should feel relatively powerless before the prevailing stratification of society.

Like the material power rooted in wealth and income, symbolic power, such as prestige or honor, is also highly unequally distributed in society. To whom do we defer and who defers to us? Which occupations are we proud to announce when asked, "What do you do?" and how many people occupy those occupations? In postmodern culture, the most important form of symbolic power is conveyed through the mass media, which creates a hyperreality that overshadows all other everyday realities. Any consideration of agency and power in postmodern culture must deal with hyperreality.

Lacking firm ground for emotional development and the agency for meaningful action in the real world of their real lives, the crowds that populate the public square of today's postmodern society look and act much as they are depicted in Orwell's novel—except that things possibly are worse than Orwell imagined. Whereas Orwell gave us the image of the "telescreen," which is both omnipresent and capable of looking into private lives and reading inner thoughts based on analysis of facial expressions, postmodern people, in contrast, look into television and find there what our expressions should be, what our inner thoughts are, and live in its world as though its lives were our lives.

According to the cultural critic Neil Postman, television is a form of "amusing ourselves to death."[47] Postman explicitly prefers Huxley to Orwell because he believes that televison is more like soma than surveillance. We jeer at images of Iraqis and cheer the use of smart bombs, but no one is truly upset; it is more analogous to cheering for Hollywood good guys and against Hollywood villains. In Ohio, Jerry Springer can be seriously courted as a potential candidate for the United States Senate because he is recognized by name and face as a television celebrity, and name recognition is half the battle in politics. The reverse is also possible: we all know who "Monica" is, and that is why she was an attractive figure for use in Jenny Craig commercials. Winning Academy Awards is on a par with being elected President of the United States, which is akin to winning the Academy Award for Best Presidential Candidate of a Major Party. Iraqis, Monica, the Titanic, Jerry Springer, or George W. Bush (a.k.a. G-Dubya) all occupy a quantitatively similar place in our wired hearts and minds. The real workings of power and knowledge and the real questions of politics, broadly construed, are homeless for those invested in a television world. But we are entertained, and that is what is important.

Like Postman, this is the way that Jean Baudrillard, a French sociologist and philosopher, analyzes postmodern culture. Indeed, Baudrillard coined the term *hyperreality*. In books such as *America* and *The Gulf War Did Not Take Place,* Baudrillard paints a picture of a social world dominated by hyper— or, roughly, television reality, in which what happens on television and in similar electronic media is more real than reality itself.[48] To exist, it has to be on television; to be meaningful, it has to be an image. To dominate the social world, this simulated reality must be felt as more meaningful than what is experienced in everyday life. For this to be true, individuals must be deluded and overwhelmed by what earlier theorists reflecting on the advent of Hollywood called the "mass deception" of "the culture industry."[49] For Baudrillard, we are thoroughly along the road to Oz, from modern to postmodern society, from real places to no place, and from Disney World to Celebration, Florida, a planned community owned and managed by the Disney Corporation as a model utopia.[50] In Baudrillard's view, we are but theme-park visitors in our own self-made (dys)utopian lives.

"Did the Gulf War happen?" asks Baudrillard. No. What actually happened in the desert between Kuwait, Saudi Arabia, and Iraq was not a war, not in the usual sense of opposing combatants engaged in sustained military conflict, although hundreds of thousands of people were purposely killed there by means of military power. "Desert Storm," however, did happen, but only on television and in the minds and souls of its consumers the world-over. Here, there was no actual human death, just technological marvels put in the service of dramatic entertainment and, secondarily, opaque foreign policy objectives. "What is America?" asks this latter-day

Alexis de Tocqueville. It is "the only remaining primitive society," without memory, without tradition, without history, and without individuals in any recognizable sense but flush with "TV Heritage," a theme for everything, and mass-produced chicken products in every pot.[51] For Baudrillard, America is the first postmodern society because it is the most far along in its clever debasement of the individual and of human life itself. Bread and circuses never looked or felt this good. America is seductive. It is what "utopia" means today.

Baudrillard intentionally exaggerates. He is presenting a "sidereal" picture of "astral" America designed to capture the excesses of postmodern culture. But nearly every leading sociological theorist lists abuses wrought routinely on the minds and bodies of everyday people. For Jurgen Habermas, the sociologist, philosopher, and Germany's leading contemporary intellectual figure, it is the "colonization of the lifeworld," in which money and power come to distort and confuse interpersonal relations.[52] For American sociologist George Ritzer, it is the "McDonaldization of society" that renders our lives unfree and meaningless components of a fast-food society.[53] For Anthony Giddens, the British sociologist and director of the London School of Economics and Political Science, it is the "runaway world" of social institutions that threatens to exceed our capacity to control and direct our collective fate and that also leaves our personal worlds vulnerable to falling through innumerable self-made cracks.[54] In any case, the picture painted by today's leading sociologists is bleak for the individual.

This leaves us with our last question, the question of social transformation. Do individuals today possess enough agency to engage in effective social change? Huxley's and Orwell's competing pictures are dystopian because they suggest the means by which utopian aspirations are thwarted and contained. Actually, it is a bit more complicated. In each work, the utopia itself is problematic. Is the total domination of nature through science, including our own nature. Is $2 + 2 = 4$ sufficient grounds for an intellectually led wholesale revolution of society? What, after all, do we aspire to as a people? What type of knowledge is necessary to realize our aspirations? Do we really want our lives to resemble Disneyland? If not, what is it that we want?

In his 1999 study, *The End of Utopia: Politics and Culture in an Age of Apathy,* the American intellectual historian Russell Jacoby argues that a significant factor in our contemporary disillusioned culture is the inability of would-be public intellectuals to offer a compelling vision of utopian possibilities.[55] In the aftermath of the universally condemned, Soviet-style communism, many of today's intellectuals, from both the political Right and the political Left, see no need for any type of dramatic, qualitative change in modern society. Many believe that we are at what Francis Fukuyama famously called "the end of history" in the sense that what we should want for the future is only more of what we already have. We are no longer aspiring to build a new and better world; we are only in the process of extending what exists. Politicians, for example, mirror this intellectual complacency because the difference between "compassionate conservatism" and calls for "universal health care" is at best slight. As such, we live in an age of political and cultural apathy, Jacoby argues, because we have already achieved what today's visionaries and public leaders regard as "utopia." In this situation, the question of utopian social transformation is moot and is replaced by calls for more "multiculturalism," more "sustainable development," and other such watered-down buzzwords announcing the incremental extension of what already obtains. Utopia increasingly appears as a society in which every ethnic group is afforded equal opportunity to get online and busily trade stocks. With nothing inspirational before us, the question of revolutionary agency is also moot. There is no perceived need for it, so whether it exists or not is a meaningless question.

The picture of today's individual in postmodern society is one in which inner lives—embodied emotions and aspirations—are fitted to objective realities—powerlessness in a mass society and a disillusioning culture dominated by cynicism. This is the normal situation for both proles and for Winston Smiths, as it were, for both consumers and producers of postmodern society. The continuation of this culture depends on our pseudo-willful, self-medicated, self-disciplined daily participation in our own small fragment of the whole. Postmodernity depends on this type of daily acquiescence. For example, even when we are aware of the facts presented in Chapter 2, it seems impossible as a practical matter to relate them to the routines of daily life. We know that choosing paper or plastic at the grocery store is too small an act to affect the course of history. We know, and are correct in perceiving, that choosing Candidate A or Candidate B will do little to shift the political direction of our mass democracy. We know, and are correct in perceiving, that these and other issues are very complicated and that others probably know better than we the relevant facts. In this situation, we feel that it probably makes more sense for us to suppress the panicky anxiety and fear that results from a robust appreciation of our dystopian situation and to adopt a cynical attitude toward the system that is itself guided day in and day out by cynicism.

Is There No Way Out?

Before leaving this survey of the small picture, I conclude with an example of a specific person's method for resisting postmodernity. The American sociologist Jackie Orr has offered what she calls an "ambivalent gift," essentially the story of her personal experience with "panic disorder" and her struggle to understand this experience in terms of the cynical society and irrational culture that stands behind it.[56] While panic disorder is usually conceived and treated as a psychological or emotional problem, Orr's "Theory on the Market: Panic, Incorporating" appeared in the journal *Social Problems* and is properly understood as a prescription for radical social change.

Orr lists the symptoms of panic disorder: "shortness of breath or smothering sensations, choking, palpitations or accelerated heart rate, chest pain or discomfort, sweating, dizziness, unsteady feelings or fainting, nausea, depersonalization or derealization, numbness or tingling sensations, flushes or chills, trembling or shaking, fear of dying, and fear of going crazy or doing something uncontrolled."[57] She also describes her interaction with a daytime talk show dedicated to the discussion of panic disorder, tells of her brushes with street crime, pictures herself holding a gun, describes her own sometimes odd behavior, and tells about her participation in experimental trials for antidepressant drugs. In her mid-20s, living in Boston, Orr is prescribed UpJohn Corporation's Xanax® to treat her symptoms.

But in her life as in her text, Orr is not satisfied to merely treat the symptoms of panic disorder; she aims to uncover its social and cultural causes. Of "liquid capitalism," as she calls it, Orr writes,

> Value becomes incorporated, really, into a new social order of words and things (ex)changed within a high-density, low-frequency, instant-cash, fine-tuned, federally-expressed, safely-sexed, user-friendly, neural-networked, home-videoed, prime-time, live-via-satellite experience of everyday life.[58]

Of UpJohn Corporation's "Worldwide Panic Project," company-funded research involving "2,000 research subjects in 15 countries" and designed to win FDA approval for Xanax as a treatment for panic disorder, Orr argues that it rendered "women-bodies as a secure, because we're panicked, site for pharmaceutical profits" and contributed to the same "circulation" of women's bodies as objects of value in liquid capitalism that characterized Calvin Klein's contractual insistence that Jose Borain maintain her "weight, hair style and color and all other features of . . . physiognomy as they are now or in such other form as Calvin Klein may from time to time reasonably request."[59] For Orr, panic disorder and its medical treatment are in such ways intimately connected to the commodification and scientific administration of bodies in postmodern times. In this view, Xanax looks like soma and UpJohn Corporation like Big Brother.

Orr took Xanax for relief from her debilitating symptoms, but she also wrote "Theory on the Market." In the former, she was engaged in a desperate attempt to survive with mind and body intact. In the latter, she was engaged in a desperate attempt to theorize the history and society that made for her isolated, but hardly unique, problem. She writes,

> In pursuing the recognizably sociological project of weaving autobiography and history, of investigating the complex cultural text(ure)s of individual consciousness and social structures, I am also trying to do something more. Or less. In contrast to most sociological techniques of storytelling, I am interested in finding a practice of writing that evokes the political imperative, but also the *impossibility* of writing our social bodies in relation of their multiple levels of determination.[60]

In this, Orr links her account to the sociological imagination (the reflexive conceptualization of history, biography, and society), announces her preference for critical theory (the evoking the political imperative), and highlights what is perhaps the central limitation of sociology as critical theory (the impossibility of writing our own cure for our social bodies). Orr is engaged in a literary struggle for meaning in postmodern times, to clarify the source of her damaged life, and therein render the combatants in the struggle open for public scrutiny. Her "collage essay," as she calls it, is a perfect expression of what, in postmodern culture, it looks and feels like to possess and put to good use the sociological imagination.

Orr is right to emphasize that the mere possession of the sociological imagination cannot prevent one from being scared to death. The sociological imagination is an ambivalent gift. It cannot promise a cure for any particular damaged life. Orr asks, "Is it possible to resist with any effect?"[61] With regard to the big as well as the small picture, this is the question of our times.

Notes

1. Stjepan G. Mestrovic, *Postemotional Society,* with a foreword by David Riesman (Thousand Oaks, C.A.: Sage, 1997), 162.
2. Aldous Huxley, *Brave New World* (Garden City, N.Y.: Doubleday, 1932).
3. George Orwell, *1984* (New York: Harcourt Brace Jovanovich, 1949).
4. "Oceania" includes far more territory than "airstrip one" (England). Orwell clearly intended for Oceania to represent the Anglo-American power bloc or what would become NATO. By describing England as an "airstrip," Orwell was underscoring its post-World War II political weakness vis-à-vis the enormous strength of the United States, which in effect used the British Isles in World War II as merely an unsinkable airstrip. It is ironic, then, that most people assume Orwell's novel depicts life in a communist society when in fact it depicts totalitarianism in the West. The main story may be set in London, but the novel's direct relevance for the United States is clearly established.
5. See abcnews.com/onair/closerlook/wnt_000403_cl_drugs_feature.html.
6. William J. Bennett, *The Index of Leading Cultural Indicators* (New York: Broadway, 1999), 229.
7. C. Wright Mills, *The Sociological Imagination* (Oxford, U.K.: Oxford University Press, 1959), 167.

8. See Chap. 2 of *Mental Health: A Report of the Surgeon General* (U.S. Department of Health and Human Services, 1999), "The Fundamentals of Mental Health and Mental Illness" section titled "Epidemiology of Mental Illness," p. 2, which can be viewed online at www.surgeongeneral.gov/library.

9. See abcnews.go.com/worldnewstonight/poll000410.html. These results are from a 15-17 Mar. 2000 random national telephone survey of 1,027 adults, with a margin of error of +/– 3 points. Of the respondents, 15 percent said that they felt really depressed at least once per week, while 17 percent felt really depressed at least once per month. Of the women respondents, 16 percent reported using antidepressants in contrast with 8 percent of men. Similarly, 30 percent of women knew a friend or close relative who used antidepressant medication, while only 19 percent of men did.

10. Immanuel Kant, "What is Enlightenment?," in *Kant,* ed. Gabriele Rabel (1784; reprint, Oxford, U.K.: Clarendon Press, 1963), 140.

11. See George M. Fredrickson, *White Supremacy: A Comparative Study in American and South African History* (New York: Oxford University Press, 1981).

12. See The Institute for Social Research, *Aspects of Sociology* (1956; reprint, Boston: Beacon, 1972), with a preface by Max Horkheimer and Theodor W. Adorno, especially Chapter 3, "The Individual," 37-53. Also see the many works of Norbert Elias, including his masterwork, *The Civilizing Process* (1939; reprint, Oxford, U.K.: Blackwell, 1994).

13. Mills, *The Sociological Imagination,* 132-42.

14. Adrienne Rich, *Of Women Born,* 2d ed. (New York: Norton, 1985).

15. See Hannah Arendt, *Eichmann in Jerusalem: A Report on the Banality of Evil* (New York: Viking, 1963).

16. Stanley Milgram, *Obedience to Authority: An Experimental View* (New York: Harper & Row, 1969). Note that the actual experiments took place from 1960 to 1963.

17. But see Milgram's response to his critics in *Obedience to Authority,* 193-202.

18. Mestrovic, *Postemotional Society,* 162.

19. Arlie Russell Hochschild, *The Managed Heart: On the Commercialization of Human Feeling* (Berkeley: University of California Press, 1983).

20. See George Ritzer, *Enchanting a Disenchanted World* (Thousand Oaks, C.A.: Pine Forge Press, 1999).

21. See Maude Falcone, "Dystopian Elements in Richard Rorty's Liberal Utopia," (Master's thesis, Michigan State University, 1997). A revised version of this thesis appears in Steven P. Dandaneau and Maude Falcone, *A Wrong Life: Studies in Lifeworld-Grounded Critical Theory* (Greenwich, C.T.: JAI Press, 1998), 195-235.

22. See Tony Walker, ed., *The Mourning of Diana* (Oxford, U.K.: Berg Press, 1999) and Jim McGuiran, "British Identity and 'The People's Princess,' " *The Sociological Review* 48 (Feb. 2000): 1-18.

23. Bennett, *The Index of Leading Cultural Indicators,* 39.

24. Data from the 1999 Eli Lilly and Company Annual Report, which can be viewed online at www.lilly.com/financial/index.html. See also www.prozac.com/general.html and abcnews.go.com/sections/dailynews/ssri000524.html.

25. Data are from the 1999 Pfizer, Inc.'s fourth quarter earnings statement and the 18 Apr. 2000 first quarter earnings release. See www.pfizer.com.

26. See www.viagra.com. This Web page is maintained by Pfizer, Inc.

27. Bennett, *The Index of Leading Cultural Indicators,* 36.

28. See "The March Almanac," in *The Atlantic Monthly,* March 2000, 16.

29. See especially Michel Foucault, *Madness and Civilization: A History of Insanity in the Age of Reason* (New York: Vintage, 1965), *The Order of Things: An Archeology of the Human Sciences* (New York: Vintage, 1966), *The Birth of the Clinic: An Archaeology of Medical Perception* (New York:

Vintage, 1975), *Discipline and Punish: The Birth of the Prison* (New York: Vintage, 1979), and *The History of Sexuality, Volume I, An Introduction* (New York: Vintage, 1980).

30. Bennett, *The Index of Leading Cultural Indicators,* 137-8.

31. Ibid., 166-7.

32. See Janet Mukway, "The AIDS Emergency," in *The Progress of Nations 1999,* which can be viewed online at www.uncef.org/pon99.

33. See Chuck Collins, Chris Hartman, and Holly Sklar, *Divided Decade: Economic Disparity at the Century's Turn* (Boston: United for a Fair Economy, 1999), 3. This also can be viewed online at www.stw.org.

34. Frank Ackerman, "The Distribution of Wealth and Power: An Overview Essay," *The Political Economy of Inequality,* eds. Frank Ackerman, Neva R. Goodwin, Laurie Doughterty, and Kevin Gallagher (Washington, D.C.: Island Press, 2000), 34.

35. See Daniel Kadlec, "Betting with Bill," *Time,* 15 Nov. 1999, 122.

36. Melvin L. Oliver and Thomas M. Shapiro, *Black Wealth/White Wealth: A New Perspective on Racial Inequality* (New York: Routledge, 1995).

37. Ibid., 86. See also Dalton Conley, *Being Black, Living in the Red: Race, Wealth and Social Policy in America* (Berkeley: University of California Press, 1999).

38. See Norman R. Yetman, ed., *Majority and Minority: The Dynamics of Race and Ethnicity in American Life,* 6th ed. (Boston: Allyn & Bacon, 1999).

39. See Kwan S. Kim, "Income Distribution and Poverty: An Interregional Comparison," in *The Political Economy of Inequality,* eds. Frank Ackerman, Neva R. Goodwin, Laurie Dougherty, and Kevin Gallagher (Washington, D.C.: Island Press, 2000), 306.

40. See U.S. Census Bureau, *The Statistical Abstract of the United States: 1999,* 119th ed. (Washington, D.C.: 1999), 484, table no. 762. See www.census.gov for current figures.

41. Collins, Hartman, and Sklar, *Divided Decade,* 10.

42. In addition to the sources cited immediately above, see William Ryan, *Blaming the Victim,* rev. ed. (New York: Vintage, 1976).

43. See William Julius Wilson, *When Work Disappears: The World of the New Urban Poor* (New York: Knoft, 1996).

44. See David Nibert, *Hitting the Lottery Jackpot: Government and the Taxing of Dreams* (New York: Monthly Review Press, 2000).

45. See Paul A. Jargowsky, *Poverty and Place: Ghettos, Barrios, and the American City* (New York: Russell Sage, 1997).

46. See Barbara Ehrenreich, *Fear of Falling: The Inner Life of the Middle Class* (New York: Pantheon, 1989).

47. Neil Postman, *Amusing Ourselves to Death: Public Discourse in the Age of Show Business* (New York: Penguin, 1985).

48. Jean Baudrillard, *America* (London: Verso, 1988) and *The Gulf War Did Not Take Place* (Bloomington: Indiana University Press, 1995).

49. See Max Horkheimer and Theodor Adorno, *Dialectic of Enlightenment* (1947; reprint, New York: Herder & Herder, 1972).

50. See Andrew Ross, *The Celebration Chronicles: Life, Liberty, and the Pursuit of Property Values in Disney's New Town* (New York: Ballantine, 1999) and Douglas Frantz and Catherine Collins, *Celebration USA: Living in Disney's Brave New Town* (New York: Henry Holt and Company, 1999).

51. Baudrillard, *America,* 7.

52. See Jürgen Habermas, *Theory of Communicative Action,* vols. 1 and 2 (1981; reprint, Boston: Beacon, 1984 and 1987).

53. See George Ritzer, *The McDonaldization of Society,* (Thousand Oaks, C.A.: Pine Forge Press, 2000).

54. See Anthony Giddens, *The Consequences of Modernity* (Stanford, C.A.: Stanford University Press, 1990) and *Modernity and Self-Identity: Self and Society in the Late Modern Age* (Stanford, C.A.: Stanford University Press, 1991).

55. Russell Jacoby, *The End of Utopia* (New York: Basic Books, 1999).

56. Jackie Orr, "Theory on the Market: Panic, Incorporating," *Social Problems* 37 (1990): 460-84.

57. Ibid., 471-2.

58. Ibid., 474-5.

59. Ibid., 476, 461, and 483.

60. Ibid., 482.

61. Ibid., 483.

4

Toward a Postmodern Sociological Imagination and a Sociological Imagination for Postmodern Times

The constant warning against premature conclusions and foggy generalizations implies, unless properly qualified, a possible taboo against all thinking. If every thought has to be held in abeyance until it has been completely corroborated, no basic approach seems possible and we would limit ourselves to the level of mere symptoms.

—Max Horkheimer[1]

Fredric Jameson, one of America's leading contemporary social theorists, has described the central problem of living life in the postmodern era as "the loss of our ability to position ourselves within this space and to cognitively map it."[2] This is another way of saying that the central problem of postmodernity is the widespread absence of a sociological imagination, which is nothing if not a type of conceptual map, an inner global positioning system. Zygmunt Bauman, another leading contemporary social theorist, is more blunt. Bauman states, "The task of providing men and women with that 'sociological imagination' for which C. W. Mills . . . appealed years ago, has never been so important as it is now, under conditions of postmodernity."[3] The urgency is apparent: if we cannot position ourselves, we are lost in space. A third leading contemporary social theorist, Charles Lemert, has argued that "the sociological imagination deserves to be taken with deeper, analytical seriousness than it has been."[4] For Lemert, the nature of postmodernity "requires a more honest attention to the imagination than most have been willing to allow."[5]

As these statements suggest, Mills remains a vital point of reference for today's sociology. Indeed, several of Mills's books, including *The Sociological Imagination,* have been issued in new editions, and Mills' biography is again a subject of considerable interest.[6] This chapter—indeed, this book as a whole—participates in this effort to reintroduce Mills's significance for today. My aim in this particular chapter, however, is to answer Lemert's call for a deeper and more analytically serious rendering of the sociological imagination, but I also include some reflections on the significance of Mills's own life and times. As always, the overriding objective is to make accessible what is arguably the most needed form of mind in postmodern times and to demonstrate its value in terms of the orientation it provides to today's most pressing inner and outer problems.

While I rely principally on Mills's *The Sociological Imagination,* it is not inconsistent with Mills to recast his famous notion in light of the forty years of social change that has occurred since his original formulation.[7] In particular, it is crucial to further specify the meaning of "postmodernity," which Mills was among the first to foresee but which he lived only to witness at its inception. The sociological imagination today is essentially the same as it has always been, but our society and culture are more resistant to elucidation with the would be possessor of the sociological imagination more in need of the powers of imagination.

What Is the Sociological Imagination?

The "sociological imagination" is the name that Mills assigned to his distillation of the form of mind lying back of what he also called the classic tradition in modern social theory. The phrase "sociological imagination" is somewhat arbitrary. As Mills notes, "the term matters less than the idea."[8] Likewise, the phrase "classic tradition" refers only to "a definable and usable set of traditions" whose "essential feature is the concern with historical social structures."[9] As I have noted, this tradition includes the works of Max Weber, Karl Marx, Emile Durkheim, George Herbert Mead, and a host of similarly luminous nineteenth- and early twentieth-century social thinkers, many of whom did not regard themselves as sociologists. But, as Mills argued, all of these classic social thinkers shared a common set of basic questions: What is the structure of this particular society as a whole? Where does this society stand in human history? What varieties of men and women now prevail in this society and in this period?[10] Although none of these classic thinkers would have used precisely these words to describe their own way of thinking, these questions derived from the possession of a sociological imagination.

Let me provide a definition of the sociological imagination using Mills's own sophisticated language, which we shall momentarily unpack. Mills described the sociological imagination as a "form of . . . self-consciousness" or as a "quality of mind" that is firmly rooted in "an absorbed realization of social relativity and of the transformative power of history." Once realized, the sociological imagination is experienced as a "transvaluation of values," which is to say, as a type of secular epiphany, "a terrible lesson" but also, wrote Mills, "in many ways a magnificent one."[11] For Mills, this type of mind or self-consciousness is built around the "co-ordinate points" of "biography, history, and society," where each is integral to the definition of the others, and where, together, they form the crux of any worthwhile study of postmodern society.[12] In Mills's view, individuals, for example, are rendered "minute points of the intersections of biography and history within society,"[13] and all classical thinkers, no matter their respective differences in analyzing individuals, treated the problem of individual experience in terms of its social and historical determination. "By means of it," wrote Mills of the sociological imagination, "orientation to the present as history is sought"; the "classic focus," he stresses, is the human experience as it is given at the "historical level of reality."[14] For Mills, the sociological imagination is becoming the "common denominator" of the postmodern period, and given the disorientation that postmodern society systematically produces, it is the "most needed" cognitive map around.[15]

Let us pause and consider each key idea in turn. What, after all, does it mean to say that the sociological imagination is firmly rooted in "an absorbed realization of social relativity and of the transformative power of history"? The notion of "absorbed realization" suggests that Mills was speaking of an internal revolution in consciousness or the birth of a new self-consciousness. That what is being absorbed is "social relativity" leads to the conclusion that he must mean a self-understanding of our own social and historical genesis, our origin in our society and its culture in a particular time and place. To realize, for example, that what we think, believe in, feel, experience, eat, desire, and aspire to all have their source outside of us (e.g., in others, such as our parents and their native language; our school chums and the rules about how to behave in this or that situation that we learned to share and together enforce against others as well as ourselves; in the values commonly held in our community, which we learned and internalized as children) is to grasp our merely contingent or accidental place in the great and diverse scheme of things. We must remember the anthropological point that we are only a small instance of the human variety. This realization—that we are the "product" of a particular society and culture—can be experienced as "terrible" because it belies our ethnocentrism and learned value of individualism, but it can also be experienced as "magnificent" because it reveals the truth of our origin as an individual in the historical reality of postmodern society and culture.

The terms *society* and *culture* can be misleading in this context. "Society" refers to a set of social institutions that exist in an identifiable way over a period of time. When we say "British society," for example, we refer to Britain's political institutions (its parliament, monarchy, Whitehall, the Magna Carta, the Foreign Office, and the rest), educational institutions (its Eaton, Harrow, Cambridge, Oxford, and so forth), sports institutions (rugby, cricket, football), and so on, all interconnected and functioning together to form an identifiable whole. British society is an ongoing set of interconnected institutions that exist in time and place but that also, in our minds, exist as a conceptual entity, such that even if someone were to burn Parliament to the ground, the British Parliament would not be any less real or effective meeting next door at Westminster Abbey. As I have stressed, society is not a thing such as buildings made of brick and mortar. Indeed, there is no such thing as "Society," only *societies,* particular forms of collective life that humans themselves, in various times and places, have brought into existence, perpetuate, change, and sometimes let die or destroy.

The same is true for "culture," which refers to the values (abstract ideals) and norms (informal rules for behavior) as well as the material artifacts (e.g., a cricket wicket) of any particular way of life. While in reality societies and cultures always exist together, we distinguish them analytically because specific societies can share similar cultures (e.g., Britain and the United States, which both value democracy, have different institutions—Parliament vs. Congress—serving as a means to realize democratic political rule) and because societal and cultural change can occur independently of one another (e.g., the institution of term limits occurs without the value of democracy changing, or divorce rates rise without a loss in the value attached to marriage). And although, through socialization, we inevitably come to regard our way of life as "natural" and all others as strange, this ethnocentrism is false: one's own culture is not superior merely because it looks and feels naturally superior from the point of view of its socialized members. Social and cultural relativity are cornerstones of postmodern social science. Social and cultural diversity and social and cultural change are inherent characteristics of our human-made world.

To use the catchphrase "product of society" is, therefore, at best only a half-truth. To avoid this half-truth, Mills immediately incorporates the central insight of the most famous revolutionary critic of capitalism, Karl Marx, which is that humans make society in addition to being made by it. As Marx once put it,

Men [or, as we would say today, people] make history, but they do not make it just as they please; they do not make it under circumstances chosen by themselves, but under circumstances directly encountered, given and transmitted from the past.[16]

Although Marx conceded that "the tradition of all the dead generations weighs like a nightmare on the brain of the living," his overriding point, the point that Mills also wanted to stress, is that *people necessarily make history.*[17] Included in the scope and scale of history making is, of course, the building, maintenance, and revolution of human societies themselves. Since it remains true that humans are the product of society, Marx's insight is that humans are the product of human-made societies. Thus we are a self-formative species. Based on our observation and study of other species, it would appear that *homo sapiens* are unique in this regard. We are the only species that has a hand in making ourselves what we are.

The "absorbed realization of social relativity and the transformative power of history," said Mills, is experienced as a "transvaluation of values." Having doffed his cap to anthropology and to Marx, Mills now echoes the thought of the German philosopher Friedrich Nietzsche. The transvaluation of values, Nietzsche's insight, indicates that the values of our birth—which we come to regard and internalize (especially as children) as natural and from this initial ego- and ethnocentric attitude toward ourselves as superior to all others we later become aware of—this primary, originating, and unavoidable attitude, we discover in maturity as false. The apparent naturalness of ourselves, society, and culture is only an appearance, the by-product of each and every accidental birth and subsequent socialization into one or another way of life. In the absorption of this understanding, we also come to appreciate the utter ephemerality of what we previously thought collectively foundational and that constituted the bedrock of our own identity. Mills noted that, with the dawning of a sociological imagination, we realize that our "mentalities have swept only a series of limited orbits" and that it is then as if we were "suddenly awakened in a house with which [we] had only supposed [ourselves] to be familiar."[18] This is the moment of epiphany, when the terrible and magnificent lessons of the sociological imagination come home to roost.

Note that this epiphany has nothing to do with any type of transcendent spirituality and is, indeed, more nearly its opposite. The inner realization of this primarily Nietzschean insight overturns our sense of self as existentially whole and grounded. It places between us and ourselves a moment of critical reflection, and it is clearly the product of a society and culture in which, as Nietzsche famously said, "God is dead." Values that are transvaluated are thus values that we must choose or reject in the absence of divine or otherwise transcendent guidance. They are *our* values, and we must accept responsibility for them. Indeed, as Bauman contends, we must accept "responsibility for the responsibility" of making moral choices because "postmodernity is the moral person's bane and chance at the same time."[19] Cultural facts, like social facts, are not fate.

We have considered the meanings of Mills's phrases, "the absorption of social relativity," "the transformative power of history," and "the transvaluation of values." From such background understandings, we can now better appreciate why Mills's chosen coordinate points for sociological thinking are history, biography, and society, and why each is always already interrelated, codefining, and in need of continuous conceptual rearrangement.

Social and cultural reality (our reality) is never firmly fixed in time and space, nor is it readily willing to disclose itself to us. Society is shrouded in illusions of our own personal and collective making, such as in our common assumption that "it" is a naturally occurring thing. In the face of so much unavoidable artifice and semblance, we must, in effect, *dis*-cover society through the use of critical imagination.

Our minds are then tasked (as well as taxed) to mediate between myriad chosen points of reference. Those that present themselves as most promising are our own individual experience (bear in mind its historical and social determination), our society (bear in mind its historical nature and its particularity among the range of human societies that exist and that have existed), and the relation between the two in an ongoing reality of history making (although we must bear in mind that history making is historical; not all societies have had the power to shape the future that American society does, at present, possess). In actual empirical studies in the here and now of this or that feature of this or that society, the possessor of the sociological imagination will be called on to relate all things large and small, impersonal and intimate, particular and universal, "from considerations of an oil industry to studies of contemporary poetry," suggested Mills.[20] In other words, although we must attend to history, biography, and society, these would be empty mental categories if not filled in with the stuff of actual life, indeed, disciplined and driven by the content and meaning of real lives. Mills simply noted, "The sociological imagination enables us to grasp history and biography and the relations between the two within society. That is its task and its promise."[21] But what a task this is, especially today, deep into the postmodern epoch.

Postmodern Extremes

Although the notion of postmodernity is today quite common, Mills was ahead of his time when he introduced the idea in 1959. For him, the postmodern epoch was distinguished from the modern age by its self-realization that more and more science and technology does not produce more and more freedom and reason; that is, increased power over nature and over the practical problems that humans confront does not and has not led to utopia, as modern people once assumed it would. Instead, increases in rationality (i.e., Weber's "instrumental rationality") have led to a new type of dystopia of uniquely modern origin and making. When Mills talked about postmodern society and culture, he had in mind the extremes of what he called "the overdeveloped societies," the rise of "the cheerful robot," and the paradoxical preparation for collective suicide in an era of unprecedented history-making powers.

The concept of "overdeveloped society" is a critical concept; it makes a judgment. Mills himself felt that it was one of his "best notions" because it was meant in part to deflate modern society's own grandiose affection for itself as bigger and better.[22] It is also a concept that Mills used in conjunction with his terminology for the poor nations of the world, which he dubbed "the hungry nation bloc." When Mills was writing, there was an additional large-scale sector of the world, the communist countries (the so-called "Second World" lying between the First and Third Worlds), which are today, with the notable exceptions of China, North Korea, and Cuba, either nonexistent or no longer constituting a power bloc. The notion of overdeveloped society, then, refers to the fundamental nature of modern, Western societies and situates this societal type in relation to the rest of the world. It is Mills's critical alternative to the no less judgmental term, *First World*.

As we have already seen, postmodern society can be deemed overdeveloped in a number of ways. It is an ecologically unsustainable way of life. This Mills could only imagine, but today we need little imagination to conceive this reality. Postmodern societies are also overdeveloped in the sense that their abundance of material and symbolic power is selfishly consumed at the expense of the vast majority of the human population. This is an ethical formulation of the problem, which gains credence from the ethical and moral principles cherished by the members of overdeveloped societies themselves. Finally, postmodern societies can be viewed as overdeveloped in the sense that their accumulation of vast wealth has not produced the way of life originally intended. Many members of the rich societies feel overworked and overwhelmed by the proverbial "rat race" of their own making. They are furthermore disquieted, if not worse than that, by the perceived intrusion of science and technology into their lives. Protests against the practice of abortion, use of fetal tissue and live animals for medical research; profanity in Hollywood films and mass marketed popular music; the downgrading of religion practices (e.g., school prayer) and moral standards of all kinds; efforts to grow organic foods and to avoid the consumption of factory-farm meat products and genetically engineered food; protests

to contain if not eliminate the American tobacco industry and its hooked dependents— all form the basis for a marginal and growing rejection of the culture of contemporary rich societies. Many members of overdeveloped societies may be obese,
but they are not necessarily happy.

Two new political divisions are thus drawn. First, although animal rights activists and antiabortion protestors are usually viewed as hailing from the extreme political Left and political Right, respectively, when we view postmodern society as an
overdeveloped society, it becomes apparent that such groups have more in common
than even they realize. Both are social movements that, in the midst of a disillusioning culture, are fighting to protect the integrity of life, as they see it, from the intrusion of instrumental science. Both social movements oppose the realization of a
Huxleyian brave new world. Still, they are extreme movements with relatively small
percentages of the population actively involved in their various protests. Even if disquieted in their own lives by the issues raised by vocal minorities, most Americans
remain politically silent.

Second, in place of the now-defunct Cold War divide between the capitalist
West and the communist East, the world is divided between the overdeveloped nations of the North and the poor nations of the South. At the 1992 Rio Earth Summit,
for example, the richest of the rich nations, which act collectively as members of the
Group of 7 or G7, collided with the G-77, a group of so-called developing (but not
overdeveloped) nations. (By 2000, the G-77 had grown to 133 members, while the
G-7 had added Russia to form the G-8.) At Rio, as at every such meeting of the North
and South, the rich nations resisted an agreement calling for drastic reductions in
greenhouse gases, which would entail a dramatic revolution in their unsustainable
way of life. Likewise, the poor nations resisted curtailment of their own plans for industrialization, especially in the absence of G-7 sacrifices, since they wanted to enjoy the fruits of modern society and since they were not inclined to bear alone the
costs of First World cultural excess. Such large-scale, worldwide political conflict
is reminiscent not only of the Cold War but also of *1984*'s presentation of a never-
ending conflict between Oceania, Eastasia, and Eurasia. The key point for Orwell
was that, members of Oceania at least, viewed these conflicts only through the
highly distorted prism of Oceanic propaganda. Similarly, most Americans probably
do not understand the North-South conflict, or if they do, they view it only from the
perspective of the richest nation in the world, the North's inner sanctum.

My allusions to Huxley and Orwell in this context are not at all out of sync with
Mills's own assessment of the political situation in the United States at the end of the
1950s. Mills coined the term *cheerful robot* to direct attention to the underlying reason for America's confused political scene and global myopia. This concept refers
to the extreme opposite of the Enlightenment ideal of the "self-cultivating man and

woman; in short, the free and rational individual."[23] Toward the end of *The Sociological Imagination,* Mills wrote,

> The ultimate problem of freedom is the problem of the cheerful robot, and it arises in this form today because today it has become evident to us that *all* men do *not* naturally *want* to be free; that all men are not willing or not able, as the case may be, to exert themselves to acquire the reason that freedom requires.[24]

> We know of course that man can be turned into a robot, by chemical and psychiatric means, by steady coercion and by controlled environment; but also by random pressures and unplanned sequences of circumstances. But can he be made to want to become a cheerful and willing robot?[25]

Mills left this question open, but he laid the greatest responsibility for the seemingly automatic, cheery mindlessness common in the mass democracies of the world at the feet of people just like himself—"the social scientists of the rich societies"—who, he thought, were committing "the greatest human default . . . by privileged men in our times" in their collective failure to even pose the trend toward the cheerful robot as a central "cultural and political question."[26]

Mills, of course, did not participate in this intellectual default. He posited indifference and uneasiness as the most prevalent psychological characteristics of his day, but he also knew that, if left unabated, these tendencies could result in the experience of an extreme panic and apathy, tending toward a "deadly unspecified malaise."[27] Many contemporary students of postmodern society readily agree; they, too, fear the ascendency of the cheerful robot in nearly the exact terms that Mills originally set out.

The Canadian social theorists Arthur Kroker, Marilouise Kroker, and David Cook provide one useful example. In their 1989 book *The Panic Encyclopedia,* Kroker, Kroker, and Cook asserted that "panic is the key psychological mood of postmodern culture."[28] They wrote,

> [In postmodern times], panic has the reverse meaning of its classical sense. In antiquity, the appearance of the god *Pan* meant a moment of arrest, a sudden calm, a rupture-point between frenzy and reflection. Not though in the postmodern condition. Just like the reversal of classical kynicism (philosophy from below) into postmodern cynicism (for the ruling elites) before it, the classical meaning of panic has now disappeared into its opposite sense.
>
> In the postmodern scene, panic signifies a twofold free-fall: the disappearance of *external* standards of public conduct when the social itself becomes a transparent field of a cynical power; and the dissolution of the *internal* foundations of identity

(the disappearing ego as the victory sign of postmodernism) when the self is transformed into an empty screen of an exhausted, but hyper-technical, culture.[29]

In this view, panic is the dominant characteristic of postmodern society because,
since Mills's day, external standards of public conduct (such as that provided by stable norms and an effective democratic polity) and the internal foundations of individuality (such as that provided for children in stable families) have been overwhelmed by the effects of a frenzied, hyper-fast paced, hyper-technical culture
(such as exemplified by television and video games), which in the end results in people who are themselves "empty screens." This is a picture of advanced, highly technological, postmodern dystopia, a far cry from the classic ideal of individuality.

Mills himself was worried that the very fact of the "overwhelming accumulation of technical gadgets" would itself hide "the ascendency among us of The Cheerful Robot."[30] In other words, he worried that we would mistake technological advancement (e.g., widespread personal computing) as an "index of human quality
and cultural progress."[31] But, explained Mills, "those who use these devices do not
understand them; those who invent them do not understand much else."[32] Today,
when virtual reality becomes more real than real, the result for the individual is dissolution into the screen. Freedom, we are told, is the freedom to sit in front of a computer screen and surf the Net. Or, as a result of technological advancement, freedom
is refined to mean carrying the computer screen in our palm so that we can look into it
whenever we wish. Rarely are we told why we should want to do this or how mere access to computerized information entails a better life. The digital revolution is instead relentlessly advanced as a value in itself and often mindlessly accepted in these
terms.

Kroker, Kroker, and Cook also mention "cynicism." What is this cynicism?
Normally we think of cynicism as an attitude that reduces all claims to transcendent
truth and meaning to a perceived basis in someone's immediate self-interest. For the
cynic, there is no ideal that is not, in truth, a thinly veiled attempt at manipulation.
Kroker, Kroker, and Cook associate this attitude with the ruling elite of postmodern
societies, whom they suggest knowingly use the public realm as a means only to further their rule through the systematic manipulation of social life. Whereas in antiq-
uity, the Greek philosopher Diogenes's "kynicism" was a protest for plain honesty
and truth against the hubris and hypocrisy of the elites of his day, in postmodern
times, Diogenes's term for his philosophy "from below" has come to mean its opposite. Honesty and truth are thought quaint characteristics that "everyone knows" will
not get you very far. In his impeachment and Senate trial, President Clinton apparently benefited from this popular cynicism because the majority of Americans were
in favor of excusing his evident dishonesty as behavior not unexpected by holders of

high political office, even the highest office. "I never had sex with that woman, Ms. Lewinsky," the President of the United States said to a bank of television cameras, jaw firmly set.

Indeed, in the German philosopher Peter Sloterdijk's 1983 formulation, today's cynicism is a "hard-boiled, shadowy cleverness" that "no longer feels affected by any critique." Today's cynicism is "reflexively buffered" from criticism because, for Sloterdijk, the cynical are, as it were, cynical about their being cynical.[33] This is regarded as what it means to be enlightened, to know that one's consciousness is riddled with falsehood and self-deception but not to care or let this self-knowledge get in the way of participating in the status quo. In this sense, President Clinton is again a good example. In defining his critics as merely political opponents out to derail his policy agenda, Clinton rendered his bald-faced lying good political gamesmanship. Sharing his basic cynicism, the majority of the American public agreed that, although the president was a liar, he was pretty good at—indeed, better than—the liars who were his opponents. "It depends on what you mean by 'is,' " said the president.

In *The Power Elite,* Mills wrote, "Blessed are the cynical for they have what it takes to succeed."[34] Succeed at what? For Mills, postmodern society concentrates unprecedented power in the hands of those few who, by virtue of their occupancy of the command positions in the vast bureaucracies of postmodern society, can set the general course of history making for all humankind. In particular, he identified the military, government, and large corporations as the sites for the most influential and coordinated forms of power, but leaders of other large-scale organizations (e.g., universities, labor unions, television networks) are also viewed as possessing extraordinary power. For what purpose, though, would this extraordinary power be used? There are numerous answers for each organizational type. For corporations, the point of the game is to maximize profits for as long as possible. For governments, there is sovereignty and legitimacy to be maintained and spheres of influence that require cultivation in competition with other nations. Labor unions seek increased membership, and for this membership—the "rank and file"—they seek increased wages and benefits and improved working conditions. Writing at the height of the Cold War, however, Mills maintained that the most significant use of modern society's vast power was its mindless and irresponsible preparation for World War III, which he, and of course, not he alone, regarded as the most extreme form of cynicism ever acted out on the stage of human history. At the same time that Mills was writing *The Sociological Imagination,* he was also writing the ironically titled, *The Causes of World War Three* (1958).

It is hard to imagine a better way to wed the problem of the overdeveloped society and the problem of the cheerful robot than in terms of the cynical use of nuclear power as a means to threaten the very continuation of human—and the better part of natural—history. Just as postmodern society's claim to superiority over other types of human society is belied by the potential actuality of this threat, so too, does its continuation in the form now of both nuclear and ecological holocaust condemn us to again ratify the dismal assessment of the prevailing state of reason and freedom.

Only, things are worse. These past forty years were a time when many did in fact seek to wrest control of the means of history making from elites, which they did, in fact, come to regard as cynical and dangerous. Mills himself, if only posthumously, became a hero and an inspiration for many average people dedicated to revolutionary social change. Despite the notable sound and fury produced by the famous generation of the 1960s, the facts of the big and small picture remain as they are. Is it any wonder, then, that 76 percent of Americans in 1964 said that their government could be trusted all or most of the time, whereas by 1996, this same figure had dropped to 27 percent.[35] These facts, too, must be gathered up into a sociological imagination. It is important to learn from the past if there is any hope of redeeming its promise.

Looking Back on Mills

What is the structure of our particular society as a whole? Where does it stand in human history? What varieties of people now prevail? These remain the key questions for today. The motivation to go on in this study should now be clear. Imagine if it were otherwise. Imagine the person who as quickly puts out of mind the significance of human population trends and species extinction as he or she does the latest factoid blurring past on the evening news. Imagine the person indifferent to his or her own future and the future of his or her unborn children and grandchildren, not to mention the whole of the human experience in these times. Or, conversely, imagine the person so attuned to the meaning of what has been stated thus far that he or she is struck by a panic that paralyzes and turns instead to an equally false cynicism, perhaps in search of at least cold comfort in the complacency that nothing, after all, can be done.

Mills himself recognized the awful demands of the sociological imagination, but he also hoped—perhaps against hope—that the possession of the sociological imagination would itself serve as "a sort of therapy in the ancient sense of clarifying one's knowledge of self" and that it would, in the end, create a sensibility that could serve so lofty a goal as the "tasks of liberation."[36]

But C. Wright Mills was an unusual person. Awful demands and lofty goals were the stuff of his life. He was born in Waco, Texas in 1916; he died in West Nyack, New York in 1962. Throughout his relatively short life (he was only forty-five years old when he died), Mills worked extremely hard and produced an extraordinary number of books, articles, and other writings, all of which (together with one book left unfinished and two just begun) form one of the most impressive bodies of sociological erudition since Max Weber. But unlike Weber, Mills also engaged in dozens of other activities, including architecture and home building, subsistence farming, photography, cooking, and motorcycle riding, and in all of these he sought to acquire expert knowledge. Why was Mills so driven? Why was he such an intensive thinker and inveterate writer, such a doer of disparate things, such a "man in a hurry," as he has been described?

There are perhaps two main reasons. At the University of Texas at Austin, which Mills attended as an undergraduate and graduate student of sociology and philosophy, one can read the following note that Mills wrote to himself, probably in the late 1950s:

> There is a great need just now to talk about realities and prospects, but also to talk about hopes, regardless of realities and prospects. For we are now at the point where all credible images of the future from—*Brave New World* to *1984*—are images of sociological horror. Hopeful interpretations are readily seen as escapist fantasy.
>
> The general danger of this—which is already widely realized—is simply the collapse of all radical imagination. The specific danger is that we abdicate all imagination to the technologists who, without the guidance provided by interplay with other cultural workmen, simply project more of the one thing they know, and end with an air-conditioned nightmare—or, after The Big Bang, at best, some kind of unpleasant tyranny. There really is not sufficient reason for such abdication, not yet at least.[37]

Here, Mills is saying that dystopian realities and prospects abound—this is an empirical fact and cannot be denied—but that the possessor of the sociological imagination cannot for this reason abdicate its task and promise to unearth what remaining real possibilities exist for a better society. In other words, part of the reason that Mills was so driven to analyze his own society in his own time was to recover and promote the utopian dimension of the sociological project, which, for him, entailed the possibility of reason and freedom becoming the general conditions for future human society and individual life. As a sociologist, he had to concede that the chances for the realization of such a society were slim, but as a "cultural workman," as he says, he felt the responsibility to fight on nonetheless.

In these same archives, one can also find an autobiographical statement that Mills wrote in 1953 when he was thirty-seven years old. Under the title "For Ought" and quoting at some length, Mills said the following of himself:

> What we ought to do is realize ourselves, but we do not know what we are until we start to realize it. 'Realization of self' is not [the] final term of ethical reflections, but merely a way station. . . . I suppose that there have been only two images of self that I have really held: images or vague ideas of what I would really like to be and

which lend positive tone to certain roles or activities by which I have tried, often unknowingly tried to act them out. I am sure that there are other ways of saying them, but in my own awareness I think of them as The Hemingway Man and The Wobbly.

The Hemingway Man is spectator and experiencer; he is also a world traveller, usually alone or with changing companions. He is the observer, who has become romantic about this experience and cultivates only one value: skill in expressing his experience. For the rest he lives well and enjoys the best, the most exciting, the most comfortable, except when he courts danger or safe nearness to it.

The Wobbly is an actor and a political man. I have never, in social reality, been either of these types, not even for brief periods, but I have acted out, often without knowing it, both of them. When I wrote *New Men of Power* I was being the Wobbly . . . about 10 or 12 years later than most. Often I have made speeches as a Wobbly, usually in what most would consider inappropriate contexts.

When I have traveled and camped out west, when I have thought about Europe . . . always when I have thought about Europe . . . when I have bought a Burberry coat and an English sports car . . . (photography goes here too) . . . I have tried in somewhat feeble ways, perhaps even ridiculous ways, to be the Hemingway Man.

In the fall of 1952 and in fact for a year or two before then I experimented with other images . . . mainly subsistence farmer, but they didn't satisfy.

But the image which unites the Hemingway and the Wobbly . . . and both of them with my 'real' occupational role as a professor of social science . . . is the image of the political writer. This the idea of the man who stands up to nonsense and injustice and says no. Says no, not out of mere defiance or for the sake of the imprudent no, but out of love of truth and joy in exercising intellectual skills. My task is to shape and work with this role in such a way as to make it more satisfying of what it does not now satisfy in the other two images, which still float in upon me, often [with me] unaware.[38]

Whether he was really part "Wobbly," like a member of the International Workers of the World (a radical American labor union of the late nineteenth and early twentieth century), or part "Hemingway Man" (i.e., like Ernest Hemingway, the American Nobel Prize-winning author of *For Whom the Bell Tolls* and *The Old Man and the Sea*, among many other notably masculine works of fiction), the main point is to realize that Mills was driven by his own struggle to figure out who he was and who he should and could be. This struggle implies many things, not the least of which is that Mills took himself and his life seriously and sometimes, as he admitted, perhaps too seriously, but nonetheless he regarded himself to be a person worthy of self-reflection and self-knowledge. And who is not worthy of this?

In the years after 1953, Mills did indeed become more and more a political writer. His last two books, for example, were *Listen Yankee* (1960), a strongly worded indictment of U.S. policy toward the Cuban revolution written in the voice of a Cuban revolutionary explaining his point of view to North Americans, and *The Marxists* (1962), an eclectic collection of the writings of various Marxian social thinkers and Mills's critical analysis of them. Mills was never a Marxist (and certainly not a Communist), but in his last years he did become a thoroughly committed and altogether vocal critic of American capitalist society and its penchant for celebrating itself as a blameless and morally unblemished participant in the Cold War. He spoke and wrote of the need for a New Left, a new political movement for liberation in capitalist societies, as often as he scorned the evident pathologies of the Communist countries of his day.

In particular, Cuba, he hoped, would remain independent and free and serve as a model for other poor nations struggling to free themselves from the suicidal conflict between the rich nations of the world, whether capitalist or Communist. As it turned out, however, this proved to be a hope against hope. Fidel Castro (who once said that he and his revolutionary comrades gained inspiration from reading Mills's *The Power Elite*; who later, after the success of the Cuban Revolution, took Mills touring 3½ days in Cuba; and who later sent a wreath to Mills's funeral) is today as he was forty years ago, effectively a dictator in a society that Mills would have never accepted as even remotely utopian.

An often lonely public figure, it would seem that all of this direct and highly public engagement with such tense and weighty political issues finally proved too much for Mills to bear. He suffered his first heart attack in 1960, just days prior to his scheduled appearance on national television to debate U.S. policy toward Cuba. Less than two years later and only a few months before the October Missile Crisis, this author of *The Causes of World War Three* and *Listen Yankee* died at his home of a second heart attack.

Mills's death occurred when he was at the apex of his intellectual reputation and political power. In retrospect, the untimeliness of his passing intermingles with both the image of Hemingway and the Wobblies because Hemingway frequented Havana and lived hard and the Wobblies, not at all adverse to perpetuating acts of political violence, were immolated by the heat of revolutionary political struggle. Similarly, but in the realm of words alone, the firebrand Mills led a fateful life, but he was compelled by the feeling that "it's the writers responsibility to orient modern publics to the catastrophic world in which they live."[39] This was another way of his speaking about the sociological imagination's task and promise.

Notes

1. Max Horkheimer, quoted in C. Wright Mills, *The Sociological Imagination* (Oxford, U.K.: Oxford University Press, 1959), 122-3.

2. Fredric Jameson, quoted in A. Stephanson, "Regarding Postmodernism: A Conversation with Fredric Jameson," in *Postmodernism, Jameson, and Critique,* ed. Douglas Kellner (Washington, D.C.: Maisonneuve Press, 1989), 48.

3. Zygmunt Bauman, "Is There a Post-Modern Sociology?" *Theory, Culture, & Society* 5: 234.

4. Charles Lemert, *Postmodernism Is Not What You Think* (Malden, M.A.: Blackwell, 1997), 160.

5. Ibid., 161.

6. The American sociologists Alan Wolfe, Stanley Aronowitz, and Todd Gitlin have written new afterwards to *The Power Elite, The New Men of Power,* and *The Sociological Imagination,* respectively, all reissued by Oxford University Press. Recent books that address aspects of Mills's biography include Kathryn Mills, ed. (with Pamela Mills) *C. Wright Mills: Letters and Autobiographical Writings* (Berkeley: University of California Press, 2000), which includes an introduction by Dan Wakefield; Guy Oakes and Arthur J. Vidich, *Collaboration, Reputation, and Ethics in American Academic Life: Hans H. Gerth and C. Wright Mills* (Urbana: University of Illinois Press, 1999); and Mike Forrest Keen, *Stalking the Sociological Imagination: J. Edgar Hoover's FBI Surveillance of American Sociology* (Westport, C.T.: Greenwood, 1999), which includes an important chapter on Mills.

7. Mills, *The Sociological Imagination.*

8. Ibid., 19, fn 2.

9. Ibid., 21.

10. Ibid., 6-7.

11. Ibid., 5, 7-8.

12. Ibid., 143.

13. Ibid., 7.

14. Ibid., 15, 128.

15. Ibid., 15, 166, and 13.

16. Karl Marx, *The Eighteenth Brumaire of Louis Bonaparte* (1852; reprint, New York: International Publishers, 1963), 15.

17. Ibid.

18. Mills, *The Sociological Imagination,* 7-8.

19. Zygmunt Bauman, *Life in Fragments: Essays in Postmodern Morality* (Cambridge, M.A.: Blackwell, 1995), 5 and 8.

20. Mills, *The Sociological Imagination,* 7.

21. Mills, *The Sociological Imagination,* 6.

22. *C. Wright Mills Papers,* Center for American History, The University of Texas at Austin, Box 4B378, in a personal letter dated October 7, 1957.

23. Mills, *The Sociological Imagination,* 186-7.

24. Ibid., 175, original emphases.

25. Ibid., 171.

26. Ibid., 176.

27. Ibid., 11.

28. Arthur Kroker, Marilouise Kroker, and David Cook, eds., *The Panic Encyclopedia* (New York: St. Martin's Press, 1989), 13.

29. Ibid., 16, original emphases.

30. Mills, *The Sociological Imagination,* 173.

31. Ibid.

32. Ibid.

33. Peter Sloterdijk, *The Critique of Cynical Reason* (1983; reprint, Minneapolis: University of Minnesota Press, 1987), 5 and 546.

34. C. Wright Mills, *The Power Elite* (Oxford, U.K.: Oxford University Press, 1956), 347.

35. William J. Bennett, *The Index of Leading Cultural Indicators* (New York: Broadway, 1999), 189.

36. Mills, *The Sociological Imagination,* 186-7.

37. C. Wright Mills Papers, The Center for American History, University of Texas at Austin, Box 4B380.

38. C. Wright Mills Papers, The Center for American History, University of Texas at Austin, Box 4B390, dated 19 Sept. 1953. Mills's spellings of "Wobbley" and "Burburry" have been changed.

39. C. Wright Mills Papers, The Center for American History, University of Texas at Austin, Box 4B389, from the *Columbia University Alumni News,* December 1950.

II

APPLYING THE SOCIOLOGICAL IMAGINATION: THREE MODELS

5

A Wrong Child

Analyzing the Unanalyzable

Art is not alone in holding the dignity of humanity in its hands.

—*Ernst Bloch*[1]

In a discussion of Theodor W. Adorno's (1903-1969) ethical philosophy, J. M. Bernstein states that, for Adorno, dignity lay in the "indigent particular."[2] Writing self-consciously "after Auschwitz," Adorno's concern was always for the small and frail—the parts of the system that did not, as a matter of course, fit smoothly or function correctly—for these had not only been the victims of the Holocaust but they had also been the grist in the mill of the eugenics movement that helped prepare the ground for the Holocaust.[3] Indeed, not just the eugenics movement but, for Adorno, the whole of modernity seemed like a machine hell bent on stuffing square pegs into round holes or, better, seeing to it that standardized round pegs became the norm. In modern society, damaged parts, or parts otherwise resistant to integration, were to be efficiently retooled or extruded lest they gum-up the works. But for Adorno, a subversive, ethical resistance to this form of rationalization entailed a defense of the seemingly irrational; a defense, as it were, of square pegs in a round hole society. While Adorno never wrote about disabled children per se (nor did Mills), the meaning of his attention to the "indigent particular" is clarified in such a study, as is the moral significance in postmodern times of what Mills called "biography."

Consider the singular case of James Lyon Bérubé, or "Jamie," who is Michael Bérubé's son and the focus of the elder Bérubé's 1996 book, *Life as We Know It: A*

Father, a Family and an Exceptional Child.[4] Jamie was born with Down syndrome. Most people know someone with Down's or some other birth defect. As Bérubé notes, "Down syndrome alone accounts for one of every 600 to 800 live births; it's one of the most common birth 'defects' on the planet."[5] In the United States, roughly 2.5 percent of children younger than the age of three experience a disability; between the ages of three and five years, the percentage climbs to 5.2 percent, and among those aged six to fourteen years, the percentage is 12.7 (but only 1.9 percent are severely disabled). For people fifteen years of age and older, roughly 24 percent have some disability, with about half of these being severe. In total, then, there are roughly 50 million people in the United States who are in some manner "disabled," about half of whom are severely disabled, while in the world as a whole, there as many as 500 million people who are disabled.[6] Jamie Bérubé is among this number. He did not choose this form of human existence; he was just born this way.

This chapter is dedicated to the following proposition: any possessor of the sociological imagination today, "after Auschwitz," must labor to understand Jamie Bérubé, the social structures and cultural patterns that determine and define "disability," and the complicated relation between the two. This chapter aims to depict such an understanding and in so doing provides one model for how the sociological imagination works in practice.

Getting to Know James Lyon Bérubé

In the interest of full disclosure, as journalists say, I should immediately note that I write these words with my own son, Patrick, sitting next to me in his wheelchair and not very happy to be watching me "work." I know this because he is frowning and fussing and smacking with his hand the clear plastic tray that attaches to his wheelchair. And then he looks cross at me and says, "play." After seven years of being with Patrick, I know that he wants me to stop working at the computer and play with him or, better still, let *him* work at the computer. I would be rather daft, after all, and probably an especially inattentive father, if I did not understand the meaning of these gestures and words. Patrick has learned to communicate many things, his being bored prominent among them.

Like Jamie Bérubé, Patrick is disabled. Patrick was born with cerebral palsy and epilepsy and experiences numerous resulting "challenges" such that he cannot feed, bathe, walk, or dress himself independently. Patrick is also probably mentally retarded, although given his physical limitations, it is difficult to measure his cognitive abilities since he cannot readily take IQ tests or otherwise communicate with much precision or complexity. Both Down syndrome and cerebral palsy are, of course, commonly thought of as "birth defects." Although such conditions can and do have considerably varying results for the person who, as it were, has them, in the cases of Jamie and Patrick, the results are very significant. But are they defining and determining? Are Jamie and Patrick really defective from birth, as the terminology implies? Should they be objects of pity? Should they be exterminated? Are they, as a result of their defective nature, wrong children? Do we even know what they are, what should be done, or what they tell us about ourselves?

These are the types of questions that Jamie poses to his father. Michael Bérubé relates the following story about Jamie. The setting is Maine's Old Orchard Beach amusement park, which the Bérubés were visiting as part of a family vacation. Michael Bérubé wrote:

> We strolled among bumper cars, cotton candy, games of chance and skill, and a striking number of French-Canadian tourists. . . . James, however, wanted nothing to do with any of the rides, and though he loves to pretend-drive and has been on bumper cars before, he squalled so industriously before the ride began as to induce the bumper cars operator to let him out of the car and refund his two tickets.
>
> Jamie finally settled in next to a train ride designed for children five and under or thereabouts. . . . I found out quickly enough that Jamie didn't want to *ride* the ride; he merely wanted to stand at its perimeter, grasping the partition with both hands and counting the cars—one, two, three, four, five, six—as they went by. Sometimes, when the train traversed the bridge, James would punctuate it with tiny jumps, saying, 'Up! up! up!' But for the most part, he was content to hang onto the metal bars of the partition, grinning and counting—and, when the train came to a stop, pulling my sleeve and saying, 'More, again.'[7]

This experience causes James's father to experience a moment of reflection apart from the immediate and usually very consuming work of taking care of Jamie at the amusement park. He feels a terrible sinking feeling as he wonders who or what Jamie really is.

> Almost as a form of emotional exercise, I have tried, on occasion, to step back and see him as others might see him, as an instance of a category, one item on the long list of human subgroups. *This is a child with Down syndrome,* I say to myself. *This is a child with adevelopmental disability.* It never works: Jamie remains Jamie to me. I have even tried to imagine him as he would have been seen in other eras, other places: *This is a retarded child.* And even: *this is a Mongoloid child.* This makes for unbearable cognitive dissonance. I can imagine that people might think such things, but I cannot imagine how they might think them in a way that prevents them from seeing Jamie *as* Jamie.[8]

Jamie often surprises his father with what he is thinking and doing, but he also remains something of an enigma, a puzzle whose inner world, whose ultimate meaning, is ineffable in some basic sense. Moreover, the gaze of onlookers in public places and the tools of conceptualization, both of which Jamie's father is expertly conversant with, provide only limited means to sort out what is going on with Jamie. In fact, they often appear as roadblocks to any true understanding of what Jamie is all about.

Later that same day, the Bérubés dined in a local family restaurant. Jamie started to pretend that he was a waiter, taking orders and retrieving the designated fare from "the kitchen," a fireplace hearth dormant in late June. Jamie's father was distracted by his interest in watching the Stanley Cup, which was playing on a television in that part of the restaurant, but he was also half-attending to his son's busy activity. As Jamie's activity crept in on his mind and as he began to understand what Jamie was doing, he was astounded, for experience tells him that Jamie does not usually engage in such highly complex symbolic play: "Can you get me . . . let's see . . . a tuna sandwich? 'Tuna!' he half-shouts in a hoarse little voice and heads back to the fireplace. Did I imagine him pretending to write that down? I must have imagined it."[9]

Jamie's play adds to his father's cognitive dissonance. He knows that most people do not know Jamie as

> the distinct little person with whom I went to the restaurant that evening—a three year old whose ability to imitate is intimately tied to his remarkable ability to imagine, and whose ability to imagine, in turn, rests almost entirely on his capacity to imagine *other people.*[10]

For most people, like the people they had encountered earlier that day at Old Orchard Beach, Jamie is invisible, and if not invisible, then merely a "retarded child," a "disabled child," or a "child to be pitied."[11] Jamie's father is therefore pushed to use this splinter in his eye, as it were, to see all the dimensions of reality laid out before him. He cannot usually do this when immersed in the minute-by-minute care of Jamie; it occurs to him, instead, "after we got back to our motel room, after New Jersey had won the Cup, after the kids were finally asleep."[12]

In this moment of reflection on the day's experience—which included the sinking feeling that Jamie was in fact "limited," the amazement with Jamie's imaginative abilities, and the recognition that Jamie is not generally recognized or understood as he really is, which is just himself—Michael Bérubé thought the following to himself:

> As Jamie was fussing about bumper cars, serving entrees to imaginary diners, and splashing in the waves, the 104th Congress was debating how to balance the federal budget by slashing programs for the disabled and the mentally handicapped; electricians and construction workers in New Haven were putting the final touches on

preparations for the 1995 Special Olympics World Games; researchers with the Human Genome Project were trying to locate the biomedical basis for all our variances; and millions of ordinary human beings, all of them women, were undergoing prenatal testing for "severe" genetic defects like Down syndrome.

Jamie has no idea what a busy intersection he's landed in: statutes, allocations, genetics, reproduction, representation—all meeting at the crossroads of individual idiosyncracy and sociopolitical construction.[13]

Jamie, a three-year-old child, has no idea (but his father does) how practical, how real, are the menacing social and cultural forces that are work at varying distances around and through him. Michael Bérubé's questions, his thinking, his imagination, is spurred on by his concern for a single human being: "Jamie has compelled me to ask these questions anew, just as I know how crucial it is that we collectively cultivate our capacities to imagine our obligations to each other," wrote James Lyon Bérubé's father.[14]

Identities and Nonidentity

I cannot possibly "know" Jamie Bérubé. Although Jamie's father is a professor of English at the University of Illinois and an extremely gifted writer, and although Michael Bérubé is also an expert analyst of the way we have in our culture commonly understood and acted toward people with disabilities, it is not, strictly speaking, possible to know someone by reading about them in a text, even a particularly moving and well-crafted text, even a text written by a father about his own son and his own family. (I cannot know Janet or Nicholas Bérubé either, Jamie's mother and older brother.) In *Life as We Know It,* Jamie appears as "Jamie," a figure of language and an image depicted in photographs. The stories that his father writes are just that, stories. They are staged, crafted, and have gone through many phases of editing.

If I were to write about Patrick as Michael Bérubé writes about Jamie Bérubé— which, in fact, I have done—it would not be Patrick that the reader comes to know but, rather, just my—or in our particular case, me and Patrick's mother's—interpretation of Patrick, what we think Patrick is, has been, and could be.[15] Ours, then, would be a gloss on Patrick, not Patrick pe se, in-himself, as he is to himself. This is unavoidable, for neither Jamie nor Patrick speak for themselves like "normally developing" children do and certainly not like parents and, needless to say, professors tend to do. Even if Jamie and Patrick did speak for themselves, the fact that they are not the authors of their own texts would place distance between them and their interpreter's representation of them. And even if they did write their own texts—someday, perhaps—it would still be their representation of themselves and not themselves, strictly speaking, that resulted from their own writing or speaking. Words on paper, utterances floating in the air, and bodies in wheelchairs or struggling with walkers are not equivalent to one another, and there is no transparent medium that sews these dimensions of reality seamlessly together.

This is to say that words are not the same type of thing as what the words are apparently making reference to. What linguistic theorists often call *the signified* refers to what we talk (or write) *about,* as opposed to what we actually say (or write). Simply, words have *referents.* We do not just talk; we talk about something. What we say or write are *signs* whose meaning is derived from their relation to other signs in a system of signs, like a language. The signified, then, is what we are trying to "signify" with signs, such as words and gestures.

For example, if I configure my hand in such a way that my middle finger is extended but all the rest are doubled-up in a fist, and I turn the back of my hand toward another person while maintaining this configuration, the other person (if he or she has learned to interpret the meaning of this gesture as I mean for him or her to interpret it as my "giving them the finger") will know that I am telling him or her something that might, depending on the situation, lead them to understand my gesture as an indication of my unfriendliness. However, if this person is not familiar with this sign, he or she may simply be puzzled by it. It will not mean anything in particular; my sign will not signify to the person the signified I was aiming at. Or if I perform this gesture to a group of students in a classroom, they are likely to interpret my having done so as a pedagogical technique, and therefore they will not understand my sign as a rebuke or insult. What is signified in this case is my object lesson in which I am not so much giving them the finger as I am giving them an example of how symbolic interaction works in everyday life. In fact, they are more likely to chuckle at my sign than be upset by it, for professors are not normally supposed to use vulgar gestures in professional settings. The transgression of this implicit prohibition often evokes mild amusement, the form that anxiety takes when no real threat is evident.

The point of this illustration is, of course, that the meaning of the gesture or any sign is not "in" the gesture or sign itself. Meaning is not sealed in a sign of any kind but, rather, is a product of many indeterminate and particular interpretations. Established and systematically learned understandings of signs and situations reduce this indeterminacy, but it is the ever-present and unavoidable possibility of indeterminacy that we need to examine more closely.

What is signified, what we are trying to communicate, and what we are aiming at with our words, utterances, or gestures—Jamie or Patrick, say—is always already different from the words we choose and greater than any words. Adorno called this the principle of nonidentity, which in this context can mean the impossibility of words—and the minds that fashion them—to identify wholly and completely with their referents. That is, just because we know words, write books, and use language to conceptualize anything or everything does not mean that we fully know what it is that we are talking about. There is always a remainder, something left out. This is especially true of indigent particulars. They stand apart and say to us in their silence, "you cannot fully know me with your words." Animals are like this, as are all natural phenomena. Disabled children who cannot speak in normal ways say this emphatically because they have human minds, and we know that they are thinking, thinking something, and perhaps thinking something about us. This is part of what makes particulars—and especially indigent particulars—so important for the would-be possessor of the sociological imagination: they teach humility.

Arrogant Categories

Jamie is, of course, a real person, not a fictional character, but he is also a real person whose reality inevitably "stands for" others such as himself (i.e., he symbolizes "the disabled"). While inevitable, this leap from real and particular to symbolic and general is fraught with danger. If the latter gains precedence over the former (i.e., if known categories come to dominant over unknowable people, if neat and clean round holes are imagined more important than the oddly shaped pegs actually existing), then conceptual or symbolic thought becomes menacing.

"Disabled" is one grouping or category. It refers to no one and to nothing in particular. It literally means, of course, to be "not-abled," presumably, to be not able to do something. But what is the something that one is not able to do? We normally think of a loss in the major senses or body functions as constituting disability, such as not being able to see or not being able to walk. We also recognize as disabled those who have limited cognitive and emotional capacities, but the boundaries are clearly murky. Is a woman disabled if she is nine months pregnant? Is one disabled if he or she is colorblind? Is one disabled if he or she can walk only with the use of a special supporting device and only then for brief periods? Is one disabled if, though unable to hear sounds with his or her ears, he or she is possessed of a sign language and is immersed in a community of similarly skilled people, such that interpersonal communication is as complex and rich as it is for those who depend on utterances as their primary means of communication? In other words, are hearing-impaired people "disabled"? Is the professional golfer disabled who, due to a rare disease, cannot walk 18 holes without experiencing severe pain? Is a person disabled if he or she does not possess a sociological imagination? Where does disability start and stop? How do we draw these distinctions?[16] Many people are surprised to learn, for example, that many members of the hearing-impaired community do not consider themselves, nor wish others to consider them, as disabled.

The concept of disability and the disabled—not to mention handicapped, crippled, crip, mongoloid idiot, differently abled, gimp, challenged, retard, handicapable, and vegetable—are expansive generalizations meant to capture an aspect of particularity common across a range of general phenomena. To "conceptualize" something means to abstract from real things to produce imaginative groups and mental categories. For example, each disabled person is unique and in fact has abilities, but if he or she is viewed as sharing in common some general characteristic or quality, some inability or inabilities, then it is on this basis and this basis alone that he or she is conceptually grouped with others. This conceptual grouping, then, is the act of an active mind. The signified does not exist outside of our conceptualization of them. In other words, my phrase "people who are disabled" is a mindful construction, not an independent reality whose meaning is fixed outside of my conceptualization or, more to the point, a collectively accepted and routinely enforced conceptualization, some bit of "common sense."

Amid the welter of things to attend to with our minds, some things are attended to and others not and some inabilities are noted and others are not. Furthermore, after we attend to something, we have to name it and understand its meaning in one or another way. Choices must be made about what to attend to with our minds (i.e., what to define, distinguish, and categorize). Choices have to be made about what to understand by what we have defined. Historically and even today, in our own culture and in other cultures as well, the boundaries for what is and is not considered—commonsensically and also legally—a disability have been drawn in as widely varying ways. The notion of the human variety includes not just the cultural diversity of the species but also the diversity in the ways that humans have understood themselves. In some cultures, what we might regard as mental illness is regarded as a sign of special spiritual power. A postmodern adult who, due to some physical or mental limitation, cannot drive an automobile faces a "challenge," whereas an inability to ride on horseback is not viewed as a disabling condition.[17]

It is, however, important to bear in mind that the people being referred to as being members of "a group" are in fact overwhelmingly different from one another and will always, in all likelihood, be perfect strangers to one another. For example, a disabled child in Outer Mongolia and a disabled child in Brookline, Massachusetts, other than their relation to one another via the alien concept of disabled child, could not be more different. Perhaps even the concept of "child" does violence to their own experience, given that the concept of "child" is historically and culturally constructed and, for the most part, the product of modern European development. Perhaps, *violence* is too harsh a term for use in this context. More to the point is the fact that only twenty-five years ago in the United States, children with Down syndrome were commonly referred to as "mongoloid idiots," even by professionals—in fact, especially by professionals, who invented the terminology.[18] Mongoloid idiots in Outer Mongolia and mongoloid idiots in Brookline, Massachusetts are not, however, really part of a group at all, at least not part of a group of disabled children worldwide because no such group exists. This is the case even though some people may conceive of them as so being and in this process may define them in ways that are both symbolically as well as materially harmful to them.

All concepts are like this: they are simplifications and distortions of what really obtains. In some varying degree, they violate the reality of every particular thing. To think of Jamie Bérubé as a "mongoloid idiot," a stigmatizing and dehumanizing concept, is damaging. But to conceptualize him as "having" Down syndrome is also potentially stigmatizing and dehumanizing, even if this label is more sterile and clinical in origin. When concepts are dehumanizing in any way, their inherent simplification and distortion can legitimize action that renders actual what before was only symbolic. For example, when disabled people were sent to the Nazi's death camps along with "the Jews," "the Gypsies," and "the homosexuals," they were not officially full-fledged human beings in the eyes of their murderers. They were defects; they were aliens. They were infections in the body politic, members of a mongrel race, and otherwise deemed unfit for life in the "New World" imagined in Nazi ideology. The symbolic dehumanization of these people paved the way for their material slaughter.

Writing in his study *The New Genocide of Handicapped and Afflicted People,* Wolf Wofensberger analyzed such dehumanizing processes under the concept of "deathmaking," which he defined as "any actions or pattern of actions which either directly or indirectly bring about, or hasten, the death of a person or group."[19] For Wolfensberger, Nazi-style deathmaking is just the tip of iceberg because subtle, indirect, and sanitized forms of deathmaking are far more common and, due to their "detoxified" appearance, much more difficult to confront. The clearing of the Brazilian rainforest is a form of such deathmaking for tropical species of plants and animals, as is the systematic production of stark inequalities in food and medicine worldwide deathmaking for hundreds of millions, if not billions, of "the wretched of the earth." But Wolfensberger is more interested in how words such as *wheelchairbound* and *birth defect* contribute subtly to dehumanization, or how comedians who make jokes about "being mental" and kids riding in "small school buses" diminish people, the least powerful among us to withstand this diminishment.

If you think about it, everything in this book, and everything in every book, is the product of some type of conceptualization presented via some language that harbors the potential for deathmaking. Books, especially high-brow books, are well suited for detoxifying reality. Intellectual jargon helps fashion a reality onto itself. When not doing battle with big words, the ease with which our eyes pass over facts, even disturbing facts, contributes to the sanitation of the realities that the facts are referencing. A scholarly book about disabled children could easily, even unintentionally, render the lives of disabled children specimens for analysis, and instill in the mind of the reader a sense of the less-than-fully-human quality of the object of analysis. Once "presented," "constructed," or "staged," signs must therefore be critically interpreted, decoded, or deconstructed by some reader. But this process—reading—is itself a sticky wicket because writing does not control or determine reading. Every book is read differently by every far-flung reader, far-flung in both time and space. Reading *Life as We Know It* means one thing to me now, but it might mean something significantly different to someone from Japan reading the book in translation a hundred years from now, or even to me next year, when I come to it with different eyes. The meaning of a person in a wheelchair today in Germany is certainly very different than what was the case fifty years ago; such a person is usually "read" differently, perhaps as an object of pity more than as an object of scorn or revulsion, but even as an object of pity, symbolically nudged toward a dehumanized status. The process of reading and writing and, generally, interpreting the meaning of all symbolic things is a process that never ends and that never produces the exact same results twice. It is also a political process, one that contributes to or resists dehumanization and, ultimately, deathmaking.

The Necessity of Conceptualization and Communication

With so much indeterminacy and danger inexorably infused in the processes of conceptualizing and communicating, should we simply give up trying to make sense of things, not to mention trying to share our understandings with others? We can analyze until the cows come home, but if we are always battling indeterminacy and running such risks with our stabs at conceptual knowing, then why think that we really know anything at all? Why take the chance of doing more harm than good? Why write books and read them if it is never certain that what is being written and what is being read match one another or form an "identity"? And what if there is a match, but it is a match that leads to the destruction of what we are talking about? In other words, with so much nonidentity afoot, isn't everything particular and unknowable except, perhaps, as a particular thing in itself and on its own terms? Are our many efforts to use conceptualization, to overshoot reality and inevitably to simplify and distort it, themselves indigent and lame and maybe even harmful or lethal?

C. Wright Mills once wrote, "The first rule for understanding the human condition is that men [or, as we would say today, people] live in second-hand worlds."[20] Mills continued,

> Everyone lives in a world of . . . meanings. No man stands alone directly confront-
> ing a world of solid fact. No such world is available. The closest men come to it is
> when they are infants or when they become insane: then, in a terrifying scene of
> meaningless events and senseless confusion, they are often seized with the panic of
> near-total insecurity. But in their everyday life they do not experience a world of
> solid fact; their experience itself is selected by stereotyped meanings and shaped by
> ready-made interpretations. Their images of the world, and of themselves, are
> given to them by crowds of witnesses they have never met and never shall meet. Yet
> for every man these images—provided by strangers and dead men—are the very
> basis of his life as a human being.[21]

This insight should help us deal with the indeterminacy and danger of the process of trying to know and communicate. As Mills noted, the absence of "solid fact" and the presence of "ready-made" images and interpretations are perfectly mundane features of human life.

For the possessor of the sociological imagination, there is no Alpha and Omega, no solid beginning and no solid end, that is experienced in human life. Everything, including ourselves, is, as philosophers sometimes say, "always already"; there is no way to simply step out of our secondhand reality and know or experience something directly or as radically "other." We ought not, therefore, be afraid of what is unavoidable and, in fact, constitutive of what we are. If our knowing has limits simply because we are human beings who are struggling to know but always already enmeshed in ongoing systems of meaning, then we may simply accept these givens and move on. We may then choose to actively pursue the knowing that we can accomplish, analyzing even what we know is, in any ultimate sense, unanalyzable. And if we have learned to be moral people, we will develop and use our concepts while being mindful of the harm that can result from damaging forms of knowing, which, ironically, often result from fear and anxiety before the unknown and unknowable. We will thus work "from within," as Adorno once wrote, to "break out" of the prevailing "context of delusion," even if we can never fully be free of where and whence we originated.[22] We will do this with a mixture of humility and urgency because urgency is demanded by the evident harms before us and humility is dictated by our self-awareness as imperfect knowing beings.

Despite his recognition that we always already live in secondhand worlds, Mills, like Adorno and every other possessor of the sociological imagination, remained an obstinate believer in conceptualization. Indeed, as we have seen, Mills advocated a form of conceptualization that would demand nothing less than the complex conceptual interweaving of history, biography, and social structure, the interplay of the most particular with the most general. Furthermore, Mills hinted that at the extremes of experience, such as in infancy or insanity, we are at a loss without our ability to conceptualize, subject to the terrors of a world experienced as flowing in as though through a breach in the levy, which, if left unchecked, will overwhelm our senses and eventually our minds.

In a sense, Mills offers us sociological conceptualization as a means to thwart the potentially damaging effects of the symbolic-constructed social world. In effect, the sociological imagination is a type of self-consciousness that holds the world at bay, if just for a conceptual instance. Our learned ability to simplify and distort what would otherwise overwhelm us is a type of conceptual shield. Who, after all, would really want direct contact with the vastly and forever unknowable but nonetheless real and threatening nature of social reality? Who, after all, would really want to know Auschwitz? Most of the people who did know Auschwitz died as a result. Better to know "Auschwitz," that is, the concept of Auschwitz. This may be a terrible lesson, as Mills said, but it is not likely to be a lethal one. In fact, the concept of Auschwitz, if properly and deeply conceptualized, may be useful to us as we struggle from within the culture that produced it in the first place, useful and necessary lest we forget how damaging concepts such as "the Jews" and "mongoloid idiots" can be.

We therefore confront a paradox. On one hand, conceptualization distorts reality and is potentially dangerous. On the other hand, we cannot break free from our secondhand world, nor would we want to since this is the means by which we make sense of the world and control our relationship to it. Is there any other way to establish an intelligent if also moral relationship to others in such a paradoxical situation?

Mimesis

I do not know Jamie, but in knowing Patrick, such as I do, and less well Patrick's schoolmates in his "special education" class, I can imagine what Jamie is like. My experience allows me to read Michael Bérubé's description of Jamie and all things relating to Jamie's and his family's experience and say to myself, "I know what he means." By this, I really mean to say,

> I do not know exactly and completely know what Jamie is all about, but I know enough to allow me to understand, not perfectly, but well enough, what he is like, and this brings me into a human relationship with him that might not heretofore have existed.

Besides, Jamie and I both live in and are a product of virtually the same society and culture. Beyond our immediate and individual experience—he lives in Illinois and I in Ohio and he is younger than I am; he is a body with an extra twenty-first chromo-

some, which I apparently lack; Jamie likes to make "lists" of anything and everything, whereas my Patrick likes the sheer fact of letters, dollar amounts, and the
groans associated with the "bankrupt" space more than the strategy displayed by
contestants on "Wheel of Fortune"—we share a lot in common. We share the same
language, breathe the same air, and go to similar hospitals staffed by professionals
who are trained in similar ways. We have both been to Old Orchard Beach and we
share French-Canadian ethnic roots. There is no congruence, just meaningful similarities, but meaningful enough, that is, to permit the best communication possible
given our inevitably human situation.

The fact that there always exists an ineffable dimension to particular experience
leads to, or should lead to, caution in every attempt "to know." Michael Bérubé even
formulates an ethical principle based on this self-awareness, which is meant as a
guide for all human beings who are compelled to conceptualize but who wish not to
suffocate the existing ineffability of the significant "other." Bérubé wrote, "Sign
unto others as you'd have them sign unto you. Pass it on."[23] This could be thought of
as a golden rule for the postmodern age, in which we are self-aware of our own participation in ongoing, secondhand worlds not of our own creation, worlds of established meaning that we must work from within but that we recognize can do as much
harm as good.

In writing his book, then, author Michael Bérubé means to affect the world of
established meaning by challenging words, such as *mongoloid idiot,* which are a
false representation of Jamie and a damaging symbol for all who are disabled or potentially disabled (which is, of course, everyone). Therefore, Bérubé's is not a simple story of a child who is an apparently wonderful, joyous, puzzling, walking, talking, frustrating, creative, demanding, imaginative, amazing presence in the Bérubé
household but is, rather, an intervention into the minds of all people who would aspire to a liberating form of social understanding and, simultaneously, to an understanding of the meaning of a liberated society. Michael Bérubé is therefore self-
consciously engaged in social and cultural critique. He is working from within,
in close partnership with the indigent particular, to change what it means to be a human being. His primary technique for accomplishing this feat is to tear down our
preconceived notion that we know what we are talking about. In this sense, *Life as
We Know It* is an ironic title.

Bérubé is hardly a lone voice in this regard. In an essay titled "The Limits of
Life," the French social theorist and psychoanalyst Julia Kristeva echoed Bérubé's
call for new and urgent rethinking about what it means to be a human being.[24] Of
"humanity," she wrote that "nobody really knows what it means any more, yet we experience a vague 'consensual' feeling when the subject of 'crimes against humanity'
crops up." Kristeva reported that therapists working with people once thought

"unanalyzable" (i.e., terminally ill patients and the severely disabled) "have been able to isolate a fundamental human anxiety: What is the norm?" For Kristeva, this fundamental human anxiety cannot be dispelled without

> an atheistic compassion of a most radical kind. . .in which the value of life is not dependent on its bio-programmable performance, but in the meaning that the patient can continuously give it himself, aided by those close to him who become fully involved.

As with Bérubé's ethical principle, Kristeva touched on what Adorno called "mimesis." In addition to conceptually analyzing something—say, wrong children or a work of art—Adorno advanced a second way of knowing where, in the words of one commentator, "the 'other' is identified with the self *by making the other like the self*."[25] This is *mimesis*, a term linked to mimicry or imitation. In mimetic knowing, one undercuts "the overly subjective nature of conceptualization by bringing forth more of the 'voice' of the object itself."[26] In other words, one makes the other comprehensible and establishes a moral bond *against* concepts that encourage arrogant categorization or even deathmaking. One listens instead of just looking; one learns from passivity and humility before "the other" previously thought mute and retarded. One comes to see "the other" not as "them," but as "me." One plays his or her games—"up! up! up!"—and makes his or her world one's own world. This may be much easier for the parent of a severely disabled child, who might simply call mimesis "love" or the knowledge born of love. But Kristiva, like Bérubé and Adorno, thought there was a more general lesson to be learned by everyone.

Kristiva wrote that "the everyday inquiry into 'what life is' " is greatly facilitated by close analysis of the "so-called 'useless citizens,' " who are "threatened with death by a more or less disguised form of eugenics." She believed that this every day inquiry was "truly the task for our times, since it is a question of deciding on the kind of world we want to live in." Kristeva continued that "in this sense, people who are ill [and disabled] and those who look after them are spearheading the cause of human dignity, which otherwise would not necessarily survive into the next millennium." The great task, according to Kristeva, is to "recognize as human someone who is at the very border of what generally is deemed human, to relate to the modest and ordinary, and not to despair." Of course, for parents of disabled children such as Michael Bérubé, this task is both necessary and unavoidable because to do otherwise is to condemn one's own child to oblivion. For those millions who live in close proximity to the "border" of humanity, Kristeva's message is not simply a question of morality and an opportunity for personal growth, it is a compelling dilemma and task. Mimetic learning and mimetic understanding are built into people's particular social roles and situations. For Kristeva, such simple acts of being with indigent others constitute a blow against the general tendency toward dehumanization, and therein lies the seeds of what she calls "hope."

World-Historical Mimesis?

If cultivating this type of hope were all that was incumbent on the possessor of the sociological imagination, life would be easier and sociology would not be so melancholy of a science after all. We would simply keep our eyes and ears open to the blind and to the deaf and set about to learn from losses of all kinds. But to our appreciation for our own conceptual limitations, for the difference and indeterminancy of the world, and for the significance of work in the borderlands of human experience, we must add historically specific analysis of a relevant history and a specific set of social structures. In the case of Jamie, we must understand that Jamie exists today as he does only because of certain large-scale social and cultural developments, just as we must understand that a life worth living for Jamie and for all kindred spirits is constantly and systematically threatened. The big picture, as it were, is dispiriting. The lessons derived from a mimetic identity with the life conditions of the world's disabled are anything but "hopeful."

According to the United Nations, there are, as mentioned above, roughly 500 million people worldwide who are labeled as "disabled." People are counted as disabled, generally, either if they experience a significant functional limitation or if they are treated as disabled in their own society. This includes, then, people who are missing limbs due to their having stepped on land mines as well as those whose cognitive abilities are deemed socially inferior in the context of their own society. Of these 500 million people, probably as many as 400 million live in the so-called Third World.[27] These latter people are, as James I. Charleton wrote, "the poorest and most powerless people on earth."[28] They represent about 12 percent of the world's human population.

Charlton's path-breaking 1998 book *Nothing About Us without Us: Disability Oppression and Empowerment* is a handy reference for those who do not like sifting through verbose United Nations studies. Charlton also includes the data from his own extensive interview research with disability rights activists in every major region of the world. Based on these studies, Charlton is able to provide a picture of life for the world's "poorest and most powerless" human inhabitants.

Drawing mainly from studies sponsored and funded by the United Nations, Charlton reports that, in the world's poorest countries, as many as 90 percent of children with disabilities die before the age of twenty, while more specifically, 90 percent of children with *mental* disabilities die before the age of five.[29] Furthermore,

Charlton reports that roughly 100 million people have disabilities due, in the first place, to malnutrition, whereas those who are injured and have resulting disabilities, such as in the particular case of spinal cord injuries, "usually die within one or two years after becoming paralyzed, often from severe pressure sores or urinary tract infections."[30] Land mines alone, worldwide, have disabled roughly 700,000 people as of 1994; this is of course exactly what land mines—the 110 million land mines estimated to exist in 64 countries—are designed to do.[31] Beyond being maimed and killed or left to wither and die, disabled people in poor societies also face, of course, severely limited opportunities for a life worth living. For example, of the estimated 2 million children who are blind in India, only 15,000 receive any education whatsoever, with most of these few being boys because in India, like elsewhere, girls are generally regarded and treated as inferior to boys. Systematic infanticide is also widely practiced in countries such as India and China.[32] Girls, especially disabled girls but also disabled boys, are regularly subjected to this form of prebirth death.

These figures are only vague indications of the state of disabled people worldwide. To them we could add facts concerning unemployment and poor health care, political marginality, and culturally defined inferiority. But this would even be true of the roughly 100 million people who are disabled by First World standards. For example, in the United States, roughly half of all people with disabilities are unemployed, and more than 87 percent of people with severe disabilities are unemployed.[33] Americans who are disabled and who are also black have unemployment rates that are closer to 75 percent.[34] In Britain, in contrast, the unemployment rate for disabled adults is only about 21 percent, although this is still three times the rate for nondisabled people.[35] In both Britain and the United States, people with disabilities who are employed, not surprisingly, typically are employed in low-paying jobs and thus receive incomes that cause them to live in poverty at rates much higher than their nondisabled fellow citizens.[36]

Statistics such as these only tell part of the story because the lives of disabled people, in both poor and rich countries alike, are also significantly affected by socially imposed invisibility and abandonment. In *Nothing About Us Without Us,* Charlton depicts this experience through his interviews with disability rights activists worldwide. Koesbionon Sarmandhadi, associate secretary of the Indonesia Disabled Peoples' Association, said, "Children with disabilities are hidden because of an inferiority complex of families," while Fernando Rodriguez, the founder of the Mobility International chapter in Mexico City, noted, "By and large, people with disabilities in Mexico are very isolated, both because of their family's attitudes and because of all the access issues."[37] Alexander Phiri, the chairperson of the National Council of Disabled Persons in Zimbabwe, said the following of his own experience:

> After my accident, my parents visited two or three times and then I was abandoned. When I was to leave the hospital, the hospital people tried to locate my parents but failed. It was clear that they did not want a child they considered useless. . . . They also did not want to deal with the social implications in their village for having a disabled child, because they would be ostracized and maybe even ridiculed.[38]

In Brazil, where there are estimated to be 30 to 40 million children who have been abandoned by their parents, disabled children and their mothers are especially vulnerable to abandonment.[39] Rosangela Berman Bieler, president of the Center for Independent Living in Rio de Janeiro, related the case of Vera Henriques in the following statement:

> Vera Henriques, married for twenty years and mother of a fourteen-year-old girl with cerebral palsy, told me that she believes the vast majority of women with disabled children are abandoned by their husbands or companions because they do not accept the child's disability and they are so poor.[40]

Apparently, the combination of culturally accepted prejudice against disabled people, patriarchy, and widespread poverty produces predictable results.

It is important here to stress "apparently produce" because, admittedly, the data presented thus far provides at best only a sketch of the lives of people with disabilities worldwide. We would want a more complete and exact empirical description, but such does not, unfortunately, yet exist. Charlton's book and several others, plus a handful of recent United Nations studies, together constitute the best research to date. This fact itself, of course, is an indicator of the relative powerlessness and marginality of disabled people. Research of the type we would want would entail the expenditure of considerable resources and imply an interest and commitment on the part of researchers and research-funding organizations.

For example, in the United States and Britain, both highly developed countries, public concern for the rights of disabled people is of relatively recent origin, and comprehensive research into their lives and experiences and into the effectiveness of social policies designed to improve these lives is more recent still. The disability rights movement in the United States, for example, usually marks its origin in the 1973 founding of the Berkeley Center for Independent Living.[41] Up until then, most political organization by and on behalf of disabled people remained at a local or grassroots level. Modeling itself along the lines of the American civil rights movement, the disability rights movement developed quickly and established many national and international organizations. As a result of this political mobilization, the United Nations designated 1981 as the International Year of the Disabled. In 1990, the Americans with Disabilities Act was passed into law, which is described by some researchers as "the most extensive piece of anti-discrimination legislation anywhere in the world."[42] The United Kingdom's history is in many ways parallel to the American experience: the United Kingdom's Disability Discrimination Act was passed in 1995. These and other legislative acts, and the international attention focused on disabled people by the United Nations, also encouraged the development of an expanding number of researchers and research organizations. A 1998 cover story in *The Chronicle for Higher Education* featured disability studies as the latest hot thing sweeping through America's colleges and universities.[43]

The invisibility and marginality of disabled people, and in addition, our studied ignorance of their lives, is a product of social and cultural oppression. But the growth, especially in the rich societies of the world, of the disability rights movement and of disability studies and the related expanding visibility, political voice, and growing knowledge of disabled people are indicators of how socially defined meanings and lived realities can and do change. In other words, our sense for the constraining nature of prevailing social structure (e.g., in terms of the adverse and lethal effects of global economic inequality) must also include an appreciation for how the mobilization of concern and power can change prevailing institutions and attitudes. The medium of this change is history or, more specifically, history making. The disability rights movement, like the civil rights and women's movements, is nothing if not an organized group of people working from within their society and culture to not only change that society and culture in ways that will improve the lives of a specific group (in this case, disabled people) but also to redefine what it means for all people to live as human beings. They seek to make history, and in so doing, make humanity.

In this regard, consider one instance of history making. It was only in 1840 that the concept of "normal" acquired its current meaning. As Lennard J. Davis, the editor of the 1997 *The Disability Studies Reader,* noted, the concept of normality as indicating "constituting, conforming to, not deviating or different from, the common type or standard, regular, usual" came into widespread usage at roughly the same time that the eugenics movement became popular in Europe and the United States.[44] Among the many supporters of eugenics were such luminaries as Alexander Graham Bell, George Bernard Shaw, and Theodore Roosevelt. The goal of the movement was to use enforced sterilization and selective breeding to eliminate people and types of people who did not contribute to the development of a "normal" and, indeed, superior human type. As Davis noted, "We have largely forgotten that what Hitler did in developing his hideous policy of eugenics was just to implement the theories of the British and American eugenicists."[45] By way of evidence, Davis noted that in 1933, "the prestigious scientific magazine *Nature* approved the Nazis' proposal of a bill for 'the avoidance of inherited diseases in posterity' by sterilizing the disabled."[46] Davis also stated that "the magazine editorial board said 'the Bill, as it reads, will command the appreciative attention of all who are interested in the controlled and deliberate improvement of the human stock.' "[47] Such opinions were as common among learned people only one human lifetime ago as was the opinion that most "races" of people in the world were inferior to those of western European "stock."

Most people today do not support an active eugenics policy against disabled people or against anyone regarded as "abnormal." Yet the fact that some 400 million people in the world who are disabled face life-threatening conditions on a daily basis belies the optimism this otherwise notable social and cultural change in rich societies might encourage. After all, inaction toward the situations faced by the vast majority of the world's poorest and least powerful people is akin to a policy of passive eugenics—what Kristeva called a "more or less disguised form of eugenics"—for to die of neglect and abandonment because your body is damaged and because your well-being is relatively unimportant is to die under the auspices of a world that is still fixated on the high value of normalcy. Deathmaking is deathmaking no matter if progress has been made or not. In other words, some people's lives are worth more than others, and poor disabled people living in poor societies are not worth, evidently, very much, if anything at all.

The fact that even the more fortunate people who are disabled and lucky enough to have been born in rich societies at a time of growing concern and positive social change for disabled people continue to face significant barriers to a life worth living (e.g., significant material inequalities, significant stigma and prejudice) should cause us to pause before any premature celebration of our progress. Progress it is, to be sure, but progress enough? The possessor of the sociological imagination could hardly accept the past thirty or so years of advancement in one corner of the world without weighing these historical changes in a comparative balance with the experience of the majority of similar people worldwide, without attending to the fate of those millions for whom time has already run out, or without looking ahead to a time soon when the problems of a dying world will significantly erode the possibilities for the inclusion of the world's hundreds of millions of disabled human beings in a true community of humankind.

The Shadow Cast by "Christmas in Purgatory"

We might pause here to recall the words of the late Burton Blatt, who was among the first leaders in the struggle to salvage the lives of people with mental retardation in the United States and who, at the time of his death in 1985, was also the dean of the School of Education at Syracuse University.[48] Blatt gained initial fame on the basis of a 1966 exposé titled "Christmas in Purgatory: A Photographic Essay on Mental Retardation," which included the photographs taken by Fred Kaplan of the conditions in America's institutions for the mentally retarded. Blatt wrote, "There is a hell on earth, and in America there is a special inferno."[49]

Following is a description by Blatt and Kaplan of one institution that they visited in December 1965:

> In each of the dormitories for severely retarded residents, there is what is euphemistically called a day room or recreation room. The odor in each of these rooms is overpowering. After a visit to a day room we had to send our clothes to the dry cleaners to have the stench removed. The facilities often contribute to the horror. Floors are sometimes wooden and excretions are rubbed into the cracks, leaving permanent stench. Most day rooms have a series of bleacher benches, on which sit unclad residents, jammed together, without purposeful activity, communication, or any interaction. In each day room is an attendant or two, whose main function seems to be to "stand around" and, on occasion, hose down the floor "driving" excretions into a sewer conveniently located in the center of the room.[50]

Conditions such as those that Blatt and Kaplan described were commonplace for disabled people locked away in institutions and "hospitals," kept at a safe distance from public consciousness and the public's conscience. Indeed, Blatt and Kaplan's exposé played a part in the deinstitutionalization movement, which put a stop to the unquestioned institutionalization of people with severe mental and physical disabilities and encouraged community and home-based care as a progressive substitute. In 1955, there were roughly 558,000 people in state mental hospitals; by 1980, this number had fallen to 140,000.[51]

At first, this deinstitutionalization movement was regarded as a progressive initiative, its point being to free thousands from de facto imprisonment and systematic neglect and encourage the assimilation of disabled people into mainstream society. The mid-1970s were its heyday. Disabled Americans started showing up in grocery stores and living in neighborhoods, and disabled kids started appearing in regular classrooms with normally developing peers. But after many significant political and policy successes, Blatt still maintained the following perspective: "As you will see, everything has changed during the past decade. As you will see, nothing has changed."[52] The conditions inside the remaining institutions were not significantly improved, nor were the lives of those who were "set free" from the institutions necessarily any better.[53]

Indeed, in the late 1990s, more than ten years down the road from Blatt's dismal assessment of the progress of his day, research suggested that roughly 40 percent of America's homeless (citizens without shelter in the richest society in the world) are affected by one or another form of mental disorder. In this regard, it would seem that Blatt and Kaplan's purgatory has simply changed venue, and it is now a kind of open air prison instead of scenes from behind the bars and in the back wards of "One Flew Over the Cuckoo's Nest" institutions. In this way, responsibility for this social problem is dispersed into thin air, except for those who possess the sociological imagination and who therefore see the straightforward connection over time between deinstitutionalization on one hand and homelessness on the other, the well-intended half solution to one hell on earth becoming the basis for another. But even for the nonhomeless, things were not good. Care given in homes, even by parents, is tenuously supported by social programs. It is difficult, for example, for the parents of the estimated 800,000 people in the United States living at home with schizophrenia and bipolar illnesses to manage a household conceived as a small-scale mental hospital.[54] An indicator of the stress caused by the "family-centered" care of a severely disabled person is the fact that, in Britain (where data are available) the divorce rate is roughly 10 times higher in families with children with learning difficulties than the national average. Disabled children are also more likely to be abandoned, physically and sexually abused, and passed over for adoption.[55]

Seen in this light, Jamie Bérubé, like my own son, is simultaneously very fortunate and very unfortunate indeed. Due to changes enacted during the course of the past thirty years, we can safely say that we have no more mongoloid idiots among us (although the concept lingers in many minds, and in this way, as a sort of nightmare, remains a hectoring presence). Jamie certainly benefits from a new and emerging language; he benefits from people stopping to consider, for example, whether it makes sense or whether it is subtly dehumanizing to say he "has" Down syndrome. Jamie has access to expensive medical and therapeutic services, which in our society are available to most professors' kids. Prejudicial attitudes are also changing and, when need be, laws are now on the books to mandate equal education and equal access to all of society's benefits and opportunities. Jamie and kids like him, not to mention adults, do not as a matter of course spend much time in institutions such as those that Blatt and his pioneering colleagues condemned by exposing them to a wide public audience. Indeed, Jamie could not have picked a better place and a better time to be born. Through the use of conceptual thinking about history and society, I know this without even being able to fully know Jamie.

But when they conjure the meaning of a child like Jamie, the possessors of the sociological imagination imagine also the mongoloid idiots of the past locked in their institutions, remember the eugenics movement, and see the disabled children today abandoned in Brazil, left in hospitals in Zimbabwe, or cared for by over-stressed parents in the lands of milk and honey. They understand, too, the broad economic, political, and cultural bases for these myriad individual, particular experiences. The sociological imagination—this type of mind that relates history and biography through an analysis of social structure and that works back and forth from the most particular to the most general—sees also many people the world over struggling to change their own lives and the situations that define their lives. Michael Berube's book fits in here, and so does the one you are reading.

The initial concern in this chapter with what we can know takes on new meaning when given practical expression in the form of knowledge sought and knowledge gained in an ongoing struggle for particular life against systematic and predictable death. Adorno's concept of the indigent particular itself takes on new weight when the flesh of particular living and actually indigent people is added on to it and then related to today's myriad forms of deathmaking. Likewise, the notion of nonidentity is deepened considerably if, instead of turning it over for discussion in a philosophy seminar, we relate it to the ongoing experience of people who, by virtue of their obstinate bodies, cannot identify with what is imposed on them as normal. In this interplay between abstract ideas and concrete human lives, we have before us what is perhaps at the heart of the sociological imagination. The sociological imagination is not just a conceptual apparatus, pure and simple. It is also a means to achieve a mimetic—humble, respectful, awe-filled—relationship to the borderland experiences of human existence, what we have also called the "liminal" aspects of postmodern experience. Wrong children, for example, can teach us this form of knowing *if* we are prepared to listen and learn. "I am not supposed to be like this, but it's okay," sing R.E.M.[56] It is, alas, a terrible and magnificent lesson.

Notes

1. Ernest Bloch, *Natural Law and Human Dignity* (1961; reprint, Cambridge, M.A.: MIT Press, 1986), 280.

2. J. M. Bernstein, "Why Rescue Semblance?," in *The Semblance of Subjectivity: Essays in Adorno's Aesthetic Theory,* eds. Tom Huhn and Lambert Zuidervaart (Cambridge, M.A.: MIT Press, 1997), 195.

3. On the idea of "after Auschwitz," see Theodor W. Adorno, *Negative Dialectics* (1966; reprint, New York: Continuum, 1987) and "Education after Auschwitz," in *Critical Models,* ed. Henry W. Pickford (New York: Columbia University Press, 1998), 191-204.

4. Michael Bérubé, *Life as We Know It: A Father, a Family and an Exceptional Child* (New York: Pantheon, 1996).

5. Ibid., 19. Bérubé also noted, however, that "80 percent of fetuses with Down's are eventually miscarried," meaning that Down's syndrome would be even more common if this were not the case.

6. Bureau of the Census, *Statistical Abstract of the United States: 1999* (Washington, D.C., 1999), 151. On worldwide estimates, see James I. Charleton, *Nothing About Us without Us* (Berkeley: University of California Press, 1998).

7. Bérubé, *Life as We Know It,* x-xi.

8. Ibid., xi-xii.

9. Ibid., xvii.

10. Ibid., xviii.

11. Ibid.

12. Ibid.

13. Ibid., xviii-xix.

14. Ibid., xix.

15. See Chapter 3 of Steven P. Dandaneau and Maude Falcone, *A Wrong Life: Studies in Lifeworld-Grounded Critical Theory,* titled "Dried Beans and Beethoven: The Art of Parenting the Ineffable" (Greenwich, C.T.: JAI Press, 1998).

16. This question is explored in detail by Simi Linton in her book, *Claiming Disability: Knowledge and Identity* (New York: New York University Press, 1998), with a foreword by Michael Bérubé.

17. For a cross-cultural overview of disability, see Benedicte Ingstad and Susan Reynolds White, eds., *Disability and Culture* (Berkeley: University of California Press, 1995).

18. As Michael Bérubé wrote, "Right through the 1970s, 'Mongoloid idiot' wasn't an epithet; it was a *diagnosis.* It wasn't uttered by callow, ignorant persons fearful of 'difference' and Central Asian eyes; it was pronounced by the best-trained medical practitioners in the world, who told families of kids with Down syndrome that their children would never be able to walk, talk, dress themselves, or recognize their parents. Best to have the child institutionalized and tell one's friends that the baby died at birth." See Bérubé, *Life as We Know It,* 27.

19. Wolf Wolfensberger, *The New Genocide of Handicapped and Afflicted People* (bound manuscript, Syracuse University, 1987), 1. See also David J. Vail, *Dehumanization and the Institutional Career* (Springfield, I.L.: Charles C Thomas, 1966).

20. C. Wright Mills, "The Cultural Apparatus," in *Power, Politics, & People: The Collected Essays of C. Wright Mills,* ed. Irving Louis Horowitz (1959; reprint, Oxford, U.K.: Oxford University Press, 1963), 405.

21. Ibid.

22. Adorno, *Negative Dialectics,* 406. Adorno's own formulation (in translation from the original German) is as follows: "Dialectics is the self-consciousness of the objective context of delusion; it does not mean to have escaped from that context. Its objective goal is to break out of the context from within."

23. Bérubé, *Life as We Know It,* 249.

24. Julia Kristeva, "The Limits of Life," viewed online (11 Nov. 1999) at www.unesco.org/drg/human-rights/pages/english/Kristeva html. All Kristeva quotations are from this document.

25. T. Sherratt, "Negative Dialectics: A Positive Interpretation," *International Philosophical Quarterly* 38 (Mar. 1998): 60, emphasis in original.

26. Ibid., 64.

27. See Charleton, *Nothing About Us without Us,* 24.

28. Ibid.

29. Ibid., 43.

30. Ibid., 43-4.

31. Ibid., 43.

32. Ibid.

33. Charleton, *Nothing About Us without Us,* 45.

34. Colin Barnes, Geof Mercer, and Tom Shakespeare, *Exploring Disability: A Sociological Introduction* (Cambridge, U.K.: Polity Press, 1999), 112.

35. Ibid., 111.

36. Ibid., 112. See also Charleton, *Nothing About Us without Us,* 45.

37. Charleton, *Nothing About Us without Us,* 85.

38. Ibid., 86.

39. Ibid.

40. Ibid.

41. See Barnes, Mercer, and Shakespeare, *Exploring Disability,* 160-4, and Charleton, *Nothing About Us without Us,* 130-6.

42. Barnes, Mercer, and Shakespeare, *Exploring Disability,* 161.

43. Peter Monaghan, "Pioneering Field of Disability Studies Challenges Established Approaches and Attitudes," *The Chronicle of Higher Education,* 23 Jan. 1998, A15-6.

44. Lennard J. Davis, "Constructing Normality," in *The Disability Studies Reader,* ed. Lennard J. Davis (New York: Routledge, 1997), 10.

45. Ibid., 19.

46. Ibid.

47. Ibid.

48. Steve J. Taylor and Steven D. Blatt, eds., *In Search of the Promised Land: The Collected Papers of Burton Blatt* (Washington, D.C.: American Association on Mental Retardation, 1999).

49. Ibid., 5.

50. Ibid., 7.

51. See Ann Braden Johnson, *Out of Bedlam: The Truth About Deinstitutionalization* (New York: Basic Books, 1990), 115.

52. Ibid., xx.

53. See Rael Jean Isaac and Virginia C. Hunt, *Madness in the Streets: How Psychiatry and the Law Abandoned the Mentally Ill* (New York: The Free Press, 1990).

54. Ibid., 250.

55. Barnes, Mercer, and Shakespeare, *Exploring Disability,* 103.

56. R.E.M., "The Wrong Child," *Green* (Warner Brothers, Inc., 1988). Lyrics by W. T. Berry, P. L. Buck, M. E. Mills, and J. M. Stipe.

6

Generation X

A Phantom Subject

Who would have thought the kids would start taking over so soon? Or that they would even want to? They were supposed to be slackers, cynics, drifters. But don't be fooled by their famous pose of repose. Lately, more and more of them are prowling tirelessly for the better deal, hunting down opportunities that will free them from the career imprisonment that confined their parents. They are flocking to technology start-ups, founding small businesses and even taking up causes—all their own way. They are making movies in and out of Hollywood, making money, spending money. Slapped with the label Generation X, they've turned the tag into a badge of honor. They are X-citing, X-igent, X-pansive. They're the next big thing. Boomers beware! It's payback time.

—Margot Hornblower[1]

Betwixt the particular and the totality, between the individual and the whole of human experience, there exists innumerable groupings, strata, and layers defined by various types of social and cultural relationships. These include but are not limited to the family, religion, and nation. There are, for example, x number of families in any single society or in the world as a whole; x number of religious orders, dominations, and cults; and x number of nations. The composition of any one of these conceptual categories is changing at every moment, and all of them are internally very complex. Some nations, for example, dominate or control their own independent state (e.g., the French people and France or Russians and Russia), whereas some are not sovereign over a distinct political territory (e.g., Kurdish people and Iraq and Turkey). With regard to religion, imagine the internal complexity of what goes under the heading "Protestant" or all the variations and subdivisions and levels subsumed under the Roman Catholic Church. Both of these latter groups, enormous though they are, are just part of the worldwide Christian community, which itself represents only 35 percent of the world's religious people. Sometimes a people, a religion, and a political territory are intimately intertwined, such as Jewish people, Judaism, and the state of Israel, which is a Jewish state even though not everyone who is a citizen of Israel is a member of the Jewish faith. Many countries, especially geographically large ones such as the United States, Canada, and Russia, are multiethnic and multireligious, and political authority in these countries is officially neutral with respect to its many subgroups and communities. The United States, for example, includes both Utah, with roughly 80 percent of its population belonging to the Church of Latter Day Saints, and Hawaii, with a population that reflects its proximity to the Pacific Rim countries of Japan and the Philippines. In other words, when sociology attends to actually existing human societies, things get complicated very quickly. In ranging back and forth from the very small and particular to the very large and abstract, the possessor of the sociological imagination cannot plow through this intermediate thicket too quickly. There is always a very real risk of oversimplifying the complexity of social and cultural relationships.

The intermediate category "generation" provides a means to explore such complexities. In this chapter, I shall demonstrate the workings of the sociological imagination in postmodern times through a study of the arguably nonexisting and hence peculiar intermediate social grouping called "Generation X." If in the last chapter our attention gravitated to the problem of wrong children and hence to the meaning of biography in postmodern times, in this chapter we shall attend especially to the problem of a generational "common destiny" and hence to the meaning of history as it intersects with biography. Although I focus on the phenomenon of Generation X, my concern is really to discuss the political and cultural significance of all post-baby boomers—Generation X, Generation Next, Generation Dot Com, The Digital Generation, et cetera, ad nauseam—and to situate this segment of the population within the historical social structures that define postmodernity. On this basis, we can then make sense of these phantom generational categories and suggest ways in which the use of the sociological imagination can help to define the political challenges squarely confronting today's "young."

What Is a Generation?

The idea of a generation seems straightforward enough. A generation refers to an age-bound cohort that shares something more than the sheer fact of being born at roughly the same time. So-called baby boomers, for example, are considered a distinctive generation for reasons that extend far beyond the fact that a bunch of children—roughly 77 million, or nearly 25 percent of the current U.S. population—were born in the years immediately following the end of World War II and continuing up until the year 1964. They are instead the famous—or, depending on one's point of view, the infamous—generation of the 1960s; politically involved and culturally innovative, they like to think of themselves as a generation decisive in overturning American apartheid, stopping the war in Vietnam, reinvigorating the women's movement, expanding personal freedom and popular artistic expression, and, in so many other ways, a generation that served as a catalyst for progressive social and cultural change. The American sociologist Todd Gitlin, who was himself a leader in the student movement of that era, has described the 1960s as "years of hope, days of rage."[2] There is no denying that the decade of the 1960s was a time of social and cultural ferment.

As suggested by the famous German sociologist Karl Mannheim (1893-1947), who wrote about generations in "The Problem of Generations," the *something* beyond mere demographics that makes a socially and cultural meaningful generation could be said to be a self-conscious, collective pursuit of a "common destiny."[3] In this light, it could be said of the generation of the 1960s, the baby boomers, that their common destiny was the expansion of individual moral freedom and democratic social relations throughout society. From the Berkeley "Free Speech" movement to the civil rights work spearheaded by the Student Nonviolent Coordinating Committee, many young people growing up in the 1960s and early 1970s were courageous activists. Many more simply wore their hair in new, longer ways and experimented with drugs, sex, and rock and roll. Innumerable acts of rebellion, overt and subtle, challenged the status quo and notably affected the dominant culture, and these acts were not strictly an American phenomenon either; generational change was experienced throughout the rich societies and was especially intense, for example, in France and Germany.

As a result of their many and various collective actions, both personal and political, this generation changed society and culture such that today we largely take for granted the freedoms they, in solidarity with one another, fought so hard to achieve. Writing in the late 1980s, Gitlin observed in reference to the American experience, "True, the country is conservative—as it was, campuses included, during most of the Sixties—but some of what it is conserving now are Sixties breakthroughs."[4] However much we may in retrospect criticize their actions and their self-understanding, and however cautious we should rightly be in overgeneralizing about any 77 million-person generation, the baby boomers did act toward their world and change it. In a meaningful sociological sense and without prejudging the value or fate of their common destiny, this generation created itself, in Mannheim's words, as a true "generation as actuality."[5]

In this regard, the notion of a Generation X is especially fascinating because it does not refer to an age-defined cohort in pursuit of a common destiny. Generation X does not, in this sense, exist. What is more, everyone knows this. Why, then, do we hear so much about it? If it does not exist, then what is it?

If the members of the so-called Generation X are known for anything, it is for their being, in Ted Halstead's words, "the most politically disengaged" generation in American history.[6] Today's young adults—the 50 million variously stereotyped "slackers, cynics, whiners, drifters, [and] malcontents" born roughly between 1964 and 1978—are important precisely because they would appear to be the very opposite of an age-defined cohort self-consciously in pursuit of a common destiny.[7] The members of Generation X would appear to be, as it were, a nongeneration or even an antigeneration. But even this formulation does not quite get at what makes this topic so elusive.

Generation X exists, if anywhere, in Baudrillard's hyperreality. It is the product of postmodern media, more a simulation of a generation than a real generation. The same is true for its younger siblings, Generation Next, Generation Dot Com, or, as it were, Generation Whatever. By their very nature, hyperreal simulations are unreal, perpetually blurring and self-devouring phenomena. Analyzing the television reality of the Gulf War, for example, can be even more difficult and disturbing than analyzing the real war itself. The analysis of U.S. patriot missiles, celebrated as technological marvels even though they never intercepted a single hostile Iraqi scud missile, can acquire a dizzying and disturbing quality, whereas actual killing and death is something most people can gets their minds around. Likewise, the serious, slow discussion of anything that appears on television or in the mass media (e.g., Monica Lewinsky's ads for "Jenny Craig" or the 23 hours of "Millennium" coverage) taxes most peoples' patience and interest. Baudrillard, like the would-be analyst of Generation X, risks nauseating the reader by trying to match the whirl of television's false consciousness in the medium of conceptually ordered printed words.

As we look more closely at Generation X, and especially as we attend to the changing social structure that, in general, sets the stage for young adults' lives in the present, we will see that it is society itself and, in particular, the emergence of hyperreality that bears the greatest responsibility for this generation's disrepair. We have already noted that this generation faces unprecedented and all together daunting challenges, but to the facts of the dying world and today's mundane dystopian everyday existence we must add the ironic twist that today's young adults must destroy the hyperreality that defines them as a generation in the first place. Only then could this cohort even have a chance to realize its latent common destiny. Indeed, this nongeneration will have to squarely confront those aspects of contemporary society that the generation of the 1960s so adored and reveled in—hyperreality and its resulting cynicism and panic—lest this generation be swallowed up by them and its political potential forever blunted and contained. Generation X does not really exist, and for this reason there is hope for today's young adults, no matter when they were born. These may not be "days of rage," but this may turn out to be a good thing.

The Origin of Generation X

It is wise to begin by fixing the origin of the Generation X phenomenon in time and space. Unlike television itself or, for that matter, the whirl of the dot-com-everything Internet, the slowness of reading and writing, and especially book reading and writing, is well suited for this task. The term itself originated with a 1980s punk band by this name but was popularized as a generational label by the 1991 publication of a novel by the Canadian writer Douglas Coupland titled *Generation X: Tales for an Accelerated Culture.*[8] Describing Coupland's first publication (which he issued at the ripe old age of thirty) as a novel is a generous characterization. Its fame, which has proven fleeting, rests not on the quality its characters (Andy, Dag, and Claire) and its narrative structure but on the fact that Coupland included an unusual series of sidebars that name and define dozens of generational terms or lingo. The most well-known of these is "McJob." Coupland also added a series of generationally specific statistics in an appendix. In other words, the very form of *Generation X,* with its generational glossary and appendix, smoothed the way for its reception as a Statement (with a capital "S") and for Coupland, although he claimed not to have anticipated or relished this role, to be made a spokesperson for young, post-baby boom adults.

Coupland's novel is also written self-consciously from within hyperreality (a.k.a., an accelerated culture, a culture that simulates television and in which television reality is more real than actual reality). In a way, Andy, Dag, and Claire foreshadow the television situation comedy "Friends" more than they aspire to a place next to Ishmael, Ahab, and the white whale in literature's pantheon of great characters. Coupland is self-conscious about his book not really being a work of literature at all. Some have termed this its "irony," although it is more plainly the case that *Generation X,* more than *Moby Dick,* was produced as an entertainment commodity, something stimulating for sale. If not necessarily explicitly tailored for mass consumption through the mass media, it was, given its McNovel form and its transparent message, perfectly constructed for this fate.

McJob, for example, is the first generational neologism listed in the book and is defined in two sentences: "A low-pay, low-prestige, low-dignity, low-benefit, no-future job in the service sector. Frequently considered a satisfying career choice by people who have never held one."[9] Not surprisingly, McJob is also the aspect of the book that members of the mass media popularized with the greatest zeal. Of course, members of the mass media often do not have time or patience for whole books nor the space to engage in their full exegesis or a large enough paying audience with sufficient attention and interest to warrant such critical attention. This is true of academic life as well, in which far more is written than could ever be read, much less read carefully and fully considered. How many undergraduates, how many faculty members, have ever read the whole of *Moby Dick*? In our accelerated culture, who has the time or patience for this? Coupland, of course, cannot be blamed for the workings of the accelerated culture of which and from which he wrote; like everything else about Generation X, this culture controlled the media reportage and it controlled him. He could not write about the whale from anywhere else other than from within the whale.

In the book's wake, a minor Generation X industry was born. The same publishing house that issued *Generation X* was soon putting out another book, *Generation Ecch!*, which criticized Coupland's presumed attempt to name, define, and speak for an entire generation.[10] The phantom *something* that the media suddenly staged arguments about was really a *nothing* construed as the latest big thing. Generation X was thus born as a fad and, like all fads, was destined to fade as its newness withered into yesterday's news. Ironically, this is the very sort of world that Coupland's novel-commodity describes. The same year not only saw the publication of *Generation Ecch!* and many similar statements, such as Daniel Strong's "Generation Hex," but also *The GenX Reader*, which collected as much of the flurry of "S"tatements and anti-"S"tatements that could be bound together for roughly $14.00.[11] It is not a book that examines the real lives of young adults, just their various representations in the mass media.

Interestingly, *The GenX Reader* concluded with a strong dose of cynical self-criticism under such titles as "GenXploitation" and "It's the Hyperreal Thing," thereby incorporating into itself an understanding of the nebulous and fabricated nature of the phenomenon that it nonetheless further contributed to by its very existence. *The GenX Reader* is a reader about nothing real. It was published by the same people—Ballantine Books—who brought us C. Wright Mills's *Listen Yankee* and *The Marxists* twentysomething years earlier.

This should cause us pause. While largely now forgotten, it was once thought that the decade of the 1990s would mirror the decade of the 1960s in that young adults were expected to coalesce in solidarity as a real generation. They would react to the conservatism of their upbringing (just as the baby boomers did to theirs) and rise up to act toward the world in ways that would alter the course of history. This notion—again, not surprisingly—was memorably articulated in a Hollywood

movie, the not especially distinguished 1990 film, "Flashback." The line was the following: "The 90's are going to make the 60's look like the 50's." The actor who uttered this money line (that is, the clip used to sell the movie in its promotional advertising), was none other than Dennis Hopper. Hopper is an actor adept at marketing
his own apparent strangeness (e.g., in ads for Nike and the National Football
League) and whose film career includes a starring role in the 1969 antiestablishment
hit, "Easy Rider." After a long hiatus from the silver screen, Hopper's career had, by
this point, been resurrected by his freakish performances in Francis Ford Coppola's
"Apocalypse Now" and the David Lynch postmodern thriller, "Blue Velvet."

"The 90's are going to make the 60's look like the 50's." That is, Generation X
was imagined as a cohort whose political coming of age would far exceed that of the
baby boomers. There was to be a new and extreme easy rider on the horizon, more
outrageous than its predecessor and so freakish that the born-again image of Dennis
Hopper was needed to sell it.

It is more the case that the 1990s made *the 1980s* look like the 1960s. Once
thought to be *only* a period of ascendent conservatism—the coldness of the Reagan
and Thatcher governments warmed only by the image of Michael J. Fox as a "Family
Ties" young conservative—the 1980s also saw many young adults protest apartheid
in South Africa, construct AIDS quilts, and rally against the threat of the second
phase of the Cold War. For example, shanty town displays protesting conditions in
South Africa were not an uncommon feature of university and college campuses.
Ecological politics also flourished: Greenpeace, Green Parties, and R.E.M.'s
"Green" all preceded the advent of "Green Day." U.S. foreign policy, including especially the internationally condemned illegal war against the Sandinista government in Nicaragua, came under sustained criticism and protest in this country, and,
as a result of the Iran-Contra Affair, nearly cost a popular president his office. It
would be a gross exaggeration to equate 1980s political activism with 1960s political activism, but there was in this decade a significant degree of critically minded political mobilization in which young adults participated in significant numbers.

In contrast, the last decade of the twentieth century did not see even a smidgen
of generational coalescence, much less generational rage. The "Battle in Seattle"
and an occasional campus protest against Third World sweatshops notwithstanding,
self-consciously generational books, movies, and popular music styles, and, of
course, the ever-present use of Generation X by marketing agencies do not constitute the collective pursuit of a common destiny. When in search of independent, au-
tonomous, and authentic political mobilizations among the young, we must concede
that things have been quiet on this particular western front. While there has been fun,
political significance, and aesthetic quality in extreme sports, Seattle's Nirvana and
Pearl Jam, the low-budget movie "Slacker" and the big budget movie "Reality

Bites," the people who are the presumed referent of the sign "Generation X" have made no political statements, unless we construe no statement as a statement in-itself. Xers, as it were, hardly even vote, and when they do, it is for candidates such as Jesse Ventura, the schlock TV wrestler turned governor of Minnesota.[12] Inside the whale, indeed.

Publishing houses, magazines, movie studios, MTV spin-offs, and Madison Avenue, however, have had a lot to say about Generation X, and what they say is quite political in its own way. These institutions, after all, have a vested interest in marketing to 50 million young consumers, the youngest of whom possess consumption patterns that are still malleable. Generation X is the sign under which marketing specialists peddle their goods and services, and the going assumption seems to be that Generation X is a passive market segment that can be won over with clever gimmicks and cynicism presented as a sophisticated irony. The idea is to make fun of serious politics, transcendent values, and cultural criticism; in effect, to celebrate stupidity and complacency as a higher form of consciousness. In this way, marketers hope to ingratiate themselves with the newest cohort of potential customers. Thus, the way to influence Xers in advertising is to criticize advertising itself (e.g., 7-Up vs. Sprite); the way to influence Xers in politics is to criticize politics itself (e.g., Jesse Ventura's self-presentation as an antipolitician action figure); the way to influence Xers in culture is to abandon any attempt to present artistic expression as having meaning beyond its commercial form (e.g., *Generation X*, "Austin Powers" movies, the ubiquitous and self-conscious product placements featured in "Seinfeld," the character of "Bart" criticizing the buying of News Corp. stock in an episode of "The Simpsons," which is broadcast on FOX, a News Corp. television network, and so on *ad nauseam*). The key is the presentation of cultural criticism that simulates the act of biting the hand that feeds culture in the first place. The result is a pseudo-authenticity. It is the outward expression of a culture in which people are cynical about their being cynical.

This process is made easier by self-appointed generational spokespersons who advocate "selling out" as a means of resistance. This is the ironic point of view articulated in the popular Reel Big Fish song, "Sell Out," which includes the lyrics: "sell out with me tonight, 'cause the record company is gonna give me lots of money, and everything is gonna be all right."[13] Thus, the way to have a breakthrough hit single in the culture industry is to write a song about writing a breakthrough hit single in the culture industry. Andrew Hultkrans concluded *The GenX Reader* with the following advice:

> This is our 15 minutes of fame. Sell out while you still have the chance. When the GenX media virus runs its course (as all do), you'll still be stuck in that McJob col-

lecting interest on irony bonds. Graying Boomers will still be gathering cobwebs in middle management, preventing *you* from getting anywhere. After all, it's attention that we've wanted all along—approval from our elder siblings. Culture Inc. is finally bent over on the stretcher, eagerly accepting our penetration. Seize the media by the hips and take the plunge.[14]

Here, politically correct taboos against explicitly sexist and homophobic (not just sexual) imagery are violated as a form of rebellion: if that is what they want, give it to them. Without the hesitation called for by political consciousness and moral conscience, participating in the pornographic, prole feed that supplies the Generation X segment of the culture industry its forward motion is a politics born of self-conscious powerlessness. Selling out is presented as the only viable means of resistance; self-debasement as unavoidable and therefore worthy of the embrace of those who possess this purportedly sophisticated insight.

In controlling society's primary medium for collective self-presentation and self-reflection, Hultkrans' Culture Inc. commands our collective mind as it defines, interprets, and distributes images that will work best for its purposes. The powerlessness and mindlessness evident in Generation X discourse is a true reflection of its current situation. The question is really whether selling out or embracing mindlessness are the only viable means of resistance to cultural and political powerlessness.

The Cultural Apparatus

Mills was himself not just a critic of "the cultural apparatus," as he called it, but was also eager to use it to his advantage, to willfully participate in the same mass media that a few decades later would bring us Generation X. He had in mind the possibility of reaching a wide audience with "his preachings," which is how he described the political pamphlets of his last years. He was increasingly unsatisfied with merely publishing. Instead, he wanted mass publicity, and thanks to the advent of inexpensive, mass circulation paperback books (such as those published by Ballantine Books, the makers of *The GenX Reader*), his wish came true. Mills, or rather, Ballantine, sold hundreds of thousands of copies of *Listen Yankee,* and Mills became, if not a household name, arguably the most famous sociologist of his day.

However, fame, per se, was not his goal. It was rather a means to an end and that end was radical politics. Mills wanted to "take it big" more than he wanted to simply be a "big shot."[15] He wanted to subvert the institutions of mass society by working through the institutions of mass society. He wanted to reach the public and change their minds, indeed, enlarge their minds, by instilling in them through demonstration of its value what we have in this book called the sociological imagination. It didn't work.

It is not just that Mills died and therefore could not shape the reception of his work with new contributions and self-criticism. Ironically, Mills's own analysis of the cultural apparatus is well suited to explain the demise of his political strategy. It is also a useful point of departure for any reflection on the ill-fated, 1960s call for "a long march through the institutions."

As modern society developed the means of mass communication—mass circulation newspapers, popular magazines, radio, television, and now the Internet—the power to shape public consciousness was increasingly concentrated in the hands of those who commanded the means of mass communication. This meant that corporations and government, mainly, would determine the content of news and the production of culture. Sometimes, if the issues were sufficiently important, economic and political elites would coordinate their management of culture, which occurred, for example, during World War II and with respect to America's understanding of the potential for nuclear war. Anyone today who watches the classic Hollywood film, "Casablanca," for example, can see it as a thinly veiled bit of wartime propaganda on behalf of the idea that the United States must fight a war in Europe and Africa against the bad Nazi's and on the side of the good French. The purpose of "Casablanca" is not to depict the tragedy of romance during wartime but to use romance and, especially, Bogart-style masculinity to sell an isolationist American public on the virtues of a particular foreign entanglement. There is nothing essential that distinguishes this film from what we would expect of Soviet or Chinese propaganda, except, perhaps, that the Yanks had Bogey and the Communists and Nazis did not.[16] Likewise, the well-documented history of civil defense and other domestic Cold War programs reveals their origin in a kind of "duck and cover" reality-management of thermonuclear weapons. When examining the popular culture of the 1950s, it is difficult if not impossible to know where Cold War propaganda stops and authentic culture starts.[17] If there was an authentic culture in the 1950s, the images of its creators (e.g., Miles Davis, Jack Kerouac, Samuel Beckett) are today used by Apple, Inc. to sell personal computers, their reputation for authentic cultural production and criticism being the very thing that makes them so valuable to today's marketers.

Moreover, the nature of the communication has also changed a great deal. At the beginning of the last century, most people were largely ignorant of events in the world and had little access to ideas and especially to critical ideas. As a result of being plugged in to the mass media in greater numbers, they increasingly became more likely to be aware of, and have an impression of, many more things than ever before. Similar to other industrial societies, the United States quickly moved from what Marx called "rural idiocy" to electronically mediated urban cosmopolitanism.

Mass communication and transportation were expanding people's worlds in ways that had never occurred before in human history, in effect, compressing time and space. They were drawing things such as Casablanca, Morocco, and Imperial Japan into the common consciousness, and as December 7, 1941 in Pearl Harbor suggests, drawing them into tangible, violence-filled relationships as well.

The fact that the new mass media were producing an increasing quantity of information and expanding horizons was never in doubt, but information is not knowledge and in fact can impede knowledge. Expanding horizons can just as easily be lost horizons. The key is the quality of this information and whether average people have the conceptual skills to make sense of it. This is the problem of the social pragmatics of knowing: people cannot be said to be free to act when they do so with minds filled with propaganda. Who is at war with whom and why? Eastasia, Eurasia, and Oceania? The result of ubiquitous propaganda is not Shangri-la; it is Orwell's Hate Week.

Mills noted that we live in an "Age of Fact," which to his way of thinking was a criticism.[18] Facts do not speak for themselves but instead require interpretation of their meaning. But the production of interpretation was itself, in Mills's view, becoming just as regimented and narrowed as the production of information. Furthermore, thought Mills, the outlets for the distribution of preinterpreted pseudo-facts were themselves also increasingly controlled from above, such that the where, when, how, and what of cultural production were as bureaucratically and undemocratically organized as any factory. Mills was trying to analyze the institutional history of Hulkrans's pithy formulation, Culture Inc.

In our time, of course, fact has eroded to factoid; radio "play lists" are determined ahead of time by market research, and so-called "independent films" can cost millions of dollars to produce. Whether we focus on bits of information or whole symphonies, the products of today's culture are, for the most part, created in ways alien to and not well understood by consumers and distributed at a faster pace through rapidly expanding and, for the most part, highly controlled outlets of distribution in addition to being interpreted by a handful of experts whose judgment of quality is secondary to their assessment of potential market value. Likewise, millions of Web sites fragment culture, and together with the forces named above, they contribute to an ever thinner cacophony of culture rather than providing the basis for a rational public education and considered public deliberation. But Mills apparently thought that he could single-handedly jam this machinery.

For a brief time, he seemed prescient. Read mostly by college students (who had time to read books), Mills quickly became a hero for the generation of the 1960s. Tom Hayden, the principal author of the famous 1962 "Port Huron Statement" (the political manifesto of the Students for a Democratic Society [SDS]), was himself an inspired student of Mills's sociology. Todd Gitlin, who authored a 1999 introduction to a new issue of *The Sociological Imagination,* was once president of the SDS. In their study *The Seeds of the Sixties,* Andrew Jamison and Ron Eyerman include a prominent discussion of Mills's influence on the generational upheaval that was brewing in the beatnik coffeehouses and quiet campuses of the late 1950s and early 1960s.[19] There is no reason to doubt the validity of their assessment.

But like so many before and after him, Mills did not sufficiently value his own analysis of the suffocating and distorting power of the cultural apparatus, that is, the mass media and its expansive accouterments and powers, what Mills called its "observation posts," "interpretation centers," "presentation depots," its "star" system, which makes celebrities out of the very few and nobodies of the rest.[20] He may have not fully appreciated that he was playing with a seductive and expanding firestorm of image-proliferation industries drawing strength from newfound technologies. The fate of the generation of the 1960s speaks to this power as well as anything else. Despite its notable production of sound and fury, the generation of the 1960s cannot be said to have internalized the sociological imagination. Instead, it is more the case that the culture industry internalized them.

What has become of the baby boomers today? Gross generalizations can be given. Demographically speaking, they are middle aged. Economically, the majority are well off, indeed, better off than any previous generation in American history. As one group of researchers note: "Financial asset holdings of baby boomers appear to be markedly higher than their predecessors."[21] Politically, they are more likely to be liberal than conservative, but they are hardly radical about their liberalism, much less are they on good terms with the radicalism of their youth. None of this is surprising or unexpected. What is striking about this generation now reaching its fifties is its childish love for the mass media, for giant television sets offering nostalgic images that depict the generation of the 1960s when they were a generation on the move. We have Oliver Stone and we have "Forrest Gump." We hear advertisers telling aging baby boomers that it is okay to buy a Cadillac because it is time for "making whoopie," and if that does not work, Janis Joplin singing "Lord, won't you buy me a Mercedes-Benz" to sell, of all things, Mercedes-Benz automobiles. For products designed for an aging population, there is Mick Jagger, who has gathered his share of moss, singing "time is on my mind." Television programs, films, political rhetoric and political success, Viagra, and even the interest in generations themselves all stem from the overwhelming market power squarely in the hands of the roughly 77 million baby boomers who are in the prime of their earning potential, and who are therefore increasingly the culturally dominant generation. The election of William Jefferson Clinton announced their rise to power.

Why is this childish? Is it not self-indulgent for Warren Beatty, a politically liberal Hollywood movie star, to think that he could produce the film "Bulworth," in which he stars as a U.S. senator who is radicalized in mid-life, and then attempt to use this film as the launching pad for a real Beatty for President campaign? Is it not childish for President Clinton to believe that he could carry on an affair with a White House intern and not be caught, or look squarely into a bank of television cameras and say with a stern voice, "I never had sex with that woman, Ms. Lewinsky," when he knew that he did but did not want to admit it? What is it, if not childishness, that leads people in their fifties to attend Rolling Stones concerts as though the spirit of rock-and-roll was not inherently youth-oriented and rebellious and therefore antithetical to its manifestation in the form of wealthy, aging sex symbols forever reprising their role as antiestablishment rebels? Billy Joel, once perhaps a sex symbol, has given this image up in favor of the role of history teacher, telling his generation, "we didn't start the fire." This song, which lists in a rap-like, rapid fire public figures from the decade of the 1960s, was used in some American classrooms to actually facilitate the teaching of real history.

The reader may disagree with these characterizations because they are clearly judgmental, but the main point is that popular culture and the culture of politics are intertwined, lacking *gravitas,* and dominated by the hyperreality so valued by the generation of the 1960s. The public life of the United States (but not just the United States) is awash in superficial images and, from a historical perspective, merely momentary sensational events without lasting significance. President Clinton was the first President of the United States to be asked, as he was on MTV, whether he wore boxers or briefs. He is also the first elected U.S. President to be impeached while in office, mainly for his having lied under oath concerning his extramarital intimate relations. Yet this event was as soon forgotten in the popular mind as a canceled sitcom from a television season past. It is of roughly equivalent cultural value to his answer to the boxer-or-brief question, which, seemingly, says it all.

In setting down to examine the phenomenon of Generation X, then, our sociological imaginations are asked to grasp a set of apparently ethereal relationships. On one hand, there is a real history of institutional change to conceive, involving in particular the growth of mass media and the eventual establishment of a new image-reality that overwhelms ordinary, day-to-day reality. In this analysis, we have stressed the power of collectively produced representations to dominate what is purportedly represented. The phenomenon of Generation X is an example of this power because no real "generation as actuality" exists, only the *simulation* of a generation as actuality. Much of the anxiety produced by the "Generation X" label, then, is the result of its unabashed banality, which is imposed from without on those who are already suffering under the weight of a difficult real reality. This creates the potential for a real type of generational conflict in which the referents of the "Generation X" label struggle for the right to use their own minds to understand themselves and guide their action in the world. In a sense, it would be a battle for reality against its debasement in the form of hyperreality. As long as everyone is watching television, however, there is no generation "gap."

Enter the "Improbable Guru" of the 1960s

The term *improbable guru* was coined by *Fortune* magazine and repeated by the intellectual historian Paul Breines to describe his surprisingly famous and influential teacher, the philosopher, sociologist, and radical political thinker Herbert Marcuse (1898-1979).[22] In addition to Max Horkheimer, Theodor Adorno, and other "Frankfurt School" colleagues, Marcuse fled Nazi repression in his native Germany and came to the United States in 1934. After an initial affiliation with Columbia University and the Harvard University Russian Research Center, Marcuse held major academic positions first at Brandeis University and then at the University of California at San Diego, where, despite the dedicated efforts of then Governor Ronald Reagan to remove him, he stayed until his retirement.

In the first two-thirds of his life, Marcuse distinguished himself as a brilliant student of Hegel, Freud, and Marx. Marcuse also wrote a book-length condemnation of the Soviet brand of dogmatic Marxism, and for several years during and after World War II, worked for the U.S. State Department's Office of War Information and the Office of Strategic Services. These last affiliations contributed to the (obviously false) charge years later that he was a secret government agent sent to undermine the student movement.

Indeed, always an independent thinker committed to radical democratic politics, Marcuse's later years saw him become increasingly outspoken and inclined to act toward the world. By the late 1960s, he was acknowledged, along with Jean-Paul Sartre, as not only a major intellectual inspiration for but also an actual partner in student-led rebellions worldwide. This old German philosopher with a talent for very complicated thoughts was certainly, as *Fortune* dubbed him, a terribly improbable guru.

Marcuse's best known book, one especially well known to the students of the 1960 generation, argued that advanced industrial civilization had produced in most people a very deep and pernicious form of *false consciousness* so elusive and confounding that it was experienced as a "comfortable, smooth, reasonable, democratic unfreedom."[23] In this 1964 book titled *One-Dimensional Man,* Marcuse analyzed the forces that he felt prevented a much needed revolutionary form of social change lying within our society's grasp.

He based his study on philosophy, but he also suggested that

> perhaps the most telling evidence [in support of his thesis] can be obtained by simply looking at television or listening to the AM radio for one consecutive hour for a couple of days, not shutting off the commercials, and now and then switching the station.[24]

The main idea of the book is that contemporary culture reduces everything to the merely technical and instrumental, to merely this one dimension of possible human experience. In this regard, Marcuse was in effect following Max Weber's criticism of the science-for-everything mentality produced by the dominance of instrumental reason. Even more than Weber, however, Marcuse did not hesitate to criticize the totality of human society, especially the so-called advanced societies that thought of themselves as beyond reproach and that, indeed, worked in such a way as to stifle critics by promising and delivering more and more technologically produced wealth and power.

In the face of such a productive if also irrational behemoth, Marcuse was firm in his commitment to the value of the second dimension of human culture, the sphere of free artistic expression, genuine human love, beauty, critical insight, and the transcendent values of reason and freedom, none of which can be obtained in the same way that production quotas are met, and none of which are ever equivalent to shopping malls overflowing with new and improved products for sale. This is why Marcuse is more an intellectual descendent of Karl Marx and not, strictly speaking, of Max Weber because Marcuse was much more a political radical than was Weber. Marcuse was always on the lookout for any real possibility for a qualitatively new, indeed, utopian, form of society and culture.

Although we can never fully attain utopia, argued Marcuse, we must strive to attain the utopias within our grasp. Marcuse was, by the 1960s, an outspoken advocate for revolution, for many achievable utopias, and for the liberation of consciousness and of the body that would be both prologue and the result of this revolution. He would follow his pessimistic *One-Dimensional Man* with such works as his *An Essay on Liberation* (1969) and *Counterrevolution and Revolt* (1972). Although he would never repudiate his own pessimistic views in *One-Dimensional Man,* he also never gave up the idea that concluded this book: "it is only for the sake of those without hope that hope is given to us."[25] Marcuse borrowed these words from his friend Walter Benjamin, a Frankfurt School colleague who committed suicide during his own attempt to flee Nazi persecution.

One of Marcuse's concepts seems to capture the essence of his distinct manner of social analysis: "repressive desublimation."[26] "Sublimation," a Freudian concept, means to transform raw biological drives for sexual pleasure and aggression into socially acceptable manifestations, say, in the form of dedication to work. A certain amount of psychic repression is needed for humans to engage in socially and culturally meaningful work, indeed, in any recognizably cultural activity. This repression can become unnecessarily onerous, blotting out real feelings and desires. Marcuse worried very much about the advent of such "surplus repression" as people became subjected to greater demands to conform themselves to machine-like performance standards in and out of work.[27] Too much repression means there is no room for individual freedom. We could become robots, although perhaps not cheerful robots.

But Marcuse also worried that, under the domination of a consumer-driven capitalism, people would be sold false forms of desublimation, which promised not real sexual gratification and not real leisure nor real outlets for the expression of aggression but only the knock-off equivalents: pseudo-sexual gratification, say, in the form of pornography or simply racy movies and advertisements, and pseudo-aggression in the form of violence-based video games.

In other words, for Marcuse, the apparent desublimation of "free love," flower children, and a steady ingestion of psychedelic drugs could turn out to be repression in sheep's clothing and not the liberation of basic human desires, their genuine fulfillment, and a resulting happiness. If sexual promiscuity, for example, is promoted as a means to distract attention from social and political issues and dissipate youthful energies, then it is plainly a form of repression. "Prole feed," as it were, can come in all sorts of unexpected packages, although this is one form that Orwell predicted, at least for the Proles. A strong if vicarious identification with sport heros, especially those engaged in collision sports such as American football, is tantamount to cheering for the lions in their match with the Christians whether one actually has seats at the Coliseum or voyeuristically views from the safety of their own living room. It is the potential for violence, not the sportsmanship or athletic competition, that makes rodeo as much as stock car racing so interesting and popular. All forms of consumption that promise happiness but merely stimulate anxiety and provide a "rush" or titillation-in-a-box constitute for Marcuse examples of repressive desublimation. Forever-delayed gratification is no better than repressive forms of immediate and base gratification, and it is in fact worse in the sense long ago expressed by the German poet Goethe when he wrote that "no one is more a slave than the one who thinks he is free without being free."[28]

It is ironic, then, that Marcuse would be the improbable guru of the 1960s generation, for one-dimensionality and repressive desublimation are the very things that this generation has—half-heartedly if not whole-heartedly—embraced. Herbert

Marcuse died the same year that Margaret Thatcher became the first female Prime Minister of the United Kingdom. Since roughly this time, we have heard little concern expressed about the satisfaction of real human needs, the promotion of genuine happiness, and the responsibility (personal as well as political) implied in the notion of hope for the sake of those who have none. Instead, booming stock markets, Christmas consumerism, and economic individualism have reigned triumphant. Today's young adults can hardly be blamed for their truncated utopian sensibilities because their's is a society transfixed by information technology, Teletubbies, and a fear of falling through an increasingly nonexistent safety net. As he approached his own biographical finality, Marcuse was not at all optimistic about the future of human existence, nor did he think he had been well understood by those who were his putative followers. If Marcuse was a guru, even an improbable one, he was also a failed guru whose teachings had fallen on ears made deaf by the more intense cacophony of today's bread and circuses.

W[h]ither the Sociological Imagination?

The advent of postmodernity relied on a set of distinctly modern institutional revolutions, including industrialization, urbanization, and bureaucratization. The media-driven, information society of the present was only possible as a result of these initial earth-shaking changes associated with the making of modern society. In other words, postmodernity required modernity's legacy. Now, however, with its technology in place, this type of culture can spread itself throughout the world, extending itself through the distribution of radios, television sets, movie houses, home and personal computers, and so forth such as to realize the always ironic notion of a "global village," if only in hyperreality. Young adults today know this hyperreality as well as, and perhaps better than, they know their real reality. Generational relationships, such as they exist, are often defined in terms of the television shows watched, the movies seen, the fashions worn, and the computer games played. It is thus a generation that is more wired together than actually together, a generation for whom the experience of solidarity is electronically mediated. Thus, the new generation confronts the task of establishing a common destiny without first having anything other than image consumption in common. Generation X and its spin-offs and sequels, if they are to be real, must emerge squarely from within postmodernity, a context of delusion if there ever was one.

This leads to ironies. The intense interest in politically engaged generations is itself a product of Generation X's immediate predecessor, the 1960s generation. This generation of the 1960s metamorphosed as they moved into a position of power *within,* not beyond or in critical opposition to, the image-dominated society of today.

That the 1960s generation has done its own selling out means that the young adults that follow them into maturity must contend with loads of hyperreal nostalgia—a kind of detritus storm—in addition to attending to the real reality before them. This may mean doing something more than selling out to the already sold out or mindlessly attempting to replicate the form of generational politics.

The example of C. Wright Mills helps to draw together these threads of analysis. If the originator of the idea of a sociological imagination, himself an incisive analyst of the cultural apparatus and a soon-to-be hero of the 1960s generation, could not successfully negotiate the postmodern situation and alter its development toward one dimensionalization, then what hope is there for today's would-be possessor of the sociological imagination, who faces, and is the product of, a much more robust canned culture of taken-for-granted delusion and official childishness? How is the Brady Bunch generation going to handle global warming, the world population crisis, and the results of species extinction? How is the space shuttle Challenger generation going to handle the worldwide AIDS crisis, Ritalin, and cyberporn? How is the Atari, MTV, and Nintendo Generation, or Pepsi Cola's Generation Next, going to take control of its own mind and confront its own powerlessness. It would seem that the original formulation of the sociological imagination may not suffice in the face of these questions. It may be that the sociological imagination must itself be radicalized.

We have already gone some way in this direction. In Mills's hands, "biography" referred simply to "the inner life and external career of a variety of individuals."[29] But we have already extended this notion by introducing the idea of indigent particulars whose inner life is ultimately ineffable and whose external career runs against the grain of socially imposed normalcy. Mills was not wholly unaware of the importance of extreme experience, but it did not serve him as a critical fulcrum for his own politics or his own activity as a cultural workman. For political and theoretical reasons, Mills was more interested in the promise of Third World revolutionaries, like Fidel Castro, than in the lives of children whose legs have been removed by land mines.

This suggests also a masculine bias in Mills's view of biography, masculine biases being not uncommon in his day. Inner lives were important inasmuch as they undergirded self-directed external careers, careers "external" in the sense of having their importance in public life as opposed to private or intimate social relations. For Mills, a "career" refers to any public role playing in which selves have careers as self-made images deployed in relation to other selves. His own aspiration to *be* a political writer, not just *work* as a political writer, is an example of what he had in mind, but this is a far cry from thinking about Jamie Bérubé, who is not likely to spark insurrections.

Can we also extend the notion of a common generational destiny? Is it possible to radicalize the sociological imagination's concern for history and history making in a way that will facilitate its power to conceive of a way out of the confinement of Generation X and Generation Whatever?

Several efforts in this regard have already been proposed. One of the most important is a notion advanced by the famous University of Illinois sociologist Norman Denzin, who advocates a "minimalist" sociology in direct and explicit opposition to a Mills's "taking it big" sociology.[30] Denzin's take-it-small approach is really an effort to achieve Mills's aims by new, indirect means. He wants today's sociology to focus its attention on "the ever elusive subject . . . the man, women, and child who cries out and sometimes goes to others for help, [who has] an occasional grasp on who she is and where she is going."[31] Denzin is especially interested in "epiphanic moments," that is, "when the subject is in-between interpretive frameworks" or in-between what Mills called "secondhand worlds."[32] Here Denzin seeks "the stories of personal trouble that ordinary people tell one another," not the stories of "self- or society-appointed experts," that is, the books written by would-be Millsian sociologists.[33] For Denzin,

> Mills spoke to an earlier generation [i.e., Denzin's]. His text [i.e., *The Sociological Imagination*] affected sociological lives and set in motion versions of the sociological imagination that are now turning back on him. The mark of a good sociological narrative is its ability to raise questions and to create challenges. Mills did this, but today we must go beyond him.[34]

Denzin's alternative is an "ethically responsive, feminist, theoretically minimalist, postmodern sociology and anthropology of existential experience that is responsive to the death of the 'social' in sociology while it opens itself to the sounds and voices of contemporary American life."[35] For Denzin, selling out is unnecessary because critique is called for when sociology "come[s] up against cultural writings which reproduce repressive ideologies that go against the grain of experience uncovered in the stories we have secured."[36] This is the heart of Denzin's response to postmodern hyperreality, where it is difficult if not impossible to write about a "fixed reality," a "world out there that can be objectively mapped by a theory or a method," including objectively mapped by the so-called sociological imagination.[37]

If Denzin were to analyze Generation X, presumably he would do so by studying young adults, probably a handful of young adults, and look for an opportunity to learn from them what their lives are really like during moments of personal crisis when they are trying to grasp who they are and what they are doing. It is difficult to speculate about what such moments would entail, but certainly they would involve experiences that occur when televisions are turned off, when young adults are given over to actual interactions with other people and with themselves. Denzin wants sociologists to report these real interactions as richly as possible and eschew the use of "thick theory," which more often than not just gets in the way of reporting on existential realities. Presumably, then, Denzin would look for the seeds of an authentic generation as actuality in such terms.

Another effort to extend Mills's formulation of the sociological imagination to postmodern society comes from Cornel West, the famous American philosopher, theologian, political writer, and professor of African American studies at Harvard University. West treats Mills as a harbinger of "prophetic pragmatism." Writing in his 1989 book *The American Evasion of Philosophy,* West argues that Mills's sociological imagination attains its ultimate pragmatic significance only when Mills's sociology is seen as thoroughly infused with a utopian spirit, as prophetic of a better world.[38] There is no doubt that Mills was heavily influenced by American *pragmatism,* the philosophy that weighs the value of ideas in terms of their potential power to shape the course of history making. There is also no doubt that Mills was "An American Utopian" (the subtitle of Irving Louis Horowitz's biography of C. Wright Mills).[39] In West's reading, there is an unavoidably spiritual dimension to the use of the sociological imagination because mustering the will to make the effort to conceptualize the totality of human experience requires a preexisting ethic of care as well as a faith in the goodness of humankind, which militates against the more easily adopted passivity of a cynical view of human potential. For West, keeping faith with Mills today means being explicit about the transcendent values that undergird even a sociological mind wedded to the transvaluation of values. The pragmatic value of the sociological imagination lies squarely in its utopian loadstar, the promise of redemption and ultimate salvation. Presumably, this is what West would recommend to members of Generation X and their younger siblings: that they act toward the world and that they do so on the basis of faith in their ability to act, faith in their power to realize a better world, and faith in the transcendent justice of such acts and such aspirations to act. West is himself an exemplar of goodwill and good acts toward woman and man.

A third and fourth example of efforts to reconfigure the sociological imagination for the postmodern world come in the form of sociology textbooks: Michael Schwalbe's (1998) *The Sociologically Examined Life: Pieces of the Conversation* and David R. Simon and Joel H. Henderson's (1997) *Private Troubles and Public Issues: Social Problems in the Postmodern Era.*[40] Schwalbe, a professor of sociology at North Carolina State University, describes his book ("half-jokingly") as an "antitext," meaning an antitextbook that eschews the "standard fare" of "safe" topics presented as though professional sociologists already have them well in hand and thoroughly understood.[41] In contrast, Schwalbe emphasizes the notion of sociologically mindful *conversations,* that is, dialogue about "where we are and what needs to be done."[42] In this view, Schwalbe's own effort to popularize the sociological imagination is construed as one voice from one man inviting others to join him on "a path to heartful membership in a conversation that ought to have no end."[43] No doubt, then, Schwalbe would welcome the participation of Generation X, Y, and Z in this conversation. Noting that "sociological mindfulness" is a "rarity," Schwalbe's book is written to prepare young adults—students, in particular—with the concepts they would need to get into the conversation.[44]

For their part, Simon, a professor of sociology at the University of California at Berkeley, and Henderson, a professor of public administration and urban studies at the University of California at San Diego, present their book as a "holistic" alternative to standard "social problems" textbooks.[45] Their book is "a full-blown application of the paradigm Mills set nearly forty years ago," a direct application of "the sociological imagination perspective" to today's "social problems in the postmodern era."[46] Chapter titles indicate the tone and content of the book and include: "the Politics of Postmodern Crises: The Scandalization of America," "Postmodern Environmental Crises: Alienation, Mass Consumption, and the Overpopulation Debate," "The American Crime Factory: The Crime-Drug Nexus," "The Medical-Industrial Complex: Problems of Health and Mental Health," and "Freedom, Reason, and the Sociological Imagination: Social Change and Personal Transformation." Simon and Henderson discuss, among other things, cheerful robots, power elites, "the American Way of (Prescription) Drugging," and at one point, the assassination of President John F. Kennedy as the topic of "Critical Thinking Exercise 4.2." Here, Simon and Henderson present conservative, liberal, and radical perspectives on this event and conclude with a thinly veiled call for what all radicals, including Simon and Henderson, are presumed to want: "revolution."[47] At the very end of their more than 500-page textbook for university social problems courses, they wrote the following:

> From a sociological imagination perspective, solutions to the problems of our age must take place on the individual, community, and societal levels. Along with a humane transformation in social character, masses of people must be encouraged to engage in collective action that will extend both economic and political democracy.[48]

This brings us quite a distance from Schwalbe's "conversation," West's "prophetic pragmatism," and Denzin's "minimalist" sociology. While each of these extensions of Mills's original formulation may capture aspects of what is essential for the sociological imagination today, do they help in the analysis of Generation X? Clearly we have already acknowledged the importance of existential experience in the form, however, of a inevitably mediated relationship with the indigent particular and not as stories told in moments of epiphany, and we have noted the malaise produced by this era of "the end of utopia," although not with reference to any transcendental values or prophetic traditions. We have also, like Schawlbe, construed the book in your hands as an invitation to participation in sociological "mindfulness" and with reference to actually existing social phenomena, like Gen X, even though there are here no invitations to any "heartfelt membership" in a mere "conversation." Since we will have occasion in later chapters to return to the work of Denzin, West, and Schwalbe and there to fully draw out the significant flaws in each approach, let us focus exclusively on Simon and Henderson's preference for a "radical" perspective. Do members of Generation X need a revolution? Does the development of a sociological imagination in the postmodern epoch logically end in a revolutionary stance vis-à-vis the status quo?

Simon and Henderson say as much. Their book is thematically arranged to "define social problems," "explain their causes," "point out the defects in other approaches," and "point to solutions that *logically follow from* the causal analysis" of these social problems.[49] If it is true that Generation X is a nonexistent simulation of a generation as actuality, a marketing tool that belies the power of hyperreality to shape the political consciousness and moral conscience of 50 million young adults in the most powerful nation on earth, and a hold-over from past sellouts that drains genuine criticism of its sting by cynically incorporating whatever critical impulse exists among the young within its workings, then does it logically follow that young adults today have no other choice than to revolt against postmodernity's electronic bread and circuses? No choice but to overturn the dominance of the mass media and its hyperreality and therein create a new space for solidarity, free thought, and authentic political action? Is this not the logical "solution" to the nauseating problem of Generation X? Is this not the common destiny presented to today's young adults?

If this were so, then studies such as Ted Halsted's (1999) *Atlantic Monthly* article, "A Politics for Generation X," wildly miss the point. Halsted argues that the solution to Xers's extreme political disengagement is the formulation of a political agenda that mirrors what today's young adults care about. So tantalizing would be this political agenda, with its "balanced-budget populism" and its "social investments," that it would easily motivate young adults, indeed, "galvanize" them as a generation as actuality, to create "the nation's next majoritarian coalition."[50] Halsted clearly has electoral politics in mind. Halsted wrote, "If Xers do eventually enter the fray [i.e., the election fray], their agenda [i.e., the one Halsted thinks they have] will transform America's political landscape [i.e., who wins elections and on what platform]."[51]

It is important to note that Halsted, aged 30 when he wrote his article, is described by the editors of the *Atlantic Monthly* as "a venture capitalist of talent and ideas."[52] As founder, president, and chief executive officer of the New America Foundation, Halsted is dedicated to helping to "launch the careers of young journalists with a demonstrated interest in politics and public policy," to "build a new set of political ideas based on innovative and pragmatic solutions," and to "train and support the next generation of public intellectuals."[53]

Halsted and his ambitious foundation raise the question Marx famously posed: Who is to educate the educator? Is it not more of the same to train would-be public intellectuals, launch their careers, and proscribe the limits of their political imagination to the established game and its "majoritarian coalitions"? What kind of politics for Generation X is this, which does not acknowledge itself as among the chief obstacles in the way of a historically meaningful political thought? It would seem that criticism of Halsted and the New America Foundation, more than revolution, logically follows from the type of analysis that flows from the free working of a sociological imagination, because the New America Foundation is clearly an obstacle to free thinking and free thinking about politics most of all.

For its part, revolution—if we can still use this term without blushing—does not flow logically from anything, including the development and deployment of the sociological imagination. There is nothing inherently wrong with participation in mainstream American politics, either. Indeed, Simon and Henderson's and Halsted's self-delusions are fundamentally the same. How is it, after all, that a form of mind, a critical self-consciousness, could translate itself into an objective radical "paradigm" or an effective "policy agenda"? There is an unwarranted leap of logic in this rush to judgment, an unwarranted and untenable leap from imagination to specific forms of condemnation, from conceptualization to causally determined political commitments. The sociological imagination cannot determine a set politics, nor does it necessarily invite revolution as the only logical response to the current situation. A Generation X possessed of 50 or 100 million versions of the sociological imagination would not necessarily constitute a revolutionary vanguard, and certainly not one with a single mind. If the members of Generation X were each possessed of a sociological imagination, then this would be a generation that thinks for itself, and it is not possible to predict what millions of self-directed individuals would do or think. A generation possessed of the sociological imagination might, for example, opt for a new and unprecedented type of self-consciousness not recognizable as a sociological imagination. This is, in large part, what makes the sociological imagination a radical form of self-consciousness in the first place: it contains no fixed boundaries. Rather, the sociological imagination is self-consciousness of impermanence, including, potentially, its own.

Radicalizing the Sociological Imagination

Of course, we are here tittering on the brink of absurdity. It is not that we are close to undermining our own representation of the sociological imagination (although we are) but that the likelihood of its popular adoption is, on sociological grounds, close to nil. It is important to underscore this observation, to constantly remind ourselves of this empirical reality. Thus, speculation along these lines is evidence not so much of political sophistication as it is evidence of sociological mindlessness. Very few people, and very few young adults especially, read *Atlantic Monthly,* and when they do, we may reasonably speculate that they are not radicalized by their reading. The same is true for social problems textbooks and, indeed, any textbooks. What is more, the politics advocated by Simon and Henderson, no less than by Halsted, are not truly radical. There is the problem of critical thinking itself becoming propaganda when it is reduced to an objective plan or political blueprint, but there is also a greater problem. Simon and Henderson's as well as Halsted's politics issue from a truncated historical consciousness in which today's humanity is at the center and all the world is its space for self-actualization. Is it not the case that the problems faced by today's young adults imply a much deeper set of concerns that do not fit easily into traditional, human-centered historical thinking? Does it not logically follow that today's young adults must engage natural history?

The dizzying effects of all the glitz and glamour of postmodern hyperreality has its antidote, perhaps, in the dreadfully slow moving and ponderously long stretches of geologic time and the infinitely spacious universe. Whereas nature used to be seen as the enemy of humankind, perhaps it can serve us well as a reminder of who we really are and where we ultimately stand. Here, the task for the would-be possessor of a sociological imagination appropriate for our times is the conceptualization of humanity as part of a natural order and a natural disorder or, simply, as part of the structured fluidity that is nature. The electronic madness of satellite-driven television and high-speed Internet connections is placed in a real, material context by remembering that humanity is but one species of millions on a roughly 5-billion-year-old planet that is situated in an expanding and confounding universe of stars moving in tension with one another. The merely simulated world of recent invention that appears more real than real is thus a tiny bubble of illusion hatched in an almost infinitely small corner of known space and time. One need not venture out to the nearest IMAX theater to experience humanity's humbling enclosure in such natural contexts; one need only turn off the television and computer, step outdoors, sit on the surface of the planet earth, and look out to the rest of what can be seen. From this position, it helps to defamiliarize our artificial human containment of this otherwise stone-cold and deadly obvious reality.

Below the manicured monocultures called lawns and rock gardens that form a thin cover over an otherwise molten monster of a planet, across from the geometric etchings of automobile veins and agribusiness fields, through the vapor trails produced by flying machines and beyond the space debris in various stages of orbit, in simple awareness of being surrounded by birds and insects and an occasional mammal, surrounded by water and numerous vital gases in one form or another, and infested by microorganisms that live in our guts and on our face, one can see and feel the elementary fact that one is but a single mortal member of a single animal species pressed by gravity onto the surface of the third rock from one particular star in a space of billions of similar stars. In reality, this tableau looks nothing like the cartoon depiction that is meant to draw viewers into watching the latest episode of "Third Rock from the Sun," and there is nothing self-evidently humorous about it. All around, we see living and dying and evidence of living and dying stretching back millions of years. If we choose to assign them proper names (e.g., Grand Canyon, Panda Bear, Pacific Ocean, "Third Rock from the Sun") and thus bring them under the control of our meaning system, then all we are doing is drawing a symbolic veil over a real reality that cannot be contained or subsumed by mere words alone. As we look at the earth beneath our feet and imagine the air that we breathe, we can then appreciate that our own mortal bodies will soon, varying with the amount of formaldehyde pulsed through our veins and the water-tight quality of our tomb, decompose into them. We can thus see our individual fate, which is in fact a common destiny for all: each and every one of us, baby boomers, Xers, the stars of "Third Rock," and everyone else, will form an identity with that from which we came: nature.

In the meantime, our temporary nonidentity with nature—the result of our being alive as mindful human creatures animated with cognitive and emotional agency—is a gap through which reason and freedom, and in addition to these, moral responsibility and political imagination, ebb and flow. It is this gap, and not some generation gap, that is truly of biographical as well as historical significance, and it is this gap that provides the basis for the pursuit of a common destiny before and beyond the grave.

Generation X's Common Destiny

In this unprecedented time of a dying world, those with the most time ahead of them to act in the world have the greatest opportunity to affect the course of human history as it fatefully intersects with natural history. They also bear the greatest responsibility for doing so wisely and with appropriate determination and urgency. Fifty or 100 years hence, people in all corners of this planet will look back at this era and most directly at those with the greatest potential for historical agency. They will look back to this era when so much was at stake and when so little was being done. They will remember that millions of young adults in the rich nations of the world sat stationary before tiny glowing screens and tapped gently on keyboards and remote controls. Video images flashed before them, windows were piled on top of windows, and virtual realities simulated deeper and deeper spaces to explore. In this projection of what we will look like to our children and grandchildren, it is hard to imagine a type of activity that is more distant or opposed to the activity of developing a mindful relationship to our earth-boundedness. It is hard to imagine life pursuits more out of sync with the demands of the current situation, lives evidencing a more gross ignorance of the entwinement of human and natural history at the end of industrial civilization.

Given the gravity of the current situation, however, it is understandable why inaction is the name of the Generation X game. The very sort of conceptualization presented here tends to diminish the will to act because it implies the need for real collective actions that cannot be imagined as realistic. In other words, it is clear that dropping out and turning on, carrying placards and gathering for farmyard music festivals, protesting university policies, marching through institutions, and storming the Bastille will do nothing of historical significance vis-à-vis the facts of a dying world. It is much easier to hope against hope that the science is simply wrong or to cling to the notion that the very network of information technology that binds and contains this generation is also the means to save it as though somehow the institution we depend on to guide our lives in every other respect is wrong in this one case, and as though the overflowing of desperate bits of information will create social solidarity, human reason, and a dispersed revolution without courageous revolutionaries willing to take risks. One might as well choose paper or plastic.[54]

I write these words sitting in front of a tiny glowing screen, tapping on a keyboard, making use of the latest word processing software. Writing books, like reading them, requires a mostly docile body passively positioned before the outdoor world. As I write these words, I am 35 years old. It is Christmas Day, 1999. I plan to check my email later. I know that what is written here will appear in a textbook, which will be marketed. This author, this book, this chapter—its means of production, distribution, and reception—are no less in the whale of the mass media than anything else.

The great challenge for today's young people is to find a way out this one-dimensional world. This means that people must develop the conceptual and emotional wherewithal to demystify hyperreality. The bogus notion of their "generational" identity must be among the first things to go. The means for this demystification, however, cannot be the mass media, which is the source of the problem in the first place. In place of postmodern false consciousness there must develop the widespread appreciation and use of a postmodern sociological imagination, which will open thought to broader realities than what television defines and create an indeterminate political future. Once oriented to the problems of this period and once focused on its "common destiny," young people must discover news means for making history. Their energy to act constructively in the world must not be dissipated through forms of repressive desublimation, nor will many disparate local actions suffice when global crises are a current reality. In other words, merely thinking globally is insufficient; we must find ways to *act* globally also. In this sense, campus protests against Third World sweatshops and the Battle in Seattle do prefigure this generation's common destiny, which is to alter the course of world history lest natural history become the only history left.

Notes

1. Margot Hornblower, "Great Xpectations," *Time,* June 9, 1997, 58.

2. Todd Gitlin, *The Sixties: Years of Hope, Days of Rage* (New York: Bantam, 1987).

3. Karl Mannheim, "The Problem of Generations," in *Essays on the Sociology of Knowledge,* ed. P. Kesckemeti (1928; reprint, London: Routedge & Kegan Paul, 1952), 303.

4. Gitlin, *The Sixties,* xii.

5. Mannheim, "The Problem of Generations," 302.

6. Ted Halsted, "A Politics for Generation X," *The Atlantic Monthly,* August 1999, 33.

7. Ibid.

8. Douglas Coupland, *Generation X: Tales for an Accelerated Culture* (New York: St. Martin's Press, 1991).

9. Ibid., 5.

10. Jason Cohen and Michael Krugman, *Generation Ecch!* (New York: Simon & Schuster, 1994).

11. Douglas Rushkoff, ed., *The GenX Reader* (New York: Ballantine Books, 1994). See also Daniel Strong, "Generation Hex," *The New York Times,* October 1, 1994, A15.

12. See Halsted, "A Politics for Generation X," 34. Halsted notes that roughly 20 percent of Generation Xers vote in nonpresidential election years (compared with roughly 38 percent of all voters). In presidential elections, 18- to 24-year-olds have never achieved greater than a 45 percent turnout. According to Halsted, Generation Xers also tend to favor "independents" over Republicans and Democrats. Only one-third of Generation Xers identify with either Republicans or Democrats, whereas 44 percent of 18- to 29-year-olds identify themselves as "independents." Thus, as Halsted reports, "not surprisingly, young adults gave the strongest support to Ross Perot in 1992 and to Jesse Ventura in 1998."

13. Reel Big Fish, "Sell Out," *Turn the Radio Off* (Mojo Records, 1996). Lyrics by A. Barrett and S. Klopfenstein.

14. Andrew Hultkrans, "The Slacker Factor," in *The GenX Reader,* ed. Douglas Rushkoff, 303, emphasis in original.

15. Compare Dan Wakefield, "Taking It Big: A Memoir of C. Wright Mills," *The Atlantic Monthly* 228 (Summer 1971): 65-71, with the depiction of Mills in Guy Oakes and Arthur J. Vidich,

Collaboration, Reputation, and Ethics in American Academic Life: Hans H. Gerth and C. Wight Mills (Urbana: University of Illinois Press, 1999).

16. Strangely, even as an astute social analyst, Todd Gitlin recalls with fondness his first encounter with "Casablanca." He wrote of his college days: "I went to Bogart movies (the two-week Bogart festival had become an exam-time institution at the Brattle Theatre [in Cambridge, Mass.]): I was overpowered by *Casablanca,* of course," which Gitlin, then anyway, understood as an allegory "about the passage from cynicism to political commitment." Gitlin, *The Sixties,* 103.

17. See Guy Oakes, *The Imaginary War: Civil Defense and American Cold War Culture* (New York: Oxford University Press, 1994) and Stephen J. Whitfield, *The Culture of the Cold War* (Baltimore, M.D.: Johns Hopkins University Press, 1991).

18. C. Wright Mills, *The Sociological Imagination* (Oxford, U.K.: Oxford University Press, 1959), 5.

19. Andrew Jamison and Ron Eyerman, *Seeds of the Sixties* (Berkeley: University of California Press, 1994).

20. See Mills's "The Cultural Apparatus," in *Power, Politics & People: The Collected Essays of C. Wright Mills,* ed. Irving Louis Horowitz (Oxford, U.K.: Oxford University Press, 1963), 405-22.

21. Richard A. Easterlin, Diane J. Macunovich, and Eileen M. Crimmins, "Economic Status of the Young and the Old in the Working-Age Population, 1964 and 1987," in *The Changing Contract Across Generations,* eds. Vern L. Benegtson and W. Andrew Achenbaum (New York: Aldine De Gruyter, 1993), 81. Note, however, that income inequality is comparatively high among baby boomers, meaning that there exist significant income disparities *within* this age group even though the group average is the highest among all age groups. Daniel Okrent offers a lightly despairing testament of an aging baby boomer in his "Twilight of the Boomers," *Time,* 12 June 2000, 68-74.

22. See Paul Breines, "Editor's Notes" and "From Guru to Spectre: Marcuse and the Implosion of the Movement," in *Critical Interruptions: New Left Perspectives on Herbert Marcuse* ed. Paul Brienes (New York: Herder and Herder, 1970), ix-xiii and 21. See also Martin Jay, *The Dialectical Imagination: A History of the Frankfurt School and The Institute for Social Research, 1923-1950* (Boston: Little, Brown and Company, 1973) and Douglas Kellner, *Herbert Marcuse and the Crisis of Marxism* (Berkeley, University of California Press, 1984).

23. Herbert Marcuse, *One-Dimensional Man: Studies in the Ideology of Advanced Capitalism* (Boston: Beacon Press, 1964), 1.

24. Ibid., xvii.

25. Ibid., 257.

26. Ibid., see also pages 56-83.

27. See Herbert Marcuse, *Eros and Civilization: A Philosophical Inquiry into Freud* (Boston: Beacon Press, 1955).

28. Johann Wolfgang Von Goethe, *Maxims and Reflections,* ed. Peter Hutchinson (London: Penguin Books, 1998), 6, originally in Goethe's *Elective Affinities* (1809).

29. Mills, *The Sociological Imagination,* 5.

30. Norman Denzin, "The Sociological Imagination Revisited," *The Sociological Quarterly* 31 (Spring 1990): 1-22.

31. Ibid., 13, 14.

32. Ibid., 12-3.

33. Ibid., 15, 7, 5, 15.

34. Ibid., 13.

35. Ibid., 2.

36. Ibid., 15.

37. Ibid., 13.

38. Cornel West, *The American Evasion of Philosophy: A Genealogy of Pragmatism* (Madison: University of Wisconsin Press, 1989).

39. Irving Louis Horowitz, *C. Wright Mills: An American Utopian* (New York: Free Press, 1983).

40. Michael Schwalbe, *The Sociologically Examined Life: Pieces of the Conversation* (Mountain View, C.A.: Mayfield, 1998) and David R. Simon and Joel H. Henderson, *Private Troubles and Public Issues: Social Problems in the Postmodern Era* (Orlando, F.L.: Harcourt Brace College Publishers, 1997).

41. Schwalbe, *The Sociologically Examined Life,* iii.

42. Ibid, 207.

43. Ibid.

44. Ibid., 6-7.

45. Simon and Henderson, *Private Troubles and Public Issues,* vii.

46. Ibid.

47. Ibid., 130-6, 134.

48. Ibid.,482.

49. Ibid., vii, emphases added.

50. Halsted, "A Politics for Generation X," 40-1.

51. Ibid., 42.

52. The editors, *The Atlantic Monthly,* 6.

53. Ibid.

54. For more optimistic, often religious assessments written by authors five and ten years my junior, see Tom Beaudoin, *Virtual Faith: The Irreverent Spiritual Quest of Generation X* (San Francisco: Jossey Bass, 1998) and Jedediah Purdy, *For Common Things: Irony, Trust, and Commitment in America Today* (New York: Knopf, 1999). Beaudoin writes of his book that it is "about impropriety and irreverence, beginning with my fundamental claim that Generation X is—despite and even because of appearances—strikingly religious" (p. xiii). Purdy writes: "We need today a kind of thought and action that is too little contemplated yet remains possible. It is the kind aimed at the preservation of what we love most in the world, and a stay against forgetting what that love requires. It is an exercise of margins against boundlessness, of earned hope against casual despair, and of responsibility against heedlessness. If it appears conservative, that is because we have begun to forget the conditions necessary to betterment. If it appears radical, that is because we have neglected the conditions necessary to conservation" (p. 207).

7

Religion and Society

Of Gods and Demons

He [Mills] was always fond of saying that there were two types of Americans worth talking to: clergymen and students.

—*Irving Louis Horowitz*[1]

What if a sociologist were to stumble across a crowded parking lot in Clearwater, Florida, where hundreds had gathered to see the image of the Madonna (*the* Madonna, not the recording artist) as it appeared in the window of Suncoast Savings Bank at the corner of State Route 13 and Blah Street? Imagine hundreds of candles lit, hundreds of dreadfully serious looking people, television satellite trucks, flowers, crowds of people crying or standing back and just staring at the image, brisk sales of T-shirts at a nearby oil-change business depicting the apparition, people in wheelchairs, people holding rosaries and praying, and police officers dutifully controlling the traffic and watching over this unusual scene. Would a sociologist, even a sociologist who was a Catholic believer, think that the Virgin Mary had made an appearance in the windowpanes of Suncoast Savings Bank? Probably not.

Or imagine a sociologist plunked down at a contest between the Dallas Cowboys and the Miami Dolphins, facing off in the National Football League's Super Bowl. There are plenty of rituals to observe; a man dressed like a stereotypical cowboy roams the sideline (he is a "mascot"); females dance and dress so as to display much of their body (they are "cheerleaders"); contestants, all males, gesture and dance after certain successful moments in the competition (they act out their "signature celebration"); and spectators wave objects or are adorned to indicate their allegiance to either the team named for a species of aquatic mammal (reputedly a relatively smart animal) or to the team named for a type of occupation involving all facets of care for a particular type of domesticated livestock (mythologized as the epitome of rugged American individualism). And then there is an interlude that is produced as a spectacle meant to instill awe, and there is the sense, widely shared and promoted, that this gathering is the most important place to be in the world at this moment. Would a sociologist see religion in this coliseum? Probably.

Or imagine weeks later in the same arena that a former football coach stands before tens of thousands of men who call themselves "Promise Keepers." Mainly Protestant Christian men, they have gathered to pledge allegiance to a specific creed, one that lists responsibilities along with privileges due to them *as men* of a particular faith. Or imagine the arena is again a football field and the "Honor Guard" is entering, carrying a cloth dyed in blue, red, and white that features stars and stripes and is hung on an ornate stick with the golden figure of a large bird perched on top. The crowd stands and on cue they collectively vocalize an organized sound. They sing this national anthem, in other words, and so pledge their allegiance to this flag, which is to say, to the sacred idea of a particular nation-state. They are displaying their nationalism, and they tend to do so even if they are not particularly nationalistic. A person carrying the flag of Timbuktu runs across the field and knocks over a young U.S. Marine, identifiable by his uniform, carrying the Stars and Stripes. The man with the sacred flag of Timbuktu stomps on the sacred flag of the United States of America. What would happen? How would a sociologist analyze this situation?

These descriptions mix real and imagined scenarios that, taken together, highlight the question of whether religion stands apart from social institutions. Is religion, any religion, truly transcendent? The examples could be multiplied endlessly and in a less ethnocentric fashion. We could imagine the conclusion to the holy month of Ramadan, as the Islamic faithful gather in Mecca and prepare to feast for three days, or we could ponder the popularity of the Dalai Lama and his Tibetan Buddhism, which in the United States has the actors Harrison Ford and Richard Gere as prominent spokespersons. Or we could examine less popular manifestations of religion, such as cults like the Branch Davidians of Waco, Texas (C. Wright Mills's place of birth) or the Church of Scientology, which counts actor John Travolta among its spokespeople but which is banned in Germany. Most sociologists would see all of these phenomena as begging for sociological explanation, that is, for explanations that use the same concepts that apply to other social practices and institutions.

In this chapter, we shall examine the nature of religion as a social institution and as a point of significant conflict between classical sociological thinking and other types of thinking common today. The aim here is not to denigrate religion but, rather, to display the workings of the sociological imagination vis-à-vis religion, understood as a universal cultural phenomenon and as a powerful, widespread, and diverse set of institutionalized social practices. Furthermore, the aim is to reflect on the meaning of this classic analysis for the structure and development of the sociological imagination itself. Why were the classic sociologists, and Mills, for the most part, nonreligious? What was their view of the future of religion? How did their view of religion affect their view of modern society and its fate? Why were they so apparently wrong about religion? Does their being wrong about religion tell us something about the sociological imagination today, in postmodern times?

In answering these questions, we shall stress the significance of what sociologists call *structural analysis*, that is, systematic thinking about how patterns of life and belief are reproduced across time and space such that social institutions—composed of roles, positions, groups, norms, values, and rituals—are created and maintained, thereby building and rebuilding society. The two preceding chapters addressed the extremes of biography (indigent particulars) and history (natural history); here we shall integrate into our tripartite demonstration of the sociological imagination the most extreme form of society, religious society, which is a social institution that thinks of itself as connected to something sacred, indeed, something that transcends society itself. Is there a postmodern form of religion? Probably.

The Classical View of Religion

There is a fair amount of agreement between how most people think about religion and how most sociologists think about religion. This is perhaps to be expected since most sociologists, at least in the United States, are themselves members of a religious community. For example, most people think of religion as something that is special or sacred. By this people usually mean that religion is something that stands apart or *should* stand apart from the merely everyday aspects of life, the profane or grittily human; something that, in contrast to everyday life, commands our respect and whose symbols evoke awe and make us feel and feel deeply. This commonsense understanding is also essentially the position on religion taken by the famous French sociologist Emile Durkheim (1858-1917).

Like Max Weber and Karl Marx, Durkheim is generally regarded as one of the foremost founding sociologists. Indeed, he is often regarded as the first true sociologist since his would-be competitors for this title never identified themselves as sociologists per se nor worked to define and establish an academic discipline called "sociology." But Durkheim did, and did so, at least in France, with considerable success.

In his last and perhaps most complex book *The Elementary Forms of Religious Life* (1912), Durkheim used his secondhand knowledge of so-called primitive tribal religious practices, which he acquired by reading anthropological descriptions, to develop an explanation or theory of *all* religions, including modern religions.[2] The heart of Durkheim's theory is this: religion is not merely a social institution, it is the "eminently social" social institution.[3]

This idea cuts in two directions. In Durkheim's view, religions stand apart in that they lay claim to a sacred realm that transcends all things social; but religious forces are human forces or, what for Durkheim is the same thing, moral forces. Indeed, for Durkheim, "the idea of society is the soul of religion," which is to say, it is really society (and not some god) that is the true object of our awe and respect and that makes us feel and feel deeply.[4] It is society, not some god or spirit, that is sacred. It is society, experienced as a totality, that brings us to our knees. Durkheim wrote:

> The concept of totality is only the abstract form of the concept of society: it is the whole which includes all things, the supreme class which embraces all classes.
>   At bottom, the concept of totality, that of society and that of divinity are very probably only different aspects of the same notion.[5]

For Durkheim, all religions are thus at base the same; "they respond to the same needs, they play the same role, they depend on the same causes." It also follows that so-called primitive religions are thus "no less respectable" than so-called advanced or modern religions and also that religion itself, as the face of society, is indeed a very special, sacred thing.[6]

Despite this special status of religion, even aspects of social life that are not in and of themselves religious contain elements of ritual and attention to the sacred and so borrow the form of religion for purposes that are not religious. The Super Bowl is not a religious event, nor is the singing of the national anthem. But these ritual aspects of American popular culture and nationalism borrow the sacred aura of religion.

In short, although they respect the sacred nature of religion, most sociologists (not all) understand religious institutions as social institutions, and most sociologists, like Durkheim, think that the religion of the Australian aboriginals and the religion of France have essentially the same social characteristics, the same basic social purposes, and the same origin in human social development. Furthermore, most sociologists understand social institutions as collective social enterprises requiring rituals to maintain their cohesiveness.

Not all sociologists, however, go as far as Durkheim and deny religious institutions what each and every one claim for themselves: in a word, transcendence, the transcendence of society and culture. From the point of view of believers in one or another religion, Durkheim's sociological theory of religion seeks to unduly confine their beliefs to the social and cultural totality; he seeks to reduce their claims to transcendence, to their having a real relationship with some sacred realm beyond the social; what is more, he seeks to reduce these claims to the merely human, to the merely profane. Whereas believers believe that there is a totality that lies beyond the social totality, Durkheim sees no evidence of this and, in fact, much evidence to the contrary. Other scientists, of course, do see evidence for God; still others do not but nonetheless retain their faith in a realm apart from society and culture.

Observable Patterns

Before we further analyze religious social institutions, it is helpful to clarify some basic empirical matters. There are roughly, as we have noted, 6 billion human beings in the world today. About 2 billion of these humans identify themselves as Christians. About 1 billion people are Muslims or adherents to the Islamic faith, followers of the God Allah and his prophet Mohammad. In other words, about one-half of the people in the world today are either Christian or Muslim. There are another roughly 1 billion people who are nonreligious. This is a diverse grouping, which includes but is not limited to atheists, free thinkers, and agnostics. Thus, two-thirds of the people in the world today are either Christian, Muslim, or nonbelievers. The remaining one-third, or 2 billion people, are primarily composed of Hindus, Buddhists, and adherents of various Chinese folk religions such as Taoism and Confucianism. There are, of course, many other very small religious groups. Sikhs, for example, account for roughly 0.4 and Jews 0.3 percent of the world population. Various tribal religions account for roughly two percent of the world's total.[7]

In the United States, the distribution of religion affiliation is quite different. Roughly eighty-six percent of Americans identify themselves as members of various Christian groups. Thus, whereas Christians make up only thirty-five percent of the world total, they are easily the dominant religious grouping in the United States. However, internal subdivisions are important in the U.S. Christian majority just as they are worldwide. Roughly fifty-nine percent of all Americans are Protestants, whereas only twenty-seven percent are Catholics. The remaining fourteen percent of Americans who are neither Protestant Christians nor Catholic Christians are composed of Jews, who represent roughly two percent of the U.S. total and other relatively small groups representing all the various religions of the world and people who do not view themselves as members of a religion.[8]

These numbers provide a gross characterization of religious affiliations. Each society has its own internal make-up, of course, and each religious category has important internal divisions. The division between the Sunni majority and the Shiite minority among Muslims is very significant. Jews are divided mainly between Orthodox and Reformed sects, but there are other groups as well. Protestants in the United States, as elsewhere, represent a highly diverse collection of smaller churches such as African Methodist Episcopal, Baptist, Methodist, Lutheran, Presbyterian, and Episcopalian denominations. Even these subdivisions have important subdivisions, such as the differences between the larger Southern Baptist Convention (16 million members), and the smaller National Baptist Convention, USA, Inc. (8 million members), and National Baptist Convention of America, Inc. (3.5 million members).[9] Although fifty-nine percent of all Americans are Protestants, the splintering of Protestant denominations and subdenominations diminishes its cultural presence, whereas the 61 million American Roman Catholics *seem* especially prominent even though their twenty-seven percent share of the U.S. total renders them today (as has been the case throughout American history) members of an American minority religion.

By itself, however, religious affiliation says little about what religion means to the people who affiliate themselves with one or another religious creed. In 1952, for example, seventy-five percent of Americans polled reported that religion "is important in their lives," and whereas this figure had shrunk to fifty-two percent in 1978, it rebounded to fifty-eight percent in 1990 and sixty-two percent in 1998.[10] In 1998, ninety-six percent of Americans claimed to believe in God or some higher being, but only seventy-eight percent were members of a religious body, and only forty percent attended a religious service at least once a week.[11] These participation rates are still much higher than those found in other advanced industrial societies, which tend to be more secular. Neither do these gross figures tell us anything about the intensity of the religious life or depth of commitment in various churches. Cults, such as the Reverend Sun Myung Moon's Unification Church or David Koresch's ill-fated Branch Davidians, manifest a more intense significance and power over members than do U.S. suburban Protestant denominations. That the United States is a society in which ninety-six percent of people believe in "God" but only sixty-five percent believe in "the Devil" probably also says something about how Americans feel about religion.[12] Fire and brimstone are less popular than the pearly gates.

Religious Institutions as Social Institutions

In examining religion, sociologists observe patterns such as those just described. Religious affiliation, participation, and the varying intensity of religious feeling— "religiosity"—are not randomly distributed across human populations. The United States is a predominantly Christian society, whereas Saudi Arabia is a predominantly Islamic society. The United States is a predominantly Protestant society, whereas Mexico is a predominantly Catholic society. American religiosity is greater than western European religiosity. What causes these patterns? To answer this question, sociologists step back from the worldview of any particular religion to grasp the whole of religious life in terms of the total history of human beings.

The vast majority of human existence, of course, transpired without any of today's religions being present. During the roughly ninety-nine percent of the time that humans have walked the earth as a distinct animal species, they have done so in gathering and hunting societies. These were small bands of people, probably numbering 20 to 50 members, who, among other things, spurned permanent settlement and practiced forms of what we would today call animistic religion. "Animism" is a concept that groups together diverse belief systems that share the idea that the world is inhabited and affected by supernatural spirits (e.g., tree spirits, bird spirits, buffalo spirits, rock spirits, ocean spirits, air spirits, the Great Spirit). But hunting and gathering societies and their animism are virtually extinct today. Most people today, especially the inhabitants of modern societies, do not swat a fly and feel as though they have killed a spiritual being. Most people do not see in rock and water anything other than inanimate objects there for human use and manipulation. Most people today do not, or at least do not seriously, practice magic, nor do they engage in ritual animal sacrifice. Nor do they worship totems, even if their favorite sports team is symbolized by one. This abandonment of animism is an important measure of the secularization—or disenchantment, despiritualization—of the world.

The largest of today's religious institutions, then, have a relatively short history. Roughly speaking, Judaism is 3,000 years old, the main Chinese folk religions are 2,500 years old, Christianity is 2,000 years old, and Islam is a mere 1,300 years old. More specific, the period from roughly 500 B.C. to roughly 300 A.D. is often described as "the axial age" of modern religious life because in this period there arose a tremendous revolution in human consciousness.[13] It was defined by a rapid movement away from animism and toward the idea of human-like gods (*pantheism*) and eventually to the idea of a single human-like god (*monotheism*). Today's dominant monotheistic religions, particularly Christianity, arose during or, in the case of Islam, shortly after this time. Why?

The American sociologist, Rodney Stark, provides one explanation for this development. In his book, *The Rise of Christianity* (1996), Stark poses the following question: "How did a tiny and obscure messianic movement from the edge of the Roman Empire dislodge classical paganism and become the dominant faith of Western civilization?"[14] In general, this was a time of relatively rapid human population increase, early urbanization, and the expansion of philosophically minded political empires, namely, the ancient Greeks and Romans. Stark argues, in particular, that

Roman cities were characterized by widespread disease, poverty, and ethnic conflict.[15] Their inhabitants were suffering great hardships. Better than the established
paganism and philosophies of the day, Christianity offered spiritual solace and encouraged material comfort for an expanding and suffering urban population. "It
grew," wrote Stark, "because Christians constituted an intense community" that was
"able to generate an 'invincible obstinacy' " to its would-be competitors and oppres-
sors.[16] Stark estimates that the total number of Christians grew rapidly in the first 300
years of the first Christian millennium, from 0 to more than 30 million by the time
that the Roman Emperor, Constantine, made Christianity the official religion of the
Roman Empire in 316 A.D.[17]

Christianity's subsequent status as the state religion of the Roman Empire also
contributed mightily to its continuing success. Once ensconced in Western culture
as the dominant religion, Christianity would wait another 1,500 years before the rise
of modern European society would disperse its teachings the world over. Of course,
Christianity also had to endure many internal conflicts, including the separation of
Eastern and Western varieties and, at the dawn of the modern age, the *Protest*-ant
Re-*formation*. Still, its worldwide prospects were rosy due to its being deeply embedded in a powerful type of society. Latin America is today predominantly Catholic because of its mainly Spanish colonizers, whereas the United States is, historically speaking, predominantly Protestant due to the hard-won political domination
of Protestant English colonizers over their mainly French Catholic and Spanish
Catholic rivals. The religion of the indigenous peoples in America, of course, was as
ill-fated as was their entire way of life.

Once established and backed by overwhelming force, Christianity could reproduce itself through inculcation of new members born into affiliated families and
through its close association with dominant political and cultural institutions. But
Christianity also appeals to those who continue to suffer, as seen in its form as Latin
America's "liberation theology." Likewise, Islam, Chinese folk religions, Judaism,
and other modern religions share histories that are intimately bound up with the
mundane facts of human social development. The sociologist who examines religious institutions worldwide sees similar developments in all human societies.

The success of religions at reproducing themselves today depends on maintaining their mass appeal while fitting themselves into the framework of modern political and cultural realities. Thus, in the United States, for example, roughly eighty percent of Roman Catholics believe that the use of contraceptives should be allowed
within the Catholic Church, and as many as fifty percent reject the doctrine of papal
infallibility.[18] A church that did not tolerate their deviation from official teachings
would risk self-annihilation. Among members of the Jewish faith in the United
States, more than a third choose to marry people who are not Jewish.[19] This, in its

own way, threatens the reproduction of Judaism in this society, but it also bespeaks a modern cosmopolitanism. U.S. Protestants, in particular, have shown themselves adept at transcending the pulpit by using television to reinvigorate and expand their constituencies, filling the airwaves with broadcasts pitched to a postmodern audience. Whether the issue is dogma versus individual freedom, ethnocentrism versus cosmopolitanism, or old versus new technology, each of these religious groups demonstrates its adaptation to modern society.

Many religions have come and gone; their failure to produce cohesion among a founding group of followers and thereafter reproduce themselves more widely owed less to their intrinsic character than to their social and cultural environment. Religion may claim to stand apart from the workings of society and culture, but in its unavoidable form as a social institution composed of social groups participating in one or another culture or subculture, it clearly does not.

Consider the following self-reflection by one well-known American Protestant minister:

> It is quite easy for me to think of a God of love mainly because I grew up in a family where love was central and where lovely relationships were ever present. It is quite easy for me to think of the universe as basically friendly mainly because of my uplifting hereditary and environmental circumstances. It is quite easy for me to lean more toward optimism than pessimism about human nature mainly because of my childhood experiences. It is impossible to get at the roots of one's religious attitudes without taking in account the psychological and historical factors that play upon the individual.[20]

In this statement, the author, who is most certainly a believer, concedes that one's socialization—that is, the learning process through which one acquires a distinctive selfhood through interaction with others and one's social environment as a whole—bears considerably on one's eventual religious make-up. In fact, the author wrote that his religious attitudes are mainly the result of his socialization. Social experience is, therefore, posited as a critical variable in religious self-development. This would mean that some societies or some groups encourage one type of religious development while others encourage something else. Therefore, the author of the statement is recognizing the sociocultural variability of religious attitudes.

Even if they are otherwise skeptical of the fruits of Western social science, sophisticated religious thinkers understand the importance of socialization for religious self-development. This is true even if they remain convinced that religion is not fully reducible to its social incarnation. Indeed, as we have noted, many sociologists are personally religious. Such is not as uncommon as one might expect. The reverse is also true: many religious thinkers are sociologically oriented. The author of the above autobiographical reflection is Dr. Martin Luther King, Jr., who, with these words, displayed less his notable belief in God and more his appreciation for an altogether secular sociological thinking.

Of Deferred Dreams and Blasted Hopes

Everyone knows that Martin Luther King, Jr. was a brilliant orator, but few people today have much familiarity with what he was talking about. Everyone knows that he "had a dream," but few people realize that he also had an analysis.

There is no doubt that King has been mythologized.[21] He is one of only three persons in the United States remembered with an official national holiday, the other two being George Washington and Abraham Lincoln. His is the only statue in the U.S. capitol rotunda honoring an African American, and a much more elaborate Washington, D.C. shrine is planned. His words, particularly his 1963 "I Have a Dream" speech, are standard fare in even elementary school curricula. Indeed, the main point of the contemporary usage of King's image and words seems to be to evoke the childlike sentiment: "Can't we all get along?"

Dr. King also, however, said the following: "There must be a better distribution of wealth, and maybe America must move toward a Democratic Socialism."[22] What the United States needed, said Dr. King in another speech, was a "radical redistribution of economic power."[23] He said these words forcefully and with great emotional emphasis, but they were not an unthinking outburst. Dr. King's appeal for a class-based social revolution was based on his learned analysis of the structure of American society. Indeed, in the last months of his life King had dedicated himself to creating and leading a "poor people's movement," which he regarded as the logical outgrowth of his work as a civil rights activist. The goal of this ill-fated social movement was simple: eradicate poverty in the United States and create an economic democracy alongside of America's political democracy. "Democratic socialism" is synonymous with economic democracy; this is what King sought for the United States in the last years of his life.

Why did King see this as a logical outgrowth of his struggle against racist attitudes and their institutionalization in race-based segregated housing, schools, and public accommodations of all kinds? Why did King also forcefully oppose U.S. involvement in the Vietnam War? He gave many specific reasons, but at base King was motivated by the Christian values of his ministry. "I am first and foremost a minister," he used to remind people.[24] King was therefore intolerant of any form of injustice anywhere, any form of systematic dehumanization, because to his mind these clearly ran counter to what humans must aspire to be: A brutal modern war waged against an essentially peasant society? An economic system that generated stark social inequality and material deprivation for millions? For King, the sacred goal of achieving human dignity for all people was far greater than the profane ideological squabbles that pitted capitalists against Communists, either at home or abroad. Although his many critics often called him a Communist in the hope of stigmatizing him and thereby delegitimizing his protests and social criticism, in truth King was critical of communism, arguing, for example, that Karl Marx had not, in his criticism of capitalist society, stressed enough the importance and value of individual freedom and of spirituality. King favored a form of democratic socialism, a political-economic system that would protect individual freedom while providing for social equality, and he favored pursuing this would-be social revolution as a spiritual quest. This analysis led him to Memphis, Tennessee, to lend his moral support to that city's striking municipal garbage workers. Thus, in a sense, this analysis led King to his death.

Most people today do not associate Dr. King with a call for a radical redistribution of economic power. They are led to fixate, instead, on his "dream." It is not surprising, then, that few people know that—in his own mind, in his own lifetime—King regarded his dream as having turned into a "nightmare." Witness the following:

> In 1963 . . . in Washington, D.C. . . I tried to talk to the nation about a dream that I had had, and I must confess . . . that not long after talking about that dream I started seeing it turn into a nightmare . . . just a few weeks after I had talked about it. It was when four beautiful . . . Negro girls were murdered in a church in Birmingham, Alabama. I watched that dream turn into a nightmare as I moved through the ghettos of the nation and saw black brothers and sisters perishing on a lonely island of poverty in the midst of a vast ocean of material prosperity, and saw the nation doing nothing to grapple with the Negroes' problem of poverty. I saw that dream turn into a nightmare as I watched my black brothers and sisters in the midst of anger and understandable outrage, in the midst of their hurt, in the midst of their disappointment, turn to misguided riots to try to solve that problem. I saw the dream turn into a nightmare as I watched the war in Vietnam escalating. . . . Yes, I am personally the victim of deferred dreams, of blasted hopes.[25]

Imagine how differently Americans would approach the King holiday every year if, instead of memorizing his dream, Americans analyzed the sociological factors underlying his blasted hopes. Imagine how surreal it is that Americans should erect a monument in their capital city to a man whose revolutionary ideas the vast majority of today's political leaders clearly scorn.

In remembering Martin Luther King, Jr.—the actual human being, not his mythical image—hear him say, "If a man hasn't discovered something that he will die for, he isn't fit to live."[26] King did not want to be a martyr; he said so, in fact, the night before he was murdered. He did not want to die for "democratic socialism" or any similar thing, but he understood the structural nature of American society and therefore he knew the risks he was taking.

Religion and Social Change

Sometimes religion binds a people together; sometimes it is a force that is used against a perceived enemy. This is the essence of Weber's theory of religion. Weber was truly an extraordinary student of worldwide religious practices, much more so than even Durkheim, whose own book on religion is mainly confined to the study of anthropological accounts of so-called primitive religions and, in particular, Australian aboriginal totemic religions. From his comparative view of the world's many religions, Weber discerned the essential plasticity of religion, that it could take many forms and lead to disparate social outcomes. For example, religion can be conservative by providing legitimacy for existing political regimes (e.g., the Christianized Roman Empire and today's Islamic State of Iran), or religion can just as easily provide legitimacy for social struggles against existing political regimes (e.g., the King-led civil rights movement, Latin American liberation theology, the Iranian Islamic Revolution that overthrew the secular Shah of Iran and established the present theocracy in Iran). Rarely, however, is religion the elemental source of either order or conflict. Predominantly Hindu India and predominantly Muslim Pakistan face one another as rivals not solely or even primarily because of their religious differences but, rather, as a result of their competition for control over disputed territory and regional political influence. Both groups had fought side by side in their struggle against British colonialism, illustrating the importance of social and political interests in determining the fundamental basis for apparently religious conflict. Similarly, sociologists tend to see the conflict between the Protestant majority and the Catholic minority in Northern Ireland as having to do more with underlying economic, political, and cultural inequalities than with theological differences.[27] Instead of forming the essential basis for conflict, religious differences tend to be a prominent medium through which basic social and political conflict is expressed.

The role of Dr. King in the American civil rights movement is a case in point. For the sociologist, King's success had less to do with his otherwise exceptional personal qualities—his skilled ministerial "oratory," say—than with the historical and structural facts of American society after World War II. In the 1950s and 1960s, a series of factors coalesced to create a sympathetic audience for King's message. The contradiction of slavery, recognized even by Thomas Jefferson and many of his colleagues at the founding of this nation-state, was resolved for the most part by the Union victory in the American Civil War. Yet the continuation of a taken-for-granted

racism combined with institutional segregation and the political and cultural oppression of black Americans to create a structural reality that did not mesh with the
official political ideology of liberty and equality for all. After World War II, black
veterans returned to an oppressive society, far more oppressive than those of England and France, for example. During this period, black Americans were also moving in large numbers from the rural states of the South, where they were concentrated
as a result of slavery, to the urban states of the North, where they enjoyed marginal
increases in social, political, and cultural freedom. Between 1940 and 1970, more
than 4 million blacks left the South and migrated to the urban centers of the industrial
North. As a result, this same period saw the percentage of African Americans living
in the South decline from seventy-seven to fifty-three, and the percentage of African
Americans living in urban areas increase from forty-nine to eighty-one.[28] The rise of
the mass media, which early on displayed to the entire society the oppressive local
and state regimes of the American South, further contributed to widespread dismay
with official segregation and race-based oppression. All Americans, for example,
became familiar with George Wallace, the infamous governor of Alabama who
stood at the door of the University of Alabama and personally denied entrance to
this university's would-be first black student.

The disparities, then, between what was *supposed* to be and what *was* were becoming increasingly evident and untenable to leading members of this historically
largest of American ethnic minority groups. Enter the Reverend, Dr. Martin Luther
King, Jr., a highly educated and articulate Southern Baptist minister who helped to
wed the venerable institutions of the southern black church and the enthusiasm for
change among society's youth—in the North as well as in the South—into a political
movement for radical social change that exploited the evident contradiction between the society's Christian and democratic self-image and its undemocratic, and
in King's reading, terribly un-Christian social institutions and practices.

The preceding clearly simplifies a complicated history and set of structural
changes in American society and, certainly, is in no manner intended to diminish the
extraordinary life of Dr. Martin Luther King, Jr. A similar story could be told about
Mohandas K. Ghandi and Malcolm X. The point is that individuals who use religion
to affect social change do so within structured societies and particular cultures that
either enhance or diminish their appeal. Many prophets have come and gone whose
timing was poor.

The Borderland between Faith and Reason

At this point, let us shift focus a bit and try to answer the questions posed at the outset of this chapter. It is one thing to empirically describe worldwide religious affiliations or to sketch historical change in religious practices and note a few ways that re-

ligion has been used to catalyze change or to conclude that religion is a social institution embedded in ongoing human cultures. These statements are really the stuff of ordinary, empirically oriented sociology. It is quite another thing, however, to return to the realm of the sacred and query religion's status and meaning for to-day's world. This is a subject that requires the sociological imagination because the sociological imagination is located at the crossroads of social structure, history, and biography—a point that is never fixed in any cognitive map alive to the always changing world—and thus transcends strictly empirical questions and observations. One can and should study facts about religion but that would always be an insuffi-cient basis on which to erect any serious understanding of religion. Indeed, one can study *any* and *all* empirical trends and never develop even the rudiments of a truly sociological imagination.

Thus it is, perhaps, no surprise then that the main founders of sociology each viewed religion as extremely important. For Durkheim, all religions contain truth, the truth of society's importance over and above individuals; therefore, in his view, "there are no religions which are false."[29] For Marx, religion is "the sentiment of a heartless world, and the soul of soulless conditions."[30] Marx meant that humans have projected their highest ideals and most humane values in the religious sphere of life. These ideals and values are, for Marx, rightly regarded as sacred and should be acted on with utter seriousness. In Weber's most widely read work *The Protestant Ethic and the Spirit of Capitalism* (1904-05), he argues that the Protestant Reformation, a primarily religious affair, was critical for the birth of modern, Western society, which is, ironically, an unprecedentedly secular form of society.[31]

The overarching irony is that neither Marx, Weber, nor Durkheim were them-selves among the faithful. Instead, each viewed the claims that each and every par-ticular religion makes for itself as essentially illusionary. For Marx, religion was "the sentiment of a heartless world" but also "the opium of the people," which is to say, a drug distributed by elites to the masses that promises them a false salvation and distracts people from the real possibilities for realizing in the here and now, as it were, the salvation of a heaven on earth. Weber spoke of the many and various clashes between the world's "gods and demons" and sarcastically remarked, "He who yearns for seeing should go to the cinema. . . . "[32] In *The Elementary Forms of Religious Life,* Durkheim wrote simply that "the old gods are growing old or already dead, and others are not yet born."[33]

But why were these classical sociologists (and many other intellectuals of their day) themselves nonbelievers? Perhaps a sociological answer is fitting. The nine-teenth and early twentieth centuries, when these three men lived, was a time of rapid social change. This was a time when human beings were explicitly and systemati-cally analyzing the power of society over the individual, realizing the interconnectedness of all living things (including natural forces but also far-flung human populations), and for the first time witnessing the explanatory power of natural and social science, which were revolutionizing the way humans would see the world, the "heavens," and the invisible forces that shaped and determined visible events in the world, natural or otherwise. Never before had humans been able to study all religions, for example, and never before had they the scientific sensibilities or means to discern the workings of natural and social forces. Another way of putting this is that never before had the totality been so revealed, the totality of nature and the totality of society within nature. This was the age of Charles Darwin, after all, and of Sigmund Freud. From natural evolution to the analysis of dreams, modern people were on the cusp of realizing, or so it seemed, the truth of all things.

Thus, while Durkheim was a child in a family that boasted a long line of rabbis, Weber had a mother who was a fervent Protestant, and Marx grew up in a family that was Jewish but whose father had converted to Protestantism for political reasons, none of these early socialization experiences could withstand the force of their learning as adults. For these three, at any rate, the power of religion to reproduce itself in the young was vanquished by the sobering effects of the new sciences of nature and of society. Thus they came to see sociology and religion as inherently opposed to one another. To them, religion represented the illusions of an irretrievable past and sociology represented the promise of enlightenment for an open and undefined future. To say to any one of them, "Why are you not Christian?" would be like asking, "Why don't you worship Ra, the Sun God of the Egyptians?" Their answer might be formulated as questions: "Why would I?" "Why would I believe in 'the something' believed in by this one particular religious community?" "Why would I ignore all the other belief systems?" "Indeed, why would I *believe* in anything, when I can *know*"? "Why would I subordinate myself to a particular religion when I can understand and explain all religion?" "Why," Marx might add, "should we believe when we can *make real* that which we say we aspire to? Why wait until we are dead to make our lives correspond to our most cherished values and aspirations?" These imagined responses are understandable, at least on sociological grounds, because never before had humans been so influenced by the scientific revolution. In this moment, not believing in a religion must have felt just as natural as believing once did for people of times past.

This nonbelieving was a significant contributor to the early development of the sociological imagination. To have ready-made answers to questions discourages the search for new answers. Why try to explain, for example, the causes of war if war and all manner of human "inhumanity" are already explained by the existence of "evil"? The ready availability and plausibility of nonscientific, transhuman answers thwarts the pursuit of empirical evidence in support of *social* theories or explanations. Furthermore, why try to promote the sociological imagination if history making is always and already under the control of a trans-social being, a god or a force, with a predetermined plan for human history? Why pursue the self-knowledge that the sociological imagination promises if the truly important relationship between the self and other exists in a sacred spiritual relationship with some great other who is not human and cannot be known in simple human terms? It would seem that, for the believer, social science in general and the sociological imagination in particular would have at the very least a curtailed significance. It certainly would lose any ultimate significance because it would be trumped by a form of knowing that purports to transcend what can be known by means of simple, human knowing.

Marx, Weber, and Durkheim agreed in the empirical observation that the modern world is the most despiritualized or nonreligious of all known human societies. For each, the basic structure of modern society and the main tenets of modern culture together worked to erode the power and meaning of religious institutions and belief systems. Science, bureaucracy, industrial capitalism, and cosmopolitan urbanism tend to undermine faith, moral bonds, and an orientation to the sacred and transcendent. The further development of modern society would, they thought, simply continue this trend toward secularization. While they conceded that there may be occasional backsliding—new gods "not yet born" or Weber's speculation that "new prophets" may arise—they all felt that, in the end, modern society and culture would stand as the first essentially nonreligious form of human collective life. Of course, we can look around us today and see how wrong they were in this prediction. The one billion nonbelievers notwithstanding, some five billion of the earth's human inhabitants remain in varying degrees entangled with the spirit of some traditional religious belief system and in some way participants in one or another religious institution.

The Sociological Imagination and Postmodern Religion

It would seem, then, that the persistence of religious belief and religious institutions in the world, even in advanced modern societies such as the United States, says something important about the make-up of the sociological imagination. It says either that most people need more comfort than the sociological imagination can offer or that sociologists have been ineffective in creating a need for sociological self-consciousness.

It is true that the sociological imagination hardly offers itself as "the sentiment of a heartless world." Furthermore, as a self-critical, empirically oriented, and essentially secular enterprise, the sociological imagination produces no new prophets or "seers," although some sociologists may be popular or modestly influential. Indeed, any claim to be high priests of humanity, members of a secular priesthood, would reveal an underdeveloped sociological imagination. Finally, applying a sociological imagination today produces a picture of society as essentially dying and dystopian, which is not a terribly attractive alternative to an ideal sacred realm. If solace is what people want, the sociological imagination offers little. Instead, just like at the origin of Christianity, today's "Roman Empire" is producing social conditions that are conducive to many Christianities, that is, any belief system that promises comfort and that motivates action against the stresses of rapid population increase, urban squalor, disease, and suffering. Mills's own response to this situation does not seem destined to reverse the popular distaste for sociology's cold comfort.

In his famous "A Pagan Sermon," for example (which he delivered at an assembly of the United Church of Canada in Toronto as well as before the First Midwest Conference of the Unitarian Church), Mills adopted a decidedly confrontational approach to established religion. He asserted that

> the average ministerial output is correctly heard as a parade of worn-out phrases. It is generally unimaginative and often trivial. As public rhetoric, it is boring and irrelevant. As private belief, it is without passion. In the world of the West, religion has become a subordinate part of the overdeveloped society.[34]

For Mills, religion had lost its sacred content and its ability to motivate and as a result had become little more than a means of "getting chummy with God."[35] To counter this perceived religious and, at base, moral indifference, Mills pursued the classic strategy of *immanent critique*. This entails using a group's own principles against them and encouraging them to live up to their own cherished ideals. (This is much the same strategy pursued by Martin Luther King, Jr. vis-à-vis the American public.) Mills concluded,

> According to your belief, my kind of man—secular, prideful, agnostic and all the rest of it—is among the damned. I am on my own; you've got your God. It is up to you to proclaim gospel, to declare justice, to apply your love of man—the sons of God, all of them, you say—meaningfully, each and every day, to the affairs and troubles of men. It is up to you to find answers that are rooted in ultimate moral decision and to say them so that they are compelling.[36]

Mills ends in the language of a preacher denouncing his own flock,

> I hope your Christian conscience is neither at ease nor at attention, because if it is I must conclude that it is a curiously expedient and ineffective apparatus. I hope you

do not believe that in what you do and in how you live you are renouncing evil, because if you do, then I must infer that you know nothing of evil and so nothing of good. I hope you do not imagine yourselves to be the bearers of compassion, because if you do, you cannot yet know that today compassion without bitterness and terror is mere girlish sentiment and not worthy of a full-grown man. I hope you do not speak from the moral center of yourselves, because if you do, then in the dark nights of your soul, in fear and in trembling, you must be cruelly aware of your moral peril in this time of total war, and—given what you, a Christian, say you believe—I, a pagan, pity you.[37]

Clearly, these ideas were not designed to ingratiate Mills to his Christian audiences, but not too surprisingly, for many they did just that. Why?

It is in the very nature of most religious belief systems to accord a special place to those who call the flock back to the moral essence of beliefs purportedly and officially held. Islamic fundamentalists, for example, just like Christian fundamentalists, know the importance of "revivals," movements characterized by extreme forms of moral exhortation designed to return wayward believers to their own self-chosen fundamental principles. Such revivals are a common occurrence in the history of religions because it is predictable that social, profane, or this-worldly influences will distract even the most dedicated believers from their attention to transcendent themes, values, and purposes. Mills, at any rate, played this role rather well even though, or perhaps because, he was a self-declared "pagan." If even a pagan can articulate a moral perspective on war—or if a merely young, black minister from the American South can win the Nobel Prize for Peace—then the challenge is clearly laid out for those who believe themselves morally superior to pagans, African Americans, and to all other lesser creatures.

Today, Mills's 1950s emphasis on "girlish" beliefs versus those "worthy of full-grown men" probably would not win him many sympathetic listeners, except perhaps among "Promise Keepers."[38] Clearly, Mills was not free of the ideological effects of culture; Mills was a product of his society and, in this instance, its sexism. Much the same is true of Durkheim, Marx, and Weber. They were men raised in cultures far more patriarchal than exist today in most modern societies (but not necessarily in Afghanistan, Saudi Arabia, India, or China). To them, enlightenment had a masculine edge, a kind of staunch, unemotional, unflinching, warlike bravado and courage. Armed with principle, they would face down the "dark night of the soul."

Perhaps the unpopularity of the sociological imagination—at least in terms of its insufficient comforting qualities—has to do with its implicit alliance with a traditional masculine character. Unlike religion, Mills-style sociology tends to suppress or implicitly devalue caring, loving, acceptance, and other charitable, humbling human feelings. Whatever else one might say about them, Marx, Weber, Durkheim, and Mills were not known for their humility. As Mills candidly admits, he is "prideful." Perhaps the classical sociological ideas about religion reflect this sin of pridefulness, which limits the value of its ideas, truth, and potential for widespread acceptance.

Let us approach the answer to the question of sociology's rejection of religious sensibilities indirectly. Early in this chapter, the question was posed, "Is there a postmodern religion?" The Polish-born sociologist Zygmunt Bauman (who has lived and worked most of his life in Britain) proposed that there is indeed a postmodern form of religion, namely, fundamentalism.[39] By "fundamentalism," Bauman means those revivalist movements worldwide that pose themselves as "an indubitably *supreme* authority, an authority to end all other authorities."[40] Fundamentalisms of all kinds offer to people a firm and uncompromising moral compass, a clear moral foundation for life that tells them what is right and what is wrong, what is good and what is bad, what a good life is and what a bad life is, and provide clear rewards and punishments for those who adhere or fail to adhere to the rules of the game. Islamic fundamentalists fit here, as do Christian fundamentalists.

For Bauman, fundamentalism is the postmodern form of religion because postmodern society creates extreme forms of anxiety that require equally extreme forms of solace. In particular, postmodern society creates an individualist consumer culture, which renders life a process of making innumerable individual choices. In a sense, one must buy one's self in the marketplace of selfhoods. What style of clothes to wear? What beliefs should I believe in? The need to make choices about everything is overwhelming. "The agonies of choice," as Bauman said, leads to unbearable uncertainty in individual lives as well as, perhaps, a vague perception of their narcissistic emptiness.[41] What would Jesus do? Thus not a return of premodern religion, fundamentalisms are, in Bauman's view, a direct response to contemporary social structure.

The imposition of strict religious moral codes, however, retains the same masculine edge as the pagan sociological imagination. Fundamentalist religion is not known for its feminine warmth. Indeed, the rise of fundamentalist religious beliefs is often, in fact, accompanied by a resurgence of sexism. This is the case in the Taliban's Afghanistan just as it is in the fundamentalist Protestant sects of the United States. In Saudi Arabia, women not only cannot vote but they also are not allowed to drive cars.

Beyond its affinity with patriarchal domination, though, fundamentalisms may also reveal a deeper weakness of postmodern society. It appears that *post*-modern individual freedom requires an *anti*-individual antidote. Of religious fundamentalism, Bauman observed that it legislates in no uncertain terms about every aspect of life, thereby unloading the burden of responsibility lying heavily on the individual's shoulders—those shoulders postmodern culture proclaims, and market publicity promotes, as omnipotent, but which many people find much too weak for the burden.

Religious fundamentalism...has 'a singular capacity to reveal the ills of society.'...With the market-induced agony of solitude and abandonment as its only alternative, fundamentalism, religious or otherwise, can count on an ever-growing constituency. Whatever the quality of the answers it supplies, the questions which it answers are genuine. The problem is not how to dismiss the gravity of the questions, but how to find answers free from totalitarian genes.[42]

Convergence at the Extremes?

If Durkheim was right that all religion has its truth, then the truth of the various fundamentalisms is that they respond to the burdens of individuality in postmodern society by promising to relieve these untenable burdens but at the cost of individual freedom itself. In contrast, the sociological imagination only adds to the burdens of individuality and promises no certain benefits at all. Which would we, as sociologists, expect to win? Is there no way out of this dilemma? Is our only choice one between "the promise" of sociology and the Promise Keepers?

We might answer this question by first recalling the quotation that began this chapter. We might presume that Mills liked to talk with students, as Horowitz reports, because they had a passionate interest in knowledge and in the future of society. (They were also, one imagines, bound by role differences to listen to his endless preachings!) But why, given his tone in "A Pagan Sermon," would he seek the company of clerics? This seems curious. Perhaps Mills liked to talk with religiously oriented folks not so much because he was raised in a Catholic home, which he was, or because he himself had a religious bone in his body, which he did not, but because religiously minded people tend to take seriously transcendent values, which Mills, no less than Durkheim, regarded as eminently social or eminently and distinctively human. They are, after all, higher values, similar in content to the values of reason and freedom that Mills, as an adult child of the Enlightenment, valued. Furthermore, the cleric's attention to the totality of a sacred realm as it stands apart from the merely profane creates a common ground with the Millsian sociologist who wishes to discuss the totality of society as it intersects with sacred cultural beliefs. Both cleric and classical sociologist, then, tend to share this orientation to absolute phenomena. Out of such a dialogue, perhaps, one could imagine a *rapproachement* between clerics and sociologists in which the chief difference that creates a difference between them—the question of which has primacy: society as the product of a God or Gods as the products of specific societies—is left off the table in favor of attention to the real needs and real prospects for human beings in this world, in the here and now. It is worth repeating Bauman's conclusion that "the problem is not how to dismiss . . . the questions, but how to find answers free from totalitarian genes."

This proposed dialogue presupposes a willingness to bracket or set aside the conflict about the nature of ultimate abstract principles in favor of cooperation in common projects and practical concerns. This reflects a more feminine ethics attentive to concrete people and their needs and less driven by the competing abstractions of science and theology. There are also practical reasons for this type of cooperation. From the point of view of the Millsian sociologist, the world as a whole is dying and dystopian. As a result, there is much suffering in the lives of many specific individuals. If the sociological imagination is, on its own, apparently insufficient solace, then who would deny others their right to seek something more? From the point of view of the cleric, perhaps especially the fundamentalist cleric, the world as a whole is dying and dystopian. As a result, there is much suffering in the lives of many specific individuals. If understanding and acting is enhanced by the adoption of a type of mind that conceives of the interrelationship between individuality and social structure within specific temporal and spatial horizons, then why not adopt it as a self-consciousness appropriate for this moment in human experience, even if, as a believer, one retains a sense for the unknowns of natural history and the unknowns of indigent particulars?

This last sentence, of course, is meant as a surprise. The question is the following: In pushing our demonstration of the sociological imagination to the extremes of human biographical, historical, and societal experience, does a postmodern sociological imagination converge with the form of a fundamentalist religious self-consciousness? Is this not the case even though, given everything else included in this chapter, the sociological imagination is a profoundly nonreligious "religious" self-consciousness? And although the sociological imagination is a far cry from actual religious fundamentalisms of all sorts, is it not the case that we can conclude this discussion of religion and society not in a state of panic or cynicism but calmly, in a state of sobriety, with an appreciation for the vexing demons of religious life and for the equally vexing gods of classical sociology?

Notes

1. Irving Louis Horowitz, ed., *Power, Politics & People: The Collected Essays of C. Wright Mills* (Oxford, U.K.: Oxford University Press, 1963), 6.

2. Emile Durkheim, *The Elementary Forms of Religious Life*, trans. Joseph Ward Swain (1912; reprint, New York: Free Press, 1965).

3. Ibid., 22.

4. Ibid., 466.

5. Ibid., 490.

6. Ibid., 15.

7. *The World Almanac and Book of Facts 2000* (Mahwah, N.J.: Primedia Reference, 2000), 659.

8. U.S. Census Bureau, *Statistical Abstract of the United States, 1999* (Washington, D.C., 1999) 71, table 89.

9. Ibid., 70, table 88.

10. Anthony Giddens and Mitchell Duneier, *Introduction to Sociology,* 3d ed. (New York: Norton, 2000), 422, and William J. Bennett, *The Index of Leading Cultural Indicators* (New York: Broadway, 1999), 175.

11. U.S. Census Bureau, *Statistical Abstract of the United States, 1999* (Washington, D.C., 1999), 71, table 89.

12. William J. Bennett, *The Index of Leading Cultural Indicators,* 176.

13. See Stephen K. Sanderson, *Macrosociology: An Introduction to Human Societies,* 4th ed. (New York: Longman, 1999), especially pp. 370-3.

14. Rodney Start, *The Rise of Christianity: A Sociologist Reconsiders History* (Princeton, N.J.: Princeton University Press, 1996), 3.

15. Ibid., especially pp. 156-8.

16. Ibid., 208.

17. Ibid., 7.

18. Giddens and Duneier, *Introduction to Sociology,* 422-3.

19. Ibid., 423.

20. Martin Luther King, Jr. from "Autobiography of Religious Development" (Crozer Theological Seminar, 1949). Available at www.triadntr.net/rdavis/mlkqts.htm.

21. See Michael Eric Dyson, *I May Not Get There with You: The True Martin Luther King, Jr.* (New York: Free Press, 1999).

22. Martin Luther King, Jr., in a speech delivered November 14, 1966 in Frogmore, South Carolina. Available at www.triadntr.net/rdavis/mlkqts.htm.

23. Martin Luther King, Jr., in a speech delivered August 16, 1967 in Atlanta, Georgia. Available at www.stanford.edu/group/king.

24. Martin Luther King, Jr., in *Redbook Magazine,* September 1961. Available at www.triadntr.net/rdavis/mlkqts.htm.

25. Martin Luther King, Jr., in a speech delivered December 24, 1967 in Atlanta, Georgia. Available at www.triadntr.net/rdavis/mlkqts.htm.

26. Martin Luther King, Jr., in a speech delivered June 23, 1963 in Detroit, Michigan. Available at www.triadntr.net/rdavis/mlkqts.htm.

27. See Stanley Lieberson, *A Piece of the Pie: Black and White Immigrants since 1900* (Berkeley: University of California Press, 1980).

28. All figures are from Norman R. Yetman, ed., *Majority and Minority: The Dynamics of Race and Ethnicity in American Life,* 6th ed. (Boston: Allyn & Bacon, 1999), 575.

29. Durkheim, *The Elementary Forms of Religious Life,* 15.

30. Marx wrote: "*Religious* suffering is at the same time an *expression* of real suffering and a *protest* against real suffering. Religion is the sigh of the oppressed creature, the sentiment of a heartless world, and the soul of soulless conditions. It is the *opium* of the people." See Marx, "Contribution to the Critique of Hegel's *Philosophy of Right*: Introduction," in *The Marx-Engels Reader,* ed. Robert C. Tucker, 2d ed. (New York: Norton, 1972), 54, emphases in original.

31. Max Weber, *The Protestant Ethic and the Spirit of Capitalism* (1904 and 1905; reprint, New York: Charles Scribner's Sons, 1958).

32. Ibid., 29.

33. Durkheim, *The Elementary Forms of Religious Life,* 475.

34. C. Wright Mills, "A Pagan Sermon," in *The Causes of World War III* (New York: Simon and Schuster, 1958), 148.

35. Ibid.

36. Ibid., 157.

37. Ibid.

38. See six sociological studies on the Promise Keepers collected in a special issue of *Sociology of Religion* 61 (Spring 2000).

39. Zygmunt Bauman, "Postmodern Religion?" in *Religion, Modernity, and Postmodernity,* ed. Paul Heelas (Oxford, U.K.: Blackwell, 1998), 72.

40. Ibid., 74, emphasis in original.

41. Ibid.

42. Ibid., 75.

III

THE SOCIAL FORCES WORKING AGAINST THE SOCIOLOGICAL IMAGINATION

8

The Degradation of the Public Sphere

The educational and the political role of social science in a democracy is to help cultivate and sustain publics and individuals that are able to develop, to live with, and to act upon adequate definitions of personal and social realities.

—*C. Wright Mills*[1]

Imagine this scene. Members of the antiabortion group Operation Rescue come to a town to protest around a women's health clinic where, among other things, abortions are performed. Perhaps a hundred people encircle the clinic. Many of the protesters are children. They disrupt traffic. They use bullhorns and chants to create considerable noise. They carry placards bearing antiabortion slogans and images of aborted human fetuses, including a detailed photographic image of the severed head of a fetus clutched in forceps. The local police are there to manage the traffic disruptions and to keep peace not only between the antiabortion protesters and those working or seeking services at the clinic but also between the protesters and others who have come to protest the protesters. There is considerable tension in the air. It is quite a scene.

Is this an example of democracy in action? Far from it, as we shall see. As Mills noted, there is no society that is "altogether democratic—that remains an ideal."[2] But what is the ideal? For Mills,

> democracy implies that those vitally affected by any decision men make have an effective voice in that decision. This, in turn, means that all power to make such decisions be publicly legitimated and that the makers of such decisions be held publicly accountable.[3]

> Democracy means the power and the freedom of those controlled by law to change the law, according to agreed-upon rules—and even to change these rules; but more than that, it means some kind of collective self-control over the structural mechanics of history itself.[4]

Note Mills's emphasis on the notions of being *vitally* affected, of having an *effective voice,* of public legitimation and accountability, of law- and rule-*making* (not just law- and rule-abiding), of power and freedom over the structural mechanics of history. In a democracy (a term from the Greek language that literally means, "the rule of the people"), individuals—reasoning, critically-minded individuals—come together in a public space to rationally debate the issues they themselves define as contentious and to make collective decisions about matters that vitally affect them. In democracy, people rule.

There is, then, an important connection between the sociological imagination and democratic society. As we have seen, the sociological imagination is conceived in terms that are consistent with Enlightenment philosophy (recall Kant's "escape from self-imposed immaturity," the philosophical idea that people—indeed, all people—should be and need to be self-aware and self-possessed—in a word, mature) developed into the sociological idea that, to be enlightened, people need the ability to conceptualize the intersection of their lives with the constraining nature of social structure in the historical epoch in which they live. How, after all, can people in modern democratic society be rational and free without this type of sociological self-understanding? On what basis can they otherwise effectively participate in history making if not through an understanding of social change? The sociological imagination and democratic society demand each other. They are mutually reinforcing and they are interdependent.

In this chapter, I aim to describe how the sociological imagination is threatened with extinction, not by individual ignorance or any other type of personal failing but by the eclipse of democratic society itself. If the space for democratic activity were ever fully degraded—if the public sphere were ever completely debased—then study of the sociological imagination would be, practically speaking, moot. We have broached this subject already, of course, but here we shall focus attention on the conflict between democracy and propaganda, the chief form of systemic deception that most directly subverts, distorts, and diminishes sociological thinking.

Propaganda Techniques 101

A sociologist looking at the scene described at the opening of this chapter would no doubt see many things of interest, but the sociologist who cares about democracy, public life, and adequate definitions of personal and social realities would give special focus to the phenomena of propaganda because propaganda is the sworn enemy of all of the above. What exactly does it mean?

As the American sociologist, Robert Jackall, explained, "The term 'propaganda' has distinctly religious origins."[5] Jackall continued,

> On 22 June 1622, Pope Gregory XV (1621-23) issued the Papal Bull *Inscrutabili Divinae* establishing the Sacred Congregation *de Propaganda Fide. . . . The new congregation's "mission," from the Latin mittere* meaning literally a "sending forth," was "to reconquer by spiritual arms, by prayers and good works, by preaching and catechising, the countries . . . lost to the Church in the debacle of the sixteenth century and to organize into an efficient corps the numerous missionary enterprises for the diffusion of the gospel in pagan lands."[6]

Jackall's description is notable for, among other things, its lack of propagandist elements. Here Jackall is specific about the origin of the concept, he explains the special meaning of unfamiliar historical terms, he quotes those whom he is trying to represent, and there is no use of emotionally or otherwise "loaded" language. Unlike the propagandist, Jackall is aiming to accurately inform and educate. His point is that the term and the idea of propaganda emerged out of the Roman Catholic Church's need to "persuade men and women all across the globe to believe in Christian doctrine or, if perchance they had fallen astray, to rekindle their faith."[7] The people who answered this call, "talented intellectuals of every sort," happily called themselves "propagandists."[8]

No one today happily calls themselves propagandists. The term has acquired a distinctly pejorative meaning. What is this modern meaning? Jackall writes that propaganda is understood today as

> the product of intellectual work that is . . . highly organized; it aims at persuading large masses of people about the virtues of some organization, cause, or person. And its success or failure depends on how well it captures, expresses, and then rechannels specific existing sentiments.[9]

Note that propaganda is conceived as the product of highly organized intellectual work; it is directed toward large masses of people; it does the bidding of organizations, causes, specific people; and, finally, it is conceived as the manipulation of existing sentiments. This, of course, is not appreciably different than the original meaning of the term. So defined, however, it is also clear that, in our time, writing such as Jackall's is uncommon, whereas what he is writing about, propaganda, is ubiquitous. Scarcely an institution or group is not this day and every day working to persuade large masses of people about something, in some direction, and via the manipulation of already existing emotional feelings.

Returning to the street scene depicted above, we might observe that everything before us is infused with propaganda. At the most superficial level, the placards and statements say simply that abortion is a grizzly, unwarranted, and immoral procedure. If one is emotionally disturbed by the image of a fetus's severed head in a pair of forceps, then one should oppose legalized abortion: that's the basic "message."

Yet there is much more to this scene than easily meets the eye. Perhaps it requires no great intellectual powers to observe that "pro-life" (like "pro-choice") is an instance of what propaganda analysts have long called "glittering generalities."[10] The technique is to use a name or idea that is widely and positively valued, a "shining ideal," and identify one's organization, cause, or person with this notion. We can suppose that most Americans are "pro-life." We value life; we devalue death. It makes sense, then, for Operation Rescue and other antiabortion groups to identify themselves with "life," to say, in effect, that the value of life is what motivates them and that this motivation is therefore consistent with what the masses of people value. Thus, when people see this group's messages, they will be more likely to identify with the group and perhaps lend their support or, at a minimum, feel sympathy for this particular cause. Pro-life groups would be ill-advised, for example, to describe themselves as "pro-repression of women."

This last definition of reality—"pro-repression of women"—is more likely what pro-choice groups would call pro-life groups and is a second and related type of classical propaganda technique, termed simply, *name calling*. Are doctors who perform abortions "abortionists" which is to say, people who abort human fetuses? This is name calling, which in this case works to dehumanize people who are medical doctors who perform abortions by equating them with just this one thing that they do. If they *do* this one thing, then they *are* this other thing. It would be less subtle, of course, to call these medical doctors "baby killers," but the point is just the same. Thus named, it is easier, for example, to imagine murdering these doctors because they are themselves understood as murderers, and in our society the murder of murders is much easier to justify on moral grounds than is the murder of physicians who, as part of their work, perform a legal medical procedure requested by consenting adults.

Name-calling and glittering generalities are propaganda techniques that are rather easy to observe and appreciate, but in the scene briefly depicted, there are more subtle and therefore perhaps more effective propaganda techniques at work. Why is it, for example, that Operation Rescue deploys so many children as part of their protest? It seems odd, on the surface, that 8- and 12-year-olds should be carrying around signs that depict the severed head of a fetus in the middle of such public clamor. Here we see the technique of "transfer" at work. A psychological transference along the lines of "fetus = potential child" is instilled in the minds of the passersby: "I see images of dead babies and that disturbs me, and I see children; I like children, and abortion kills potential children; abortion is therefore bad and wrong." The very fact of the children's presence becomes a kind of object lesson for the propagandists. Of course, it is unlikely that anyone would self-consciously make these mental connections but that is a key source of power behind this and every propaganda technique. The primary appeal is always to the emotions, to the existing sentiments of the masses of people, which quickly and imperceptibly translate into rudimentary if also powerful moods and dispositions. The point, after all, is to persuade, not inform or educate. The message does not have to make sense to qualify as effective propaganda. Indeed, messages that do not make sense may be more effective.

In addition to name calling, glittering generalities, and transfer techniques, we could also observe that this scene is just that, "a scene," a kind of literal as well as figurative carnival. The protesters are not local people at all but members of a cross-country caravan, stopping in town after town to create street theater on behalf of their cause. They work to affect a build up of excitement among their local sympathizers and concern among their local opponents. They may send advance teams much as political candidates do. They want coverage in the local newspaper or on local television as well as follow-up coverage after they have gone. They want to stir up controversy and bring attention to themselves so that when they actually enact their premediated protest, they will have the attention of a mass audience, the manipulation of which is the essence of their mission. Propaganda that no one sees or hears about is not effective propaganda.

One thing Operation Rescue wants their hoped-for audience to see is their own group's comradery, dedication, and enthusiasm. They are on a "band wagon," as it were, and implicitly, they want others to envy their participation in a righteous but exciting social movement. They are part of an "operation" to "rescue" children. From the point of view of the humdrum 9-to-5 existence, the very fact of so many families happily crisscrossing the country together is an implicit appeal to join in. This is the bandwagon technique of propaganda and is seen in any appeal to follow the crowd. Its success depends on the targeted audience's sense of social isolation and boredom with their own lives. This technique appeals especially to individuals with a diminished ability to stand apart from what is often called peer pressure.

Of course, as a set of techniques, propaganda can also be used to resist as opposed to create peer pressure or resist or create any emotional response for any purpose whatsoever. Tobacco companies target young people with special forms of propaganda, and the government funds counterpropaganda depicting teens who choose not to smoke cigarettes. These public service advertisements (or PSAs) are trying to create a bandwagon for not smoking: "Everyone's *not doing it!*" Examples of bandwagoning are potentially endless. Presidential candidates who win the first political primary in New Hampshire invariably say that they are "on a roll," implicitly telling future voters and campaign contributors, "Get on my band wagon or be left behind." "Don't waste your money or votes on the loser; go with the winner." This technique is so commonly understood and expected that members of the media just as invariably report that Candidate X is trying to lay claim to political momentum as though pointing out the manipulation, which is usually only half-heartedly trumpeted anyway, will somehow serve the public interest and therefore ennoble the journalistic profession.

When all of these techniques are marshaled together, they constitute an additional propaganda technique: card stacking. The idea is to stack the various implicit appeals in such a way that no other conclusion appears reasonable or justified—in our case, that abortion is wrong and should therefore be criminalized. Presumably, no one likes to look at the severed head of a human fetus; the negative emotional response is therefore predictable or "stacked" in favor of the propagandist's cause. Everyone values life; everyone likes children. Everyone is attracted to comradery and excitement. Card stacking seamlessly blends these messages together. When displayed to the average passerby, television viewer, or newspaper reader the hope is that many will be emotionally affected in the manner anticipated. It is hoped that relatively few people will pause to analyze these messages, as we have done, or to notice what is *not* being said or what is only half-true. Complexity is the enemy of effective propaganda; simplicity is its friend. Card stacking, like all propaganda, depends on the absence in the targeted audience of anything like a sociological imagination. It assumes an audience that is sociologically stupid and therefore more easily manipulated, duped, or, speaking more antiseptically, persuaded.

One might immediately assert, however, that most people are not successfully persuaded by groups such as Operation Rescue. This is true. It is not as though Operation Rescue is besieged by throngs of mindless people who, when the caravan comes to town, immediately throw down what they are doing and join up. People do not watch television commercials and then immediately head to the nearest shopping mall to buy the last thing being advertised. They do not vote for political candidates based solely on the candidate's propaganda.

This is not necessarily evidence of the unimportance of propaganda. It is just as likely that many people are reacting to one message on the basis of a counter-message. What if instead it is the case that propaganda is at war with itself, its basic techniques widely used by opposed organizations, causes, and persons, with ubiquitous and very subtle effects? Pro-choice advocates may dismiss pro-life advocates without any more independent thought than pro-life advocates use in dismissing them. A thick cloud of diffuse propaganda may not predictably serve any particular interest at any predictable time, but it may have an extraordinary social consequence nonetheless. Alas, a society whose public sphere is dominated by a diffuse propaganda, by myriad warring persuasion artists and "spin doctors," is not the same thing as a democracy.

The Public Sphere and Mass Media

At this point, the reader might reasonably protest that an Operation Rescue carnival is hardly an apt metaphor for the normal everyday workings of contemporary society. This case stands apart from the normality of everyday life. Perhaps another case would be appropriate, one that is less easy to decode and therefore more revealing of the forces of a diffuse, ubiquitous, and more insidious propaganda. Consider, then, the case of global warming.

How are average citizens to learn about global warming? In truth, there are many complicated aspects to the analysis of this phenomenon, so complicated that it would be difficult for anyone to understand them other than an expert in climatic science. Technical, scientific knowledge is the key to understanding the phenomenon and yet most people (including political leaders, journalists, and sociologists) do not possess the skills or training necessary to analyze the science that focuses our attention to the phenomenon in the first place. What is more, this is true about most, perhaps even all, social problems. Behind each there stands a body of expert knowledge that, by definition, only experts are qualified to create, interpret, and debate. How many people, for example, understand the intricacies of how poverty is measured in the United States? Many sociologists have only a passing familiarity with this topic. Most people do not know the first thing about how poverty is measured in the United States. They are thus in no position to rationally debate the quality of this measure or to understand what the resulting numbers mean, nor are they likely even to have a good guess about the nature and extent of poverty as reported to them through mass media, so disconnected are they from the production of knowledge. Most people know, however, that there is something called global warming, there is something called poverty, and that experts generally, and politicians and journalists in particular, do not always agree about anything having to do with either of them. In this situation, how can a citizen know anything of importance about anything that is important?

Clearly, average citizens must rely on experts and their interpreters to faithfully and skillfully communicate the meaning of otherwise confounding technical information. It is no good to try to become an expert in all things, since this is, obviously, impossible. A few rare individuals acquire expertise in more than one field. The former head of the U.S. Food and Drug Administration, Dr. David Kessler, is, for example, both a medical doctor and an attorney, but few people can aspire to be medical doctors or lawyers, much less both. Even Dr. Kessler's expert knowledge of medicine and the law, naturally, had its limits. He was not a heart surgeon nor was he qualified to arbitrate labor disputes. At best—*at best*—we can aspire to master one or two areas of expertise. For the rest, which is nearly everything, we must rely on others to share their expert knowledge in a way that we nonexperts can understand, make judgments about, and then act on. This assumes that the expert knowledge that is being communicated is, in the first place, reliable.

Thus, between experts and citizens there lies an important strata of actors whose job it is to interpret, distill, report, convey—some might say, "dumb down"—scientific or technical knowledge for the rest of us.[11] More important, there is also a whole range of communication technologies that act as media through which information must pass and that shape that information in the process. Reading a book is a significantly different experience from watching a television program, for example. With a book, one can go at one's own pace, read the end and then the beginning or read the entire thing repeatedly. A reader is actively using his or her mind, pushing his or her own thoughts along by the application of energy to the obstinate text. In contrast, television viewing is a relatively passive experience. The flow is not normally in the viewer's control (other than via "channel surfing"), and television is dominated by images instead of written text, images that are experienced as washing over the viewer instead of being coldly and reticently affixed to a page. One watches television; one reads a book. In short, mass communication technologies, like all technologies, are not neutral. Rather, technologies demand certain forms and deliver content appropriate to these forms.

We can imagine how this process looks. It is reported that the great British economist John Maynard Keynes visited President Franklin Delano Roosevelt in the White House to explain to the president his new theory of how a modern market economy worked, why it could get itself into a pickle called the Great Depression, and what the president might do to turn things around. Keynes used graphs and charts and numbers to make his point, but the president reportedly had little use for them. Keynes's technical presentation was confusing. Roosevelt already had his mind set on a massive government intervention into the stalled economy, and Keynes's theory, however elegant and subsequently influential, meant little except as a possible intellectual justification for what Roosevelt had already thrown his government behind, the New Deal.

Roosevelt himself famously used radio broadcasts dubbed "fireside chats" to popularize his decisions. He did not grab Keynes's charts and hit the road for one-to-one presentations with every American citizen he could get his hands on. This would have been impossible, of course. Instead, Roosevelt appealed to America's sentiment for leaders who identified with the high value of home and hearth and instilled in the fearful and agitated public a much-needed calm consistent with an evening by the fireplace. He projected his soothing yet authoritative voice to an audience situated safely in their homes but fearful for their social existence. Although he was not a dictator, his was the propaganda of a benevolent, paternalistic dictator. At the same time, across the Atlantic, real dictators were using the same technology for their own political goals. Although they would appeal to different existing sentiments and marshal them for their own ends, Hitler, Goebbels, Stalin, and Mussolini were mastering the political uses for this new medium of mass communication. Years later, H. Ross Perot, the independent billionaire candidate for president, used charts, graphs, and numbers in paid television broadcasts to inform the electorate of the facts, as his charts and graphs depicted them. He was rather successful, and he received more votes than any independent candidate ever had before him. Perot noted, for example, that the economy of Arkansas was not much bigger than that of a medium-sized business firm and, at any rate, was dominated by chicken production, suggesting that the people of America would be unwise to elect Bill Clinton, the Governor of Arkansas ("chicken man") and instead should look to a real businessman for leadership, such as himself. He also used numbers to disparage his other main opponent, then-President George Herbert Walker Bush, who had said that, in effect, the production of potato chips and microchips was of about the same value in terms of jobs and economic development, to which candidate Perot, who made much of his money in the computer industry, displayed charts, graphs, and numbers pointing out the relative value of microchips over potato chips. This made for good television because these notions were simple, oft repeated, and memorable.

Is "the medium the message," as Marshall McLuhan famously suggested? Keynes *lectured* Roosevelt. Since the President was not a student and the White House was not a classroom, Roosevelt's disinterest was perhaps predictable. Roosevelt *spoke to* Americans as they sat anonymously in their homes. His voice—not his image—was in play; his chats were literally not "in your face" affairs. An intimacy was therein effected, ironically an intimacy that Keynes's face-to-face lecture apparently did not produce. Perot was visually entertaining, as is demanded by television. His charts were colorful pictures, symbols of hard facts more than the real thing. His wisecracking manner was also entertaining, symbolizing his down-to-earth, straight-shooting, Texan persona. In one presidential debate, Perot even made fun of his large ears, directing the television audience's attention to the appearance of the messenger rather than to the content of the message. The form of the media — lecture, radio, or television—drives the content.

Of course, most of us never get the chance to have an expert such as Keynes visit our home and explain her or his theory. Most people do not have access to the mass media like Roosevelt did by virtue of his office and Perot did by virtue of his wealth. Instead, most people simply depend on mediated forms of communication for their knowledge of the world. What is the quality of this information? Is it affected by the media in which it is conveyed? Does it provide sufficient basis for democratic decision making? Specifically, is there evidence of propaganda at work in today's highly mediated public sphere? In the case of global warming, the answer is particularly clear.

The news magazine with the largest U.S. circulation is the venerable *Time,* which was founded in the 1930s by the famous Henry R. Luce and the less famous Briton Hadden. It is a self-described weekly news magazine that is part of the world's largest media empire, Time-Warner, Inc., which includes Warner Brothers, Turner Broadcasting, HBO, *Fortune* and twenty-two other mass-circulation magazines, and America Online. *Time,* however, has always been Time, Inc.'s flagship publication. What is the nature of *Time's* coverage of global warming?

In its 8 November 1999 "Beyond 2000" special issue, featuring what *Time* trumpeted on its cover as "100 Questions for the New Century," question twenty-one was "How hot will it get?" James Trefil is the author of this two-page section.[11] He is described as a "George Mason University physics professor and author of *101 Things You Don't Know About Science and No One Else Does Either.*[12] The content of Trefil's answer was aptly (and predictably) conveyed in his opening paragraph.

> Not so long ago, people talked about global warming in apocalyptic terms—imagining the Statue of Liberty up to its chin in water or an onslaught of tropical diseases in Oslo. Recently, however, advances in our understanding of climate have moved global warming from a subject for a summer disaster movie to a serious but manageable scientific and policy issue.[13]

In this single paragraph, an expert assures the nonexpert reader that, yes, once the reader might have been understandably worried about global warming, but thanks to today's expert knowledge, which contradicts yesterday's expert knowledge, there is no need to worry because the problem is such that managers of science and public policy have, or will have, things well under control. The statement also gently suggests that average people are easily duped by sensationalism ("summer disaster movies") and can only imagine a problem in terms appropriate for children (how flooding might, even humorously, affect a national landmark). For one paragraph to do all this is the mark of excellent popular writing. It is also propaganda.

There is, of course, more. As we read on, we learn that "the greenhouse effect is nothing new; it has been operating ever since the earth formed"; that predicting today's special, human-caused form of warming is not "simple"; that "there are nagging doubts even among researchers"; that scientists have at best "a fuzzy view of the future"; that climate science is "a frustrating field"; that the "greatest imponderable of all" is "how we will respond to the threat of climate warming"; and that it "makes no sense," therefore, "to overreact to the prospect of global warming, but it makes no sense to ignore it either."[14]

What reader could come away from this formulation without a sense of calm? After all, the worst thing one could do is overreact. What is called for by this interpretation is a kind of balanced concern borne of an acknowledgment that things are complicated and uncertain, but we should have confidence in our collective ability to manage this problem just as we manage other problems.

While not tendentious, the quotations thus far presented from Trefil's article are nonetheless selective. There is more that is important to relate. In his eighth paragraph of eleven paragraphs in total, Trefil stated the following:

> The most authoritative predictions about future warming come from the Intergovernmental Panel on Climate Change, a worldwide consortium of more than 2,000 climate scientists. The current forecast is that by 2100 the earth's temperature will go up 1 to 3.5° C (2° to 7° F), with the best guess being an increase of 2° C (4° F).[15]

Professor Trefil continued by interpreting what these numbers mean. The following appears his ninth paragraph:

> At the lower end of this predicted warming range, the temperature rise would take us back to the conditions that existed between A.D. 950 and 1350, when the climate was 1° C (2° F) warmer than it is now. This time period is regarded as one of the most benign weather regimes in history. To find temperature swings at the upper end, you have to go back 10,000 years, to when the earth was exiting the last Ice Age. Temperatures during the Ice Age were 5° C (10° F) cooler than they are now, and there was a series of incidents during which global temperatures changed as much as 10° F in a matter of decades. If that were to happen now, expanding oceans

might flood coastlines and generate fiercer storms. And as weather patterns changed, some places could get wetter and some dryer, and the ranges of diseases could expand. Civilization has seen—and endured—such changes in the past, but they may come much more swiftly this time, making it harder to withstand the jolts.[16]

According to this expert, then, we *will* experience the affects of global warming in this century, but this might mean we enjoy a climate not unlike "one of the most benign weather regimes in history" or perhaps something more like it was "when the earth was exiting the last Ice Age." Even if "we"—and it is unclear who Trefil has in mind—are unlucky and the coin comes up tails instead of heads, the worst case scenario entails only that "some places could get wetter and some dryer," and "civilization" can certainly endure that. Yet he warns that the changes might "come much more swiftly this time," but even if they do, it will only make things "harder," not impossible.

Again, even as Trefil faithfully cites the IPCC data and predictions, which all knowledgeable people must, his interpretation is designed to dampen-down any extreme reactions. He must acknowledge that civilization is threatened by global warming, but he wants to stress the importance of "prudent policy" as "wise insurance in an uncertain age," nothing more.[17] Therefore, he curtails any in-depth exploration of what it means to say that we may well be steaming toward a situation resembling the earth when it exited its ice age.

Trefil is not the only author who gets a shot at answering question twenty-one. Included on the two-page spread is also a sidebar by Michael D. Lemonick, whose credentials are not listed, but who is a staff writer at *Time*.[18] In his shorter, five-paragraph statement, Lemonick's main point is that "According to some respected scientists, there's a chance that global warming could plunge us into, of all things, an ice age."[19] Lemonick notes that if things go badly instead of coming up rosy, the earth could cool by "as much as 8° C (17° F)," that this scenario could be upon us with "astonishing speed," and its results would be "unimaginably devastating."[20] His final line is the following: "The lingering uncertainty about whether our relentless production of greenhouse gases will keep heating our planet or ultimately cool it suggests that we should make a better effort to leave the earth's thermostat alone."[21]

Combined, then, we have on two pages of *Time* a range of possible global temperature fluctuations for the next 100 years running from 17° F down to 7° F up! At the extremes of these expert scientific predictions, we have interpretations such as "unimaginably devastating" and thoughts concerning threats to "civilization," but in the main, the two articles counsel moderation, as in "leave the earth's thermostat alone" and enact "prudent policy." In addition to the two texts, the layout for the story includes various color graphics. Two depictions feature globes mapped with the countries of world. One globe is on fire, and the other covered in ice. This is the total of *Time*'s study of global warming, at least on this day.

This last point is crucial. It is not as though *Time*'s November 8, 1999, coverage is in fact *Time*'s coverage. Officially, *Time* has no position on global warming or on anything else for that matter. It is a news magazine that prides itself on including a variety of viewpoints, although it does so without explicitly acknowledging that viewpoints are what it is offering. Each news article is presented as though it were authoritative, and there is never the option for a reader, especially a competent, competing expert, to publish a response, except in the form of very brief letters offered in the carefully pruned Letters section. *Time*'s official editorial position was reasserted, for example, in a January 24, 2000, letter to readers by the managing editor and editor-in-chief, occasioned by the then-anticipated merger with America On-Line.[22] Readers were assured that the increasing size of *Time*'s corporate structure would have no effect on its dedication to the goal of being "honest in our judgments and truthful in our reporting." The letter claims that "a respect for journalistic independence has been part of our company's values for so long that it's encoded in our DNA." Finally, and in further explanation of the logic of this editorial position: "In a world filled with countless sources of information old and new, the ones most likely to succeed are the ones with the most credibility."

But, of course, all this sidesteps the important questions. Editorial decisions are by necessity made all the time, but how? Based on what values or politics? Who decides what is covered and which experts are hired to cover it? Who creates the format for this news? An editor need not, for example, explicitly quash a journalist or expert's story if one hires journalists and experts who have already demonstrated their "balance," and one does not have to compromise one's values (or DNA) if one's values are selected so as to mesh with an unstated political point of view. It is not difficult to imagine, then, an editorial staff having its prized integrity and eating it too.

So, for example, the readers of *Time* are not supposed to be puzzled when they read in the December 13, 1999, issue a story about global warming that is significantly different than the one from an issue just six weeks prior.[23] Presumably, this is evidence of journalistic independence, but it is really more complicated than that. In this later two-page article, titled "Greenhouse Effects," the main idea is captured in a running-head statement: "Global warming is well under way. Here are some telltale signs." There is no attribution of authorship for this story, which is dominated by a stylized map of the world depicting twenty-seven instances of evidence in support of the assertion that global warming is "well under way." Interestingly, in this article it is said only that "scientists predict that the planet's temperature could rise as much as 6.3° F (3.5° C) over the next century, and we are already seeing heat waves, melting polar ice and rising seas." According to the text, the map is drawn from the combined efforts of seven environmental activist groups, has been "reviewed by a team of scientists," and is offered to *Time* readers as an "advance look at the highlights *of the map*" (emphasis added). Here there is no special hint of caution, although the focus is on the map and not on what the map is, as it were, talking about. Instead, the main point is to convey the idea that *Time* readers are privy to an "advanced" understanding of global warming.

If we step back a moment and analyze these data, what can we say? Any average reader of *Time* (and this represents a relatively educated audience), would have to be perplexed. These articles present a variety of data, which, in this case, disagree with one another, as well as a variety of viewpoints and interpretations. One might conclude that global warming is happening or likely in some fashion to happen, but just flipping through the magazine and reading quickly and uncritically (and without any additional information), one would not probably come away with anything more than a vague sense that "this could be bad." If the reader were already predisposed to dismissing "all this global warming nonsense," then this reader, too, could take comfort in the fact that scientists themselves are not entirely sure what is going to happen, and besides, the problem is quite manageable. Stated differently, the encouraged range of reactions run from vague discomfort to confident dismissal, with most readers being encouraged to adopt a moderate, bland middle ground. In all cases, however, readers have no firm expert knowledge to guide them, and the editors of *Time* are clearly not planning on taking a stand one way or the other.

If we apply even simple propaganda analysis to these documents, we can see how clever these typical documents are. Is there card stacking here? Yes in the sense that readers are lead by half-truths, absent information, and biased interpretations to a particular range of emotional responses; but no in the sense that, as a *mass*-circulation magazine, *Time* is not interested in adopting an evident, consistent, much less narrow political stance because that could constrict its market of readers not to mention alienate corporate advertisers or future corporate advertisers. *Time*'s apparent editorial neutrality is thus critical to its credibility and to its short-term business interests. That this stance also has the effect of confusing readers with competing "messages" about what is the most pressing and already mind-boggling human issue matters less, it seems, than maintaining the veneer of value neutrality and thus positioning itself so as to capture the largest possible market for its product. The cards may be stacked, but not so much in favor of one or another particular politics or judgment as in favor of *Time* itself as a going concern. In the editorial letter cited earlier, this is described in utter seriousness as a "church-state wall . . . established to protect those of us on the edit side from corporate influence."[24] This wall, however, is breached when credibility is defined in terms of market power. The editors do not say that they are going to tell the whole and unadulterated truth regardless of whether it puts them out of business or even weakens their magazine's mass appeal. This, alas, would be unthinkable.

Are name calling and glittering generalities at work here? Since the 1950s especially, Americans have been taught that extremism of any sort is bad. Fascism and communism are both extremist political regimes, one of the Right and one of the Left, and both are deemed equally bad. The United States, in contrast, is a moderate country featuring a "mixed economy" and both liberals and conservatives. When then-candidate for president Senator Barry Goldwater said in 1964 that "extremism in the cause of liberty" was justified, he lost in a landslide. A counter slogan used by Johnson supporters was "In Your Guts, You Know He's Nuts." Barry Goldwater expressed fundamental political and moral convictions and was labeled "nuts," while Lyndon Johnson, who soon would aggressively prosecute a disastrous war in Vietnam, positioned himself as a bastion of level-headed moderation. This was a winning strategy then as it is now. *Time* has itself been a leading proponent of this value of moderation over the years. What does this really amount to? In this usage, moderation is literally conservatism in the sense that gradual social reform through established institutional channels is implicitly deemed the only legitimate form of social change, at least in and for the United States. In lesser countries, perhaps, extremes are more understandable and thus, if always distasteful, at least tolerable. When a writer employed by *Time* judges something "extreme," this is to be understood as a form of name calling, and when an author writing for *Time* calls for "prudence," this is to be understood as a glittering generality.

The politics of this type of propaganda are clear: it supports a society dominated by elites who oppose radical changes in society. These elites may be liberal-conservatives who accept the need for gradual change through elite-controlled institutions, or they may be conservative-conservatives, who, in most matters, prefer things the way they used to be and work to see gradual change occur, as it were, in reverse. Balanced viewpoints mean, in fact, support for the status quo. George Herbert Walker Bush once expressed this well in his oxymoron, "status quo plus."

We can see transference through oxymoron everywhere in these documents, as when the nonexpert reader is directed to be simultaneously skeptical of experts because even *they* are not sure and divided in their opinion. *Time*'s experts, of course, present a balanced view. Thus, the reader is to identify with this balanced view and thereby think of themselves as balanced in their views. They are to avoid extremism, embrace moderation; they are to "take a look at this potentially troubling global warming thing, but not get too upset by it either." The appearance of reasonableness is therefore transferred to the reader. If the propaganda techniques work properly, the result should be a mass audience that thinks of its newly acquired views on global warming (and everything else) as reasonable. There will be variation in response, but this has more to do with the individual reader's existing sentiments about global warming. If the reader is younger and better educated about ecological problems, we might expect relatively more concern. If the reader is older and perhaps therefore less knowledgeable about global ecological problems, we might expect less concern. If the reader is otherwise more inclined to conservative-conservative American politics, less concern—liberal-conservatism, more concern. In any case, the framework of analysis and the form of its presentation and interpretation demand a balanced view from the reader, who must either identify with the authority behind the text or be left with the nonauthority of their nonexpert individual opinion. If they choose this last route, they are in this definition of reality marginal, on the fringe, outside the pale, and not to be taken seriously.

In this way, *Time* defines the boundaries of credulity for the mass American audience, or so it tries. The editors of *Time* engage in a form of probably more or less unconscious *self-censorship.* Given its long history of so doing, this self-censorship is probably rooted in their DNA or tied to their mission to sell as many copies of *Time* as possible. What else could they be expected to do? Why would the corporate management of Time-Warner hire editors who would do otherwise?

Beyond Time

Our focus on *Time* is, of course, more or less arbitrary. The form and content of all mass media are essentially the same. An analysis of the historically somewhat more liberal *Newsweek,* owned by the *Washington Post,* would not produce significantly different results. Likewise, our focus on global warming is arbitrary in the sense that the same type of analysis could be offered about any substantive topic treated in the mass media. The point extends beyond global warming and one national news magazine. Rather, it is a point about the degradation of the public sphere in contemporary society.

In this regard, it is perhaps useful to discuss a book by another type of journalist, Ross Gelbspan, who is currently self-employed. The title of his 1998 book is *The Heat Is On: The Climate Crisis, the Cover-Up, the Prescription.*[25] The nature of Gelbspan's book is conveyed by its chapter titles, which include the following: "Climate Change Is Here. Now," "The Battle for Control of Reality," "A Congressional Book Burning," "After Rio: The Swamp of Diplomacy," and "The Coming Permanent State of Emergency." Gelbspan also includes an appendix titled "A Scientific Critique of the Greenhouse Skeptics." Just from this litany, one can see that Gelbspan pursues his topic with a sense of urgency. Before being published as a book, Gelbspan's central thesis was excerpted in *Harper's* magazine, an even more venerable American publication than *Time* but with a fraction of *Time*'s circulation. The back jacket of his book also features praise from major U.S. newspapers. Regardless, Gelbspan's book has had little or no effect on the production of global warming propaganda, but it is still worth a look.

Gelbspan wanted to immediately tell his readers that the mass media are not their friends, that the primary means by which they understand momentous issues such as global warming is failing them. For this purpose, he began with the story of Dr. Rodolfo del Valle, "an Argentine scientist who [in 1995] witnessed the disintegration of the . . . Larsen ice shelf in Antarctic."[26] Gelbspan reported del Valle's experience.

> On the twenty-third of January, they called me over the radio and said, "Rudi, something is happening, the ice shelf is breaking. An enormous crack had opened from the edge of the shelf on the Weddell Sea up to the mountains," said del Valle, who heads the earth sciences department at Argentina's National Antarctic Institute. Flying six thousand feet overhead in a light plane, del Valle saw that the ice shelf, up to a thousand feet thick in places, was beginning to break up into smaller icebergs. "It was spectacular because what once was a platform of ice more than forty miles wide had been broken up into pieces that looked like bits of polystyrene foam . . . smashed by a child."[27]

Gelbspan started a new paragraph, one sentence long, in which he reported del Valle's reaction to this discovery: "The first thing I did was cry."[28] Gelbspan wants the reader to realize that experts such as del Valle are crying over what is happening to the world. This is not reported in *Time*. Between Dr. del Valle in Argentina, flying above the once proud Larsen Ice Shelf, and the average American dependent on the mass media, there is a huge gulf indeed.

Gelbspan continued with del Valle's experience. He noted that del Valle and his colleagues predicted that the ice barrier as a whole would crack in ten years, but it actually occurred only two months after their prediction. These scientists were again disturbed and upset not at their inability to predict but at the implications this melting had for global warming trends. del Valle reported, "Recently I've seen rocks poke through the surface of the ice that had been buried under six hundred meters of ice for twenty thousand years."[29]

This personal experience of but one expert from Argentina is, for Gelbspan, a metaphor for the collapse of the public sphere in the rich societies of the world, particularly in the United States. This, after all, is one experience worth knowing about, and yet no one seems to know about it.

Gelbspan is just a journalist, so he has to rely on experts, such as Dr. del Valle, to convince his readers of the fact of global warming. He also relies on experts for information about the social consequences of global warming. Consider the following example:

> Long before the systems of the planet buckle, democracy will disintegrate under the stress of ecological disasters and their social consequences. Two different men independently expressed this chilling insight to me—William Ruckelshaus, the first head of the EPA and now CEO of Browning-Ferris Industries; and Dr. Henry Kendall of MIT, the recipient of the 1990 Nobel Prize for physics, who has devoted his retirement to the study of critical global trends.[30]

At first, Gelbspan thought this notion "seemed irrelevant to the climate crisis."[31] But then it came to him: "If we alter the balance of natural relationships that support our lives, those changes will ripple through the complex relationships that make up our society."[32] Later, Gelbspan invoked Orwell and concluded that "this much is true of totalitarianism: it usually begins with the lies."[33]

Interestingly, Gelbspan's main target for criticism in his book is not the government or even the mass media so much as it is large corporations, particularly those that dominate the worldwide oil and coal industries. Gelbspan charges these industries with having instituted a "campaign of deception," a "mystification campaign," and an "assault on our sense of reality."[34] He details and documents this propaganda campaign. His, then, is an "exposé." His book is a work in the critique of a specific instance of propaganda, in which, as Gelbspan showed, a few dissenting scientists are lavished with industry-provided research funds and their points of view constantly promoted and touted. It is an instance of propaganda in which a tiny minority of expert opinion—which happens to support the status quo and therefore the short-term business interests of oil and coal industries in particular—is weighed as equally significant, for example, in congressional deliberations, as are the findings of the IPCC, a consortium of 2,000 climate scientists from around the world whose only paymaster is the United Nations.

This is not all there is to Gelbspan's analysis. He attributed the fact that most people do not understand this most pressing social issue not primarily to propaganda in general or to the efforts of fossil fuel providers of the world but to what he regards as the greater problem: mass denial.

> The experience of Dr. Daniel Goodenough, of the Harvard Medical School, provides an illustration. Recently, the medical school mounted a series of three seminars on human health and the global environment. The first seminar was overflowing with energetic, aware, and concerned young medical students. Inexplicably, however, the second seminar was only half full. At the final seminar only half a dozen students showed up.

> When the perplexed Goodenough asked the students why attendance had fallen off so sharply, their responses were identical. The material was compelling, they said, but it engendered overwhelming personal reactions. The problems were so great—and the ability of the students to affect them so remote—that they could deal with their feelings of frustration and helplessness and depression only by staying away.[35]

Harvard Medical School students overwhelmed? Feeling powerless? This is not what one would expect of those among the world's best and brightest, most energetic and concerned, and most likely to occupy positions of authority and prestige in society. The facts in the case are, apparently, paralyzing even for young would-be elites. Gelbspan thinks what we need is "ethical maturity."[36]

If there really were a mass market for real global warming news, then probably *Time* and all the rest would provide it or at least much more of it. If Gelbspan's book had sold millions instead of languishing in obscurity, perhaps all mass media outlets would have had to respond differently to their mass audience's growing awareness and sophistication. If average people had the time to learn and reflect about this problem, then presumably public opinion would be different and not just "different" but of a different quality. Gelbspan concluded his book with a series of at least minimally hopeful scenarios and policy suggestions, but we have to attend to what is really happening or not happening. We have to look closely at social structures that shape the real powerlessness felt even by the relatively powerful. Gelbspan is well aware of the forces working against "ethical maturity" and so is driven in the end to rely on faith in his fellow human beings. He wrote,

> Perhaps people are so fragmented, so alienated from one another, that they would shrink from the challenge and block out the message. Such self-imposed ignorance could speed our descent into a more brutish and storm-battered existence. But I don't think they would react that way. I think if most people were exposed to the truth and given a channel through which to act, they would choose responsibility over selfishness. I think if they truly understood what is happening to the earth, there would be an outpouring of will and courage.[37]

This may be true, of course, but what is really important are the forces that fragment and alienate in the first place, that systematically screen out certain messages, block exposure to the truth, and deny individuals channels for meaningful political action.

Theorizing the Degradation of the Public Sphere

Who reads Gelbspan? Almost no one. That is the issue for sociologists. The usual sociological treatment of the degradation of the public sphere either identifies actual enemies of public awareness in the here and now, as Gelbspan did when he detailed the propaganda campaign waged by the oil and coal industries, or looks past these actors to the larger historical context. Both strategies are important and bear important intellectual fruits, but the latter, less common approach is where the fruit hangs heaviest on the vine. Indeed, one of the heaviest of all living social theorists is Jurgen Habermas.

Often described as Germany's leading intellectual, Habermas is both a renowned philosopher and sociologist. In his first book, *The Structural Transformation of the Public Sphere,* Habermas detailed the history of the public sphere in modern times and gave special attention to its degradation over the course of the twentieth century.[38] In a moment of apparent frustration, Habermas once said: "Of course, I too look at American television. When I see debates between presidential candidates, I get sick."[39] Habermas followed this comment immediately by saying, "But we at least have to explain *why* we get sick, not just leave it at that."[40] Explaining "the whys" of social life is what social theory is about.

For Habermas, "the world fashioned by the mass media is a public sphere in appearance only."[41] The appearance given by, say, televised "town meetings" is that of a town meeting, but in reality it is only a television format. Even the organizers and participants are self-conscious of this fact. Presidential campaigns, for example, debate with each other over the formats, knowing that their candidate might create a better appearance in one or another format. In the 1992 presidential campaign, Bill Clinton was good at affecting the appearance of being a nice, warm person in the town meeting format, whereas President Bush was not. The Clinton campaigns therefore sought as many of these formats as possible. When Bush once looked at his watch during a town meeting style debate with Clinton, this was treated as a symbol of his élitism, his distaste for, or at least discomfort with, interacting with average people. This charge was, of course, thoroughly irrational. In effect, President Bush mistakenly enacted propaganda for the Clinton campaign. Within the irreality of television formats that mimic or merely simulate a real public sphere, irrationality is treated in all seriousness as rationality, and rational candidates must subordinate themselves to this irrationality if they are to successfully manage their public images.

What is the nature of the audience presupposed by televised town meetings? Clearly, this audience is conceived of as consumers of television. The format of the faux town meeting is not appreciably different from an episode of "Oprah," nor is the audience treated any differently from the audience viewing a soap opera or talk show. Here we see a sham public sphere that, for Habermas, has "taken on the traits of a secondary realm of intimacy" and that results in candidates, for example, becoming little more than media personalities toward whom the audience feels sympathy or, in the case of President Bush looking at his watch in the middle of the "debate," feels rejection.[42] Everything is carefully staged to affect the audience's sentiments, and the audience responds appropriately by playing along, telling the commentators afterward, in effect, how the candidates "made them feel" or whether, in their opinion, the candidate did a good or bad job of creating an appearance that pleased or displeased them.

In such a society, there is little space for citizens to participate in effective democratic self-governance. There are few places for citizens to gather and discuss matters that vitally affect them. There are increasingly few places at all outside the home and workplace—what sociologist Ray Oldenburg calls "third places"—to gather for even simple conviviality.[43] Such a society renders the mass of its citizens powerless before the hyperreality of a fictive public sphere and therefore effectively disengages from the means of history making. A democracy is not a society in which citizens watch public debate on television or, more to the point, consume television political coverage, nor can one learn to be a citizen this way. The popularity of the television program "Politically Incorrect," which features celebrities debating public issues, is an indication not of the vitality of American democracy but of its metamorphoses into a hyperreality and thus its degradation as a lived reality.

Why has the public sphere in our time become a realm of intimate television illusion? Why are politicians celebrities and celebrities potential politicians? Why do so many people treat public life as a spectator sport? Habermas explained these phenomena in terms of the structural transformations of the public sphere, which he thinks has lead to a refeudalization of society.[44] As the term implies, *refeudalization* renders erstwhile democratic citizens serf-like political subjects.

For Habermas, two main social forces threaten the public sphere: capitalism and bureaucracy. They are equal enemies of free and rational democratic participation.[45] Capitalist economics is driven by the profit motive. The bottom line for business firms is the perpetual and limitless increase of their profits, not the cultivation of reason and freedom for all. Similarly, the administration of life, particularly through state bureaucracies, squeezes the liberties enjoyed by citizens and, in the extreme, renders citizens consumers of impersonally delivered services or clients under welfare state supervision. Neither the capitalist market nor the bureaucratic state provides for an open public sphere; rather, both distort and degrade it. Structural trends in both institutional spheres exacerbate this process.

Beginning in the late nineteenth century and continuing until today, capitalism changed from an economic system populated by innumerable small and relatively powerless firms locked in competition with one another to an economic system dominated by a very few large and powerful corporations. In 1997, for example, General Motors enjoyed sales revenues that were greater than the gross domestic product of Norway or Saudi Arabia.[46] In the United States today, the top 500 indus-trial corporations control roughly seventy-five percent of industrial sales, assets, and profits.[47] Similarly, the largest 500 corporations worldwide control roughly one-third of all manufacturing exports and three-fourths of all trade in technology.[48] Just the top 300 transnational corporations control roughly one-quarter of the world's productive capital.[49] By virtue of their accumulation of economic power and their tendency to cooperate rather than compete with one another, a handful of corporate giants have accrued considerable political power as well. The means of this control over the democratic process are both overt and subtle.

The most obvious form of corporate political influence is found in their contri-butions to political campaigns. Candidates for important high-level public offices regularly spend tens of millions of dollars in their efforts to get elected, and the per-sons or entities who fund these campaigns expect special consideration ("access") when their interests are affected by political decisions. Thus, it is important to know who pays the piper. According to the American sociologist Jerome L. Himmelstein, "In the early 1970s there were twice as many labor PACs [political action commit-tees] as corporate and trade association PACs . . . [but] by the early 1980s business PACs outnumbered labor PACs by more than four to one, and outspent them by more than two to one."[50] Indeed, corporate PACs today outspend every other competing interest group in the United States, not just labor unions. This process is as overt a form of political influence buying as is allowed by law. Both major political parties receive tens of millions of dollars from corporate interests.

More subtle, though, corporate capital wields influence over the democratic process because the whole of society is dependent on corporate assets. Giant corpo-rations provide jobs (and hence incomes) and pay taxes that fund government ser-vices, and in these ways contribute mightily to the stability of society. Large firms can therefore demand and regularly receive tax breaks. They can effectively shape labor and environmental protection laws to suit their private interest in profit maxi-mization. They can threaten city, state, and even the national government with their legal right to dispose of their assets as they choose—to move their factory to the next town, to the state with a more favorable "business climate," or even offshore, which means to another country. Likewise, giant corporations can deny wage increases and resist demands for improved working conditions and enhanced benefits. If General Motors (GM), for example, can shift its automobile production to Mexico or China—which, to a great extent, it has—then communities and workers in the United States who are dependent on GM jobs have little choice but to acquiesce be-fore GM's demands for special consideration.[51] Politicians know this and as a result do GM's bidding in an effort to "save American jobs" and protect their community's (and state and nation's) tax base. When this cannot be accomplished (e.g., when large corporations are intent on securing the benefits of cheap labor, low taxes, little environmental or labor regulation, and suppressed unionization in Third World countries), American politicians—the majority of them, anyway—support free trade agreements that facilitate worldwide capitalist expansion. The passage of the North American Free Trade Agreement (NAFTA) in 1993 and the extension of Most Favored Nation (MFN) trading status to China in 2000 occurred despite widespread opposition of labor and environmental groups.

Corporate groups and firms also use advertising to shape public opinion, and they use lobbyists to bring their issues and concerns before politicians. They fund think tanks and, as Gelbspan demonstrated, even individuals whose research supports their interests. Indeed, the largest and most dominating institutions of the mass media—television networks, cable companies, newspapers, radio stations, movie companies, and book publishing houses—are themselves capitalist firms, each and every one in business to turn a profit. General Electric owns NBC, Disney owns ABC, and SONY owns Columbia Pictures. We have already discussed the Time-Warner empire. The concentration of power in the mass media is so rapid that it is difficult to keep track of who owns what.

The problem is that a capitalist society is not the same thing as a democratic society. For Habermas, the concentration of capitalist economic power and influence, both overt and subtle, contributes to the degradation of the democratic public sphere. Indeed, the very principle of capitalism—with its instrumental and self-interested profit motive—is at odds with the essential principle of democracy, which is free communication and universal participation for the common good. As Habermas stated, "Between capitalism and democracy there is an indissoluble tension; in them two opposed principles of societal integration compete for primacy."[52] Capitalists pursue their self-interest, but citizens in a democracy pursue the public interest. In a capitalist society, capitalists rule. In a democracy, however, the people are supposed to rule.

Everything we have noted about capitalism is, for Habermas, equally true of state bureaucracies, indeed, any large bureaucracies. The basic principle of bureaucratic administration is as instrumental and self-interested as the profit motive. The defining purpose of an impersonal, hierarchal, machine-like organization—a "bureaucracy," which literally means "the rule of officials"—is to control its environment (its suppliers and its consumers, its inputs and its outputs) and, internally, to funnel decision-making power to its top positions. Bureaucracies are therefore both externally and internally undemocratic. They do not operate in a society of people but, rather, as components of an impersonal social system. They do not allow free and equal participation of all in decision making. Instead, bureaucracies are like a disciplined military organization more than a free democratic public sphere.

Labor unions are a good example. They are not profit-oriented corporations, but they are no less internally undemocratic and, in their workings, corrosive of the public sphere. This is ironic because, at their inception, labor unions were the organizational invention of workers involved in a grassroots social movement. They were once the very embodiment of democracy; indeed, they represented the expansion of democracy into the otherwise undemocratic capitalist economic system. But in the course of their development, particularly in the last half of the twentieth century, labor unions have become bureaucratized. The United Auto Workers (UAW), America's largest industrial union, has roughly 700,000 members.[53] While the UAW is on paper a democratically organized institution, its individual members—the "rank-and-file"—have no effective voice in the operation of their union, little knowledge of the issues confronting the union's top officials, and little choice when it comes to accepting or rejecting contract offers. Contracts are negotiated by an elite team of expert negotiators and lawyers. "Strike votes" are taken, but they are symbolic exercises meant to demonstrate rank-and-file discipline more than they are free elections with an unpredictable result. The top leadership are themselves elected, but the delegate and delegate convention selection process is so complicated and restrictive of rank-and-file participation that, for all intents and purposes, such elections are rarely if ever contested and still less is their outcome ever in doubt. Union members can attend membership meetings, but few ever do, and if they do, parliamentary procedures and by-laws are used by the officers in charge to blunt or co-opt their participation. Union members can read their local union newspapers, but these are not the product of a free and independent press; they are instead vehicles for official union propaganda. This same scenario applies to all large unions and to bureaucratic organizations generally. The Democratic party is no more "democratic" than is the Republican party; the UAW is no more democratic than GM; X State University is no more democratic than the University of Y.

Parallel to the case of GM, decisions and actions taken by the UAW affect more people than just its own membership, none of whom have a voice in the union's decisions. When a union strikes against an employer, especially when a giant union strikes against a giant employer, entire communities are affected. Other businesses and workers whose livelihood depend on the flow of spending from union wages, for example, can find themselves out of business and out of work. Consumers can find products and services unavailable. When police and teacher unions strike, public safety is reduced and kids go without education. When United Parcel Service workers go on strike, packages go undelivered. When airline pilots strike, flights are canceled and passengers stranded. Sometimes the effects of strike actions can become so harmful or potentially harmful that the state uses its supreme authority in society to prevent or forcibly resolve labor disputes. President Reagan, for example, fired striking air traffic controllers rather than negotiate a settlement. This was more a matter of intrabureaucratic struggle—a struggle between the state's authority to maintain social order and the authority of a particular public service union to advocate for the rights of its members—than it was an issue for democratic decision making. There was no public vote to decide the fate of the air traffic controllers, no formal discussion by the citizens of the country on the merits of their workplace grievances. There was, however, extensive media coverage and public opinion polling, which is to say, the televised appearance of a democratic public debate.

This brings us back to Habermas's perspective on the degradation of the public sphere. In a society dominated by the self-interested and impersonal workings of capitalism and bureaucracy, the mass media create the illusion of a common and personally meaningful society. This is its chief power and function. Many small towns in New England still hold real town meetings in real town meeting halls, where citizens gather and add their voice to the process of self-governance. But most Americans must settle for the semblance of this quaint local reality manufactured for mass consumption, the result being a simulated postmodern society that is democratic in name only.

Sociology and Democracy

In his discussion of democracy and the public sphere in *The Sociological Imagination,* C. Wright Mills conceded that "democracy is . . . a complicated idea about which there is much legitimate disagreement."[54] He also anticipated that readers will be tempted to say, " 'Well, here it comes . . . an ideal so high that in terms of it everything must seem low.' "[55] Sociologists such as Mills and Habermas are steadfast in their commitment to the democratic ideal of a society in which people participate in genuine self-government. This is because reason and freedom do not flourish in capitalist and/or bureaucratic societies, only in democratic societies. Since the cultural meaning of sociology—its "promise"—depends on the effective and free use of reason in human affairs, Mills concludes that sociology needs democracy in order to flourish. What is the point of having a sociological imagination if there is no space—no public sphere—for its use in confronting the issues and troubles of the age? Moreover, the reverse is also the case: democracy needs sociology in order to reestablish itself against the forces that diminish and degrade it. Only if citizens can identify and confront the corrosive effects of capitalism and bureaucracy can they act to democratize their society by reinvigorating or, if need be, reinventing spaces for public life to flourish. In this way, sociological theory is essential to the prospects for a democratic future.

Of sociologists, Mills wrote that "we are acting as if we were in a fully democratic society, and by doing so, we are attempting to remove the 'as if.' "[56] The promise of sociology, in other words, is equivalent to the promise of democracy. They go
hand in hand. For Mills, the popular adoption of sociological thinking about self and
society represents "the best chance," indeed, in postmodern times, "the only
chance," "to make reason democratically relevant to human affairs in a free society."[57] Mills wrote these words in 1959, more than 40 years ago. Habermas first theo-
rized the decline of the public sphere in 1962. Today, the forces that threaten democracy and with it the promise of sociology are more extreme and Mills's "as if" increasingly remote. This is the case even if—or perhaps, because—we have come to
regard television town meetings and "Politically Incorrect" as perfectly mundane,
entertaining features of society. As if to compensate for the increasing powerlessness of today's citizens, the circuses of public life have become increasingly manic
and base. Ubiquitous and ephemeral postmodern propaganda mirror the extreme
concentrations of economic power and bureaucratic organization in postmodern society.

A severe critic of President Kennedy and *The New York Times,* one can only
imagine what Mills would have thought of President Clinton and "Politically Incorrect." Even such comparatively tame phenomena as televised U.S. presidential debates leave Habermas feeling sick. "Throughout history," Gelbspan reminded us, "it
has been philosophers, religious leaders, and revolutionaries who have asked us to
reexamine our values, our relationships, our purposes, and the way we live."[58] But he
adds, "Now we are being asked by the oceans."[59] This signals our place in
postmodern society.

Notes

1. C. Wright Mills, *The Sociological Imagination* (Oxford, U.K.: Oxford University Press, 1959),
192.
2. Ibid., 188.
3. Ibid.
4. Ibid., 116.
5. Robert Jackall, "Introduction," in *Propaganda,* ed. Robert Jackall (New York: New York
University Press, 1995), 1.
6. Ibid.
7. Ibid.
8. Ibid.
9. Ibid., 2.
10. The following terms are adapted from The Institute for Propaganda Analysis, "How to Detect
Propaganda" (originally published in 1937), in *Propaganda,* Jackall, 217-24. I use these concepts in
part because I recall being taught about them in the eighth grade. I have seen them discussed in public

school textbooks for third graders as well. Although they are revealing, they are supposed to be, in other words, part of our American common sense.

11. James Trefil, "How Hot Will It Get?" *Time,* November 8, 1999, 113.

12. See, for example, Katharine Washburn and John F. Thornton, eds., *Dumbing Down: Essays on the Strip Mining of American Culture* (New York: Norton, 1996).

13. Trefil, "How Hot Will It Get?" p. 112.

14. Ibid., 112-3.

15. Ibid.

16. Ibid., 113.

17. Ibid.

18. Michael D. Lemonick, " . . . And Then How Cold?," *Time,* November 8, 1999, 113.

19. Ibid.

20. Ibid.

21. Ibid.

22. Norman Pearlstine and Walter Isaacson, "The Merger and Our Journalism," *Time,* January 24, 2000, 8.

23. "Greenhouse Effects," *Time,* December 13, 1999, 78-9.

24. Pearlstine and Isaacson, "The Merger and Our Journalism."

25. Ross Gelbspan, *The Heat Is On: The Climate Crisis, the Cover-Up, the Prescription* (Reading, M.A.: Perseus Books, 1997).

26. Ibid., 1.

27. Ibid., 1-2.

28. Ibid., 2.

29. Ibid.

30. Ibid., 153.

31. Ibid.

32. Ibid.

33. Ibid., 169.

34. Ibid., 7, 9, 9.

35. Ibid., 172.

36. Ibid., 176.

37. Ibid., 194.

38. Jürgen Habermas, *The Structural Transformation of the Public Sphere* (1962; reprint, Cambridge: MIT Press, 1989).

39. Jürgen Habermas, "Concluding Remarks," in *Habermas and the Public Sphere,* ed. Craig Calhoun (Cambridge: MIT Press, 1992), 468.

40. Ibid.

41. Habermas, *The Structural Transformation of the Public Sphere,* 171.

42. Ibid., 172.

43. Ray Oldenburg, *The Great Good Place: Cafes, Coffee Shops, Community Centers, Beauty Parlors, General Stores, Bars, Hangouts and How They Get You Through the Day,* 2d ed. (New York: Marlowe, 1997).

44. Habermas, *The Structural Transformation of the Public Sphere,* 175-6.

45. See Jurgen Habermas, "The New Obscurity: The Crisis of the Welfare State and the Exhaustion of Utopian Energies," *Philosophy and Social Criticism* 11 (Winter 1986): 1-18.

46. Neva Goodwin, "Corporate Power: Why Does It Matter? Overview Essay," in *The Political Economy of Inequality,* eds. Frank Ackerman, Neva R. Goodwin, Laurie Dougherty, and Kevin Gallagher (Washington, D.C.: Island Press, 2000), 101. See also William Greider, *One World, Ready or Not: The Manic Logic of Global Capitalism* (New York: Simon and Schuster, 1997).

47. Dan Clawson, Alan Neustadtl, and Denise Scott, "Business Unity, Business Power," in *The Political Economy of Inequality,* 118.

48. Goodwin, "Corporate Power: Why Does It Matter? Overview Essay," 101.

49. Ibid.

50. Jerome L. Himmelstein, "The Mobilization of Corporate Conservatism," in *The Political Economy of Inequality,* 132.

51. I am drawing here from my own research on this phenomenon. See Steven P. Dandaneau, *A Town Abandoned: Flint, Michigan, Confronts Deindustrialization* (Albany: State University of New York Press, 1996) and Steven P. Dandaneau, "Critical Theory, Legitimation Crisis, and the Deindustrialization of Flint, Michigan," in *Illuminating Social Life,* ed. Peter Kivisto (Thousand Oaks, C.A.: Pine Forge Press, 1998), 151-82.

52. Jürgen Habermas, *The Theory of Communicative Action, Vol. II, Lifeworld and System: A Critique of Functionalist Reason* (1981; reprint, Boston: Beacon Press, 1987), 345.

53. I am again drawing here from my own research on this phenomenon. See Dandaneau, *A Town Abandoned.*

54. C. Wright Mills, *The Sociological Imagination,* 188.

55. Ibid.

56. Ibid., 189.

57. Ibid., 194.

58. Gelbspan, *The Heat Is On,* 171.

59. Ibid.

9

The End of History

We tend to forget that our reality, including the tragic events of the past, has been swallowed up by the media. That means that it is too late to verify events and understand them historically, for what characterizes our era and our *fin de siecle* is precisely the disappearance of the instruments of this intelligibility. It was necessary to understand history when there was still history.

—*Jean Baudrillard*[1]

History would appear to be something that cannot have an "end," but history itself has a history. Its beginning occurred roughly 5,000 years ago, when people first began to record events and experiences. This record was kept in writing. Before the advent of writing and written history, humans lived in pre*historic* times—a period that encompasses the vast majority of human existence. In prehistoric times, there was no objective, written record of passing events or particular human experiences. In this world, continuity with the past was maintained orally through spoken tradition and rendered objective only through artifacts, the human-made objects used in the creation of a distinctly human way of life. Since then, however, humans have kept a record of events and experiences. Moreover, humans have made creating history—creating and institutionalizing an objective and collective memory of the past—increasingly important to the workings of society and the experience of human culture. Today, thousands of historians—but also archeologists, paleontologists, sociologists, anthropologists, journalists, geologists, and so forth—labor to create an accurate and meaningful record of the past, and "history"—the ongoing result of these efforts—is a required subject in every school.

While history had a beginning, this chapter addresses the idea that, in our time, history is at its end. I do not mean to reiterate the idea of apocalypse, the notion that human society and culture could be extinguished. We have already examined this meaning of the "end of history" in Chapter 2 under the rubric of a dying world. Apocalypse lingers, however, in the background not because it is a possibility, which, as Chapter 2 argues, it is but because it is a major feature of today's popular consciousness. Beyond the pulpit, where apocalypse is a staple ingredient in many theologies, a list of recent book titles indicates the extent and complexity of contemporary machinations over the meaning of the "end of days": *Postmodern Apocalypse: Theory and Cultural Practice at the End* (1995), *Apocalypse Now and Then: A Feminist Guide to the End of the World* (1996), *The End of the World? A New Look at an Old Belief* (1997), *Is the World Ending?* (1998), *Apocalypse Pretty Soon: Travels in End-Time America* (1999), and even *After the End: Representations of Post-Apocalypse* (1999). Asteroids-hit-earth movies and millennial fears also suggest popular concern with apocalyptic scenarios. As a result of its embedded theological moorings and its currency in popular culture, the idea that history could end is familiar to most people.

The ultimate purpose of developing a sociological imagination, however, is to facilitate participation in history making, not history ending. By developing an awareness of social structure as the media through which social change occurs, the possessor of the sociological imagination gains orientation, as Mills said, "to the big ups and downs of the societies in which they live" and, based on this awareness, conceives the "intricate connections between the patterns of their own lives and the course of world history"[2] The sociological imagination is therefore grounded in "the historical level of reality," which means in a version of reality that discerns the observable, ongoing, and inherently fluid interconnections between individual lives and social institutions.[3]

Our challenge, then, is to develop a sense for history making in a postmodern epoch defined by a pervasive sense of ending—of being *post* or coming after x, y, and z. If Baudrillard is correct, how can we make history when history has become unintelligible and therefore beyond our grasp? Is it possible to develop a clear orientation to the past and future while living "after the end" in a "post-apocalypse" world? What if, as I have argued in Chapter 8, mass media dominate today's public sphere and, as a consequence, work to undermine popular historical memory by transposing it into the History Channel? What if historical knowledge were conveyed primarily via Ken Burns's pseudo-documentary format? What if asteroids-hit-earth movies were a product of postmodern propaganda that mystify our attempts to locate ourselves in history and, from this orientation, gain perspective on our real—not fictive or fantastic—historical predicaments? What if, in other words, the media, through which historical knowledge was made part of everyday life, were themselves damaging of history and set against the development of a historical sensibility? Could we not then better appreciate Baudrillard's otherwise odd-sounding concern that history is now beyond our grasp, irretrievable?

Likewise, what if even the versions of history that intellectuals produce are so grandiose that our individual participation in history making seems moot? When history making is conceived as transcending individuals, we cannot position ourselves in time and space and, with this cognitive map, search for the means to participate in today's arguably much-needed radical social change.

For the student of the sociological imagination, mere simulations of historical knowledge or versions of history that do not account for individual experience are inadequate because they fail to provide individuals with effective orientation to the challenges confronting humanity at present. The second meaning of the end of history—beyond apocalypse—is precisely this: the end of a meaningful popular understanding of history that could provide political orientation to the issues and troubles of our age. This is the specific problem addressed in this chapter. The realization of an end to an everyday historical understanding would spell the demise of the sociological imagination and, along with it, the promise of a democratic and enlightened history making.

A Brief History of Time and Space

Before we directly address this subject, it is necessary to make sure that our sociological imaginations are loosened up and geared to think through a number of unavoidable abstractions. Analysis of "history" at the end of history can easily confound. At one level, it is not wise to presume a great deal of popular historical knowledge extending beyond what is contained in TV Heritage. This is the nature of the postmodern condition. We will therefore work from within our history-in-a-box situation toward the point in which historical illusion meets reality. But a deeper mystification is also potentially in play, and we must deal with this first. The problem is a false commonsense view that time and space—the coordinate points of history—are invariant or ahistorical. Let us first address the historical nature of time and space and use this proposition as preparation for an analysis of today's postmodern time-space experience.

Anthropologists inform us that people living in different cultures have had fundamentally competing conceptions of time and space. Painting in broad strokes, gathering and hunting societies existed in spaces limited to a known world, which to our view is a very limited patch of earth. Similarly, time in hunting and gathering societies is not experienced in terms of a linear and irrepressible passage through

seconds, minutes, hours, days, weeks, months, years, decades, centuries, and mil-
lennia but, rather, in terms of the cycles of the earth, its sunups and sundowns, its cir-
cle of seasons, and its seeming timelessness as a whole. Agrarian societies also measure time in these terms but add the cycles of planting and harvesting. Agrarian
people look at the earth and see it as recalcitrant, unwilling to yield its fruits, and so
conceive space as something to conquer and in so conquering this space, produce a
sense of place, this place for cultivation and permanent dwelling. With the industrial
revolution came "clock time," which is rooted in a mechanical means of measuring
passing moments and that was used to regiment work and, indeed, all social life.
Similarly, industrial society subjected space to processes of rationalization, in
Weber's sense, meaning to bring space under scientific control. Peering down at the
surface of the earth from an aircraft reveals farm fields cut in geometric shapes and
cities laid out in grids. The aircraft itself is perhaps passing through a country's "air
space," which is conceived as part of a political territory whose boundaries are not to
be violated without permission.

This change from a hunting and gathering society to an industrial society is not,
however, a story of progressive movement toward "the truth" of time and space.
Competing conceptions and experiences of time and space survive even in a globalized world dominated by linear clock time. For individuals, there is still a biological
time and with it a sense of ashes to ashes and dust to dust, the final resting place for
every body. There is also the notion about the relativity of time, thanks to Einstein,
which causes us to fathom time in terms of mass. Indeed, atomic clocks tell us that
time is progressing at a slower pace at the edges of the earth's atmosphere than on the
surface of the planet. And on that surface, the vast country of China not only uses its
own ancient calendar to measure the passage of years but also eschews use of the
world's standardized time zones. These competing concepts and measures of time
coexist in an uneasy and often disturbing tension with one another.

Modern capitalism, for example, presupposes a view of human life in which
one's potential to work is measured in flat, linear time. How many hours do we labor? On this work day? During this work week? What is the pay we receive? Per
hour? Per diem? How much free time do we have? When will we retire? How much
time are we allowed on break? on vacation? for holidays? Do we punch in and punch
out at the same time every day? If we are regularly late, how will this affect the pay
we receive for the time of our lives, which we must, for the most part, sell on the labor
(time) market, where we contract out, or rent, our labor time to a would-be buyer of
our labor (time)?

From the point of view of the capitalist, we could add other questions, consider-
ing fiscal years versus calendar years, quarterly profit reports, and time-and-motion
studies designed to erase every "wasted" motion from the workday. We might add
consideration of businesses' interests in protecting their ability to buy more or less

labor time any time they choose and in any place they choose in accordance with the dictates of "the market." The free market is an amazing time-space machine.

In general and beyond free markets, time and space are socially organized and culturally conceived, and they represent primary media through which societies are integrated and regulated. Furthermore, they set a framework for the meaningful enactment of individual human lives because every human life has its time-space geography. Where do we call home? Do we leave our home to travel to a workplace? How long, measured in time and space, is our commute? Have we gone abroad? Have our bodies been propelled through the sky at 100, 300, 600, or 2,000 miles per hour at 1,000, 10,000, or 40,000 feet of altitude? Have we ventured to the depths of an ocean or left the earth's atmosphere? Every biography can be mapped in such terms. Generalizing, every society produces *patterns* of time-space experience in accordance with their existing time-space machines, their systems of institutions, and every society renders these experiences meaningful in one way or another.[4]

Today's version of capital punishment in the United States is effectively a sentence of maximum loss of time. In cases of normal incarceration, the criminal is forced to "do time" in "confinement." In the case of the death penalty, this basic idea is merely extended, not qualitatively changed. For some crimes, the penalty is 5 to 10 years. For others, it is *all* one's remaining time. This explains why the condemned are not mercilessly tortured for as long as possible (a former technique of punishment) but are instead rendered lifeless as calmly and antiseptically as possible, usually through the injection of a lethal toxin. The point is not to cause these people suffering but to take away all their remaining time. Of course, once made into a corpse, there is no need to confine them, so the death penalty is also a type of erasure of the need for a place, the creating of corporal voids, a democratically legitimized method of making human absences, in which we say, in effect, "your time and space is up."

The history of time and space reveals their social determination and hence their potential historical plasticity. This means also that, like the versions of history they frame, competing conceptions of time and space are the stuff of social conflict. As the geographer and sociologist David Harvey argued:

> Beneath the veneer of common-sense and seemingly "natural" ideas about space and time, there lie hidden terrains of ambiguity, contradiction, and struggle. . . . How we represent space and time in theory matters, because it affects how we and others interpret and then act with respect to the world.[5]

For the possessor of the sociological imagination, it is essential to be self-aware of how time and space are represented in social theory. If no particular version of space and time is natural or invariant, then each has its own history and therefore its own relationship to social power.

Is it possible, for example, for history to "end" in the sense that a society could perpetuate itself in a placeless, bodiless, timeless present? Is it possible to issue history a death sentence, to take away its time and to erase evidence of its spatial existence? In Orwell's fictional "Oceania," the "memory hole" is a technological device used in the Ministry of Truth. Historical documents are to be placed in the memory hole, and the memory hole will then consume them in their entirety and forever. Winston Smith's job is therefore not only to rewrite history in accordance with the current demands of the day but also to destroy the previously fabricated histories of Oceania so that they will not cause any friction with its latest version of its history. When one day at work Winston Smith comes across a photograph of people who he remembered as "unpersons" (i.e., people who never existed), he is troubled and begins to think in proscribed ways. Winston even starts to keep a diary, which is also taboo in Oceania, and he tries very hard to remember his childhood, although this is made difficult by the blur of a constantly changing past and the many official warnings on the dangers of false memories. Winston ends up being tortured, for all of this and more, but especially for having the temerity to conceive of Oceania's history as having, as it were, not ended.

This is the stuff of a dystopian novel, of course, not sociological analysis, or is it? Is it possible to empirically discern the quantity and quality of a society's historical awareness? Is it possible to assess the abilities of individuals to have memory, and the quality of that memory, not just in terms of its accuracy but also in terms of its content, of what types of phenomena one is more or less accurately remembering? Do we remember, for example, what did not happen in history, what specific groups of people aspired to but failed to achieve? Do we remember not only what did happen and understand why it happened but also why so many paths were not taken? Do we have the technology to render people nonpersons? Do we rewrite history in accordance with current political demands? As Orwell has his character, O'Brien, the torturer, tell Winston, the tortured, the best way of maintaining the status quo is to control history, and the best way to control history is to obliterate the capacity for individuals to have memory or at least a memory they trust. In a totalitarian society, history is rewritten so that it causes no friction with the present; no one should have the instruments of history's intelligibility to judge the latest version as a forgery.

A society without memory is a society without the capacity for judgment. A society without judgment is a society in which the rational making of history is moot. Postmodern societies have created the means to learn more about history than ever before—through carbon-dating techniques, more numerous anthropological and archeological investigations, and an expanded awareness of the dilemmas surrounding historiography. We have also created and enlarged the means to recreate and falsify history and to promote the absence of a nonfalsified memory. As the mass media develop their reach and their sophistication, our collective ability to grasp the full complexity of history, both its actuality and its unrealized potentialities, is threatened with extinction.

As Mills stresses in *The Sociological Imagination,* the relevance of history depends on the type of society that produces its history. We make history not just in the sense of making our future but also our past. No less than for time and space, what history comes to mean for us is determined by our society's ability to make it not only intelligible but also practically meaningful. History therefore does not simply exist any more than does time and space; it is a contested terrain whose winners and losers catalogue the development or the debasement of the human uses of reason and freedom. If a society puts history under the control of undemocratic elites, then the prospects for democracy, and for the public uses of the sociological imagination, are themselves brought under control. In the quotation that opens this chapter, Baudrillard argues that we are already in such a condition, a society in which, as Mills said, "the ideas of freedom and of reason have become moot."[6] A central challenge for the possessor of the sociological imagination today is to proceed as if Mills is wrong by producing for ourselves an adequate sense of time and space, and from this, a sense of "the present as history" that facilitates the effective use of reason and freedom in our individual lives.[7]

In the remainder of this chapter, we shall examine two examples of the debasement of historical awareness in our present epoch and query as to their significance for the sociological imagination. In the first case, we examine two books. One is a relatively popular statement written by a former U.S. State Department employee and noted conservative intellectual, Francis Fukuyama. His 1992 book is titled *The End of History and the Last Man.*[8] We will then juxtapose this work with a book written by a leading sociologist and historian, Immanuel Wallerstein. His 1999 book is titled *The End of the World As We Know It: Social Science for the Twenty-First Century.*[9] In both Fukuyama and Wallerstein's books, we find versions of the end of history that overshoot individual lives and leave us lost in an elusive postmodern space. Our next case will be a discussion of Oliver Stone's 1991 film *JFK* and Spike Lee's 1992 film *Malcolm X,* both of which, at least on the surface, treat critical political figures and events in recent American history. They are also failed attempts to recover that history, if by this we mean the truth about this history. They are better conceived in terms of the paradoxes of history making in a period in which the past is rendered as a media simulation because it is increasingly irretrievable by normal historical means.

Fukuyama and Wallerstein: Taking It Too Big

Fukuyama originally proposed his thesis of the end of history in 1989. This was the year when the Soviet Union and its eastern European satellites collapsed. This was the year of the "velvet revolution" in Czechoslovakia (which is now two countries), the year when the Berlin Wall was breached (helping to create one country where two previously existed), and when communism, like so many statutes of Lenin, was in one country after another toppled over. Instead of singing along with Jesus Jones, whose popular song of this period announced his "watching the world wake up from history," Fukuyama announced its end. Why?

In Fukuyama's reading, communism was at this point the chief and, indeed, the only significant rival of Western "liberal democracy." Fascism and monarchy were vanquished. Communist leaders had long predicted that communism would "bury" liberal democracy because History (emphasis on the capital "H"), they thought, was on their side. They argued incessantly that human progress inevitably would lead to their form of society, or at least to its ideal, a classless society in which the people enjoyed equal control over their lives. But actual history (small "h") and their actual societies did not bear out this grandiose claim. As the events of 1989 suggested, it was liberal democracy that had buried communism, and as communist nations fell apart, their citizens seemed to embrace the ideals and institutions of Western liberal democracy. For Fukuyama, it is in this sense, and this sense alone, that history has come to end: as an ideal, liberal democracy cannot be surpassed. It is *the* utopia for all people everywhere, and we are on the cusp of realizing this ideal as never before in all of human experience. Thus as the world becomes increasingly, and inevitably, liberal democratic, humanity will have before it no additional grand historical projects, no "History" to be made. This is a simple version of Fukuyama's overarching perspective.

Fukuyama does not merely assert the end of history; he provides two types of arguments in support of this thesis. First, modern natural science, he says, gives human history "directionality and coherence."[10]

Modern natural science discovers objective natural laws. Armed with the knowledge of natural laws, modern humans are able to develop powerful technology, which, among other things, "confers decisive military advantages on those countries that possess it."[11] In a sense, historically speaking, right makes might. Countries that do not possess vibrant centers for the development of modern natural science are doomed in competition with those that do. Technology also, however, "makes possible the limitless accumulation of wealth, and thus the satisfaction of an ever-expanding set of human desires."[12] The chain of Fukuyama's argument is easy to follow: liberal democratic society produces science and technology, which produces military and economic power, which vanquishes rival types of society. Fukuyama draws the following conclusion:

> This process guarantees an increasing homogenization of all human societies, regardless of their historical origins or cultural inheritances. All countries undergo-

ing economic modernization must increasingly resemble one another: they must unify nationally on the basis of a centralized state, urbanize, replace traditional forms of social organization like tribe, sect, and family with economically rational ones based on function and efficiency, and provide for the universal education of their citizens.[13]

Fukuyama continues,

Such societies have become increasingly linked with one another through global markets and the spread of universal consumer culture. Moreover, the logic of modern natural science would seem to dictate a universal evolution in the direction of capitalism. The experiences of the Soviet Union, China, and other socialist countries indicate that while highly centralized economies are sufficient to reach a level of industrialization represented by Europe in the 1950's, they are woefully inadequate in creating what have been termed complex "post-industrial" economies in which information and technological innovations play a much larger role.[14]

Modern natural science thus empowers societies that develop it and gives them a competitive advantage in military and economic competition. In the end, they win because they are armed with the truth, the truth produced by modern natural science.

This argument deals with the triumph of the "liberal" side of liberal democracy. By "liberal," Fukuyama does not mean the use of government power to create social justice, particularly greater social equality; this distinctly American notion of liberalism was created by FDR's attempt to save liberal democracy in the 1930s through the New Deal. Fukuyama is instead using this term in its original eighteenth and nineteenth century meaning to refer to the philosophy of individual freedom, particularly freedom *from* tyrannical rulers and states. In this sense, the leaders of the American Revolution were primarily liberals fighting unjust colonial rule. Our ideals of the freedom of speech, press, religion, and assembly, then, are originally liberal ideals realized through weak and limited governments; governments, that is, held in check by such things as "The Bill of Rights."

Modern natural science was born from free inquiry, and its fruits, as Fukuyama argues, guarantee the success of any society that is structured so as to allow this individual freedom to flourish. The same is true in economics, where free markets (free, that is, from state control) are those that best encourage innovation, efficiency, and the resulting production of desired forms of wealth. Free scientific inquiry and free markets work to produce powerful and successful societies—modern liberal societies.

What about the "democratic" in liberal democracy? Here, Fukuyama introduces his second line of argument to support his thesis of the end of history. Fukuyama relies on the philosophy of G. W. F. Hegel. Fukuyama's reading goes something like this: Hegel argued that humanity's progressive movement toward the realization of its potential for reason and freedom is driven primarily by a "struggle for recognition."[15] By this, Hegel meant that human beings desire to be recognized by other human beings as beings of equal dignity and worth, and in the eyes of a universal history, all are equal before all, and every "I" represents one instance of a universal "we." For Fukuyama, democracy is a political system in which all are recognized as equal, where "I"'s and the "We" converge in a system of equal recognition. Modern democracy, then, is the product of a long history of struggle for equal recognition, a desire that is a "motor of history." In our time, "Liberal democracy replaces the irrational desire to be recognized as *greater than others* with a rational desire to be recognized as equal."[16] For Fukuyama, the desire for democracy has become rational in that we now realize our unavoidably noneconomic, nonmaterial interest in equal recognition.

Liberal democracies, then, combine the best of both worlds: power and wealth in addition to human dignity for all. There seems nothing within them that could be called a fundamental contradiction, and therefore liberal democracy presents itself as a stable form of society. Fascist or communist regimes may produce powerful and wealthy societies, but free capitalist societies are even more powerful and more wealthy; they are better structured to take advantage of the fruits of modern natural science. Furthermore, neither totalitarian societies nor monarchies and other forms of autocratic rule provide for mutual and equal recognition for all people. The only system that wins in historical competition, and the only one that is today globally recognized as the best of all possible worlds is liberal democracy. No alternative can be imagined. "The *ideal* of liberal democracy [can] not be improved upon"—and thus History (big "H") has reached its conclusion.[17]

Fukuyama is not naïve. He is not arguing that the future will bring no problems, no serious conflicts. His point is only that we will cope with these problems and conflicts in terms of the type of society that we already have and that these conflicts and problems will not cause us to devise a radically new form of society. Nor does Fukuyama argue that the world today is wholly and thoroughly liberal democratic. It obviously is not; thus much of the future will be played out in terms of the continuing conquest of liberal democracy in *all* corners of the globe. There may be backsliding as well, but it will be of a temporary sort. Backsliding, in Fukuyama's view, will be met with the overwhelming force of liberal democratic power and sentiment.

What about the second half of Fukuyama's title, "the last man?" This is taken from Nietzsche and refers to the type of human being who would exist at the end of history. Essentially, these last people would be satisfied because both their material and nonmaterial desires would be met. They would enjoy the fruits of wealth and power, and they would enjoy equal recognition. Stated differently again, they would be fat and happy. They would have all the computers and access to infinitely more numerous World Wide Web ages than they could desire and also a sense of dignity, esteem, and a feeling of being as fully and equally human as the next guy. For Fukuyama, this is a troubling but perhaps unavoidable consequence of the end of history. It is troubling because such people would be formed outside of the type of struggles that have defined the human experience to date and would have no knowledge of daring and risk or the exhilaration and zest for life associated with them.

Fukuyama's book caused quite a splash. Although usually considered a work by a conservative intellectual, Fukuyama's book also struck a cord with leftist intellectuals. Indeed, one of the most startling things that occurred during this period was that all over the world, former socialists and Marxists stood up and declared defeat. Instead of proffering alternatives to liberal democracy, they contented themselves, at best, with advocating new versions of FDR's "American liberalism." The mainstream American political spectrum—ranging roughly between Fukuyama's liberalism, which we usually call "conservatism," and FDR's liberalism—has become the world's political spectrum. The big political questions thus run along these lines: how free should our free markets be? How much social inequality should we allow capitalism to create? How should we deal with instances of unequal access to jobs and consumer goods and still-lingering forms of unequal recognition? How can we best integrate the rest of the world into our system? How can we deal with the consequences of so much success? The end of history thus coincides with an "end of ideology." If *the* ideal society is upon us and widely acclaimed or at least begrudgingly accepted, there is no need to argue about ideals. Ideological debates go the way of the telegraph and typewriter.

Now let us address Wallerstein's book *The End of the World as We Know It*. This is a collection of essays that were delivered as speeches during Wallerstein's 1994-1998 tenure as the president of the International Sociological Association. As Wallerstein explains, the title plays on the ambiguous meaning of "as we know it," which refers both to what we have known about the world and how social scientists have come to know it.[18] What was the president of the International Sociological Association telling his social science comrades between 1994 and 1998? That the world as we know it (in both senses) is about to end. Let us look closer.

Following the French historian Fernand Braudel, Wallerstein argues that history is divided into "four different kinds of social time," but for the most part social scientists perceive "only two of them," the two that are not very important.[19] These are "episodic time," the time of mere events that follow one after the other, and a transcendent or "timeless time," which is what is implied in any search for basic and invariant social laws. Braudel derided both, calling the former the mere "dust" of history, and, saying of the latter, "if it exists, [it] can only be the time period of sages."[20]

Like Braudel, Wallerstein advises that we pay much greater attention to the two other types of time, "structural time" and "cyclical, middle-range time," "the time of cycles *within* structures."[21] What does this entail?

Wallerstein is famous for having been primarily responsible for devising the ill-named World Systems Theory, which is not a theory of world systems but a general perspective that suggests that all social scientists should take as their "unit of analysis" the whole of all societies as they form "historical systems."[22] These historical systems are difficult to fathom in part because they exist in structural time, which is to say, they come to exist, reach equilibrium, and disintegrate over relatively long stretches of time. In Wallerstein's view, for example, the modern world system (which is the latest historical system) is roughly 500 years old and, like all historical systems, is defined by "an ongoing division of labor that permits it to sustain and reproduce itself."[23] The modern world systems' "division of labor" is the "capitalist world-economy." Other historical systems include the Roman Empire and the Maya of Central America. The point, though, is that social science will be blind to the essential makeup of any given object or unit of analysis unless it sees this part in terms of the whole, the whole historical system. Wallerstein, for example, speaks of the rise and fall of communism as a mere "interlude" in the ongoing workings of the capitalist world-economy.[24]

When Wallerstein writes about the end of the world as we know it, then, he means the end of the modern world system or, synonymously, the end of the capitalist world economy. He also means, of course, that social scientists ought to attend to this level of historical time, lest they misunderstand everything that is happening. And much is happening, for Wallerstein believes that the capitalist world economy is in a "terminal crisis" and is "unlikely to exist in fifty years."[25] We cannot know what type of world system will arise to take its place, thinks Wallerstein, but we can expect things to get much, much worse than they already are before things get better, if that ever happens.

Why? Why does this leading social scientist think we are in a terminal historical crisis that will determine nearly everything about our lives for the foreseeable future? He gives several reasons. First, Wallerstein observes worldwide "deruralization," the movement of people from rural areas to urban areas.[26] This is significant because it means that the world is running out of a pool of workers willing to endure the hardship of industrial work for minimal wages, which is the life-blood, as it were, of expanding "profit levels." In a world capitalist economy, expanding profits are the name of the game. If profit cannot be expanded, then the worldwide economy (and the historical systems' defining division of labor) will be thrown into a crisis. A second reason is also related to profits. Ecological devastation is usually paid for by all the people of a society via their governments. These are called the "social costs" of capitalist expansion.[27] Taxpayers, not businesses, pay to clean up toxic wastes, for example, to remedy the ill-health caused by pollution. But as the worldwide capitalist economy continues to grow (which it must do in order to achieve constantly expanding profits), ecological problems will continue to mount, and Wallerstein foresees that it will soon become impossible to cover these costs, socially or otherwise. Third, worldwide democratization has an unintended consequence, at least from the point of view of a capitalist world system: people do not hesitate to make "popular demands" for such things as universal health coverage and other expensive social rights.[28] As these demands increase, the system is further stretched to meet them, lest it surrender its legitimacy in the eyes of the people. A system no longer widely viewed as legitimate is a system in crisis. Finally, Wallerstein views the collapse of communism and with it the impoverishment of left-wing political ideology not as the crowning moment of victory for the capitalist world system but, rather, as "its greatest danger."[29] Without any future alternative to inspire the masses of people to tolerate their present hardship within the system, their only route to a better life is to subvert the system, perhaps through nonparticipation in its workings or what Wallerstein calls the " 'anarchistic' tendencies of the dangerous classes."[30] "Analytically," writes Wallerstein, "this is the road back to feudalism," by which he means the delegitimation of democracy returns the world to a state of balkanized fiefdoms competing against one another for their particular survival.[31]

Based on his analysis, Wallerstein develops a sense that history and society as we have known them for 500 years are coming to an end. As for the immediate future, he writes,

> I . . . expect considerable turmoil of the kind we have already been seeing in the 1990's, spreading from the Bosnias and Rwandas of this world to the wealthier (and assertedly more stable) regions of the world (such as the United States).[32]

How this period of "turmoil" will play itself out is, however, uncertain or indeterminate. Science cannot tell us that. It will depend on what actual people will do, what type of choices they will make, and how they will come to understand what is happening to them. In this last point, Wallerstein finds reason for a cautious optimism. He writes, "If we were certain of the future, there could be no moral compulsion to do anything."[33] He claims to be "ready to struggle with [i.e., against] those who, under whatever guise and for whatever excuse, prefer an inegalitarian, undemocratic world."[34]

The similarities between Fukuyama and Wallerstein are as striking, perhaps, as the obvious divergences. Both share a sense of history's ending and both define this ending in terms of a long and difficult to imagine process of development. In both of these long views, the specifics of particular people's lives tend to fall under gross categorizations like "last man," or they simply blow away as "dust." Both are also focused on the nature of today's "political economy," which is to say, the nature of the modern economic and political systems as they intersect and stabilize one another. Liberal democracy and the capitalist world economy are both very large-scale units of analysis describing roughly the same thing: today's worldwide dominant form of political economy. Both authors are also worried what the immediate future will hold, and, finally, both have a lot to say about what the collapse of communism means for the future of modern social development.

The divergences, however, are even more clear. Although both are concerned with the immediate future, they conceive of this period in fundamentally different ways. For Fukuyama, it is, as it were, the time after the end, after the final victory of liberal democracy, after the end of history and the end of ideological struggle. For Wallerstein, the immediate future it is not the end of all history (that is for the "sages" to discern) but just the end of the last 500 years of history within boundaries of this last historical system. One result of this divergence is that it is the pessimist about today, Wallerstein, who is cautiously optimistic about the future as a time of potential creativity and liberation, while it is the optimist about today, Fukuyama, who is pessimistic about the future as nothing more than the boring return of the ever-same. Politically, Fukuyama is a defender of the status quo, despite his misgivings, while Wallerstein is a radical, looking to a qualitatively better future historical system. Indeed, in Fukuyama's scheme, Wallerstein's very existence is anomalous because radicals are supposed to have capitulated, whereas in Wallerstein's scheme, Fukuyama is the anomaly as a person declaring victory at the precise moment when defeat is most clearly on the horizon.

Is one or the other perspective correct and the other false, or one more correct and the other more false? We are talking about the end of history, after all, and that seems a rather important topic. What is more, both authors are talking about our lives now, or between now and fifty years from now, so there is urgency and self-interest at stake as well. Contra Fukuyama, our position in this book is that the world is dying and dystopian. If Fukuyama were correct, we would not urgently need a sociological imagination today because most if not all of our problems would be strictly technical. We would need instead a good many social engineers adept at extending our basic social structure to meet the problems of tomorrow and perhaps a few philosophers and extreme sports instructors to get us through life as "last men" regardless of whether we are women or men or something else. Fukuyama asserts that there are no fundamental contradictions in liberal democracy, but we have argued in contrast that "liberal democracy" (in this book, postmodern society and culture) is both unsustainable (stands in contradiction, as it were, with nature) and neither very liberal nor very democratic. Rather than see the end of history and, along with it, the end of ideology, as an achievement, we have cast the degradation of utopian thinking as a prime symptom of a one-dimensional society and a disillusioning culture. That fundamentally divergent views of the same history coincide is itself, perhaps, evidence of how confounding is the search today for adequate historical orientation.

Rejecting Fukuyama does not mean that this book is construed in Wallersteinian terms either. We have stressed that the collapse of this historical system, after all, harbors the potential for the end of all historical systems, and no possessor of the sociological imagination can quickly skim the meaning of this fact for the biographies of those fated to endure the end of the world as we know it. Where Wallerstein attends primarily to structural and cyclical time, our focus is on the type of mind that must exist within individuals whose biological clock is ticking and whose bodies are "trapped" within postmodern spatial configurations. This book, in a sense, is written by and for "the dust" of history, potentially "last men" in an empirical sense. When Wallerstein does attend to the lives of ordinary people, which is rare, he conceives them in terms of objective powerlessness and the socially imposed "fear"—primarily expressed in terms of crime and ethnic conflict—that results from the larger crisis of the historical system.[35] As seen from his grand historical perspective, ordinary people's lives are the determinant variable in an equation whose independent variable is the capitalist world system. He views individuals, in other words, as primarily the powerless product of social structure. No less than Fukuyama, Wallerstein therein elides the dynamic intersection of biography and history. Since his theory of today's crisis conceives our epoch in grand temporal and spatial terms, he is led to treat the intricacies of biographical experience as irrelevant. While there is no doubt much to be learned from Wallerstein's long view, the possessor of the sociological imagination must blend this view together with equally valid individual, embodied experiences of time and space, equally valid levels of history and history making, and must proceed as if the intersections of history and biography remained vital. Wallerstein is primarily interested in developing an objective social *science;* we are primarily interested in developing in individuals a sociological *imagination.* For that, one has to go where people live.

Stone and Lee: Taking It Too Small

It is the end of the world as we know it, but do we "feel fine," as R.E.M. ironically proposed? Well, we might at least feel better if we were at an R.E.M. concert or watching a movie. But maybe not, if the film in question were Oliver Stone's *JFK* or Spike Lee's *Malcolm X.* Both of these well-known American filmmakers have made careers of upsetting their audience, particularly through their depiction of controversial political issues and events. Both Stone and Lee act as popular historians of such subjects as race, war, and race wars. They make Hollywood movies, but their real interest is in making history. By "making history," we mean making versions of the past, making the versions of the future, and attending to the process of history making itself. Oliver Stone and Spike Lee are masters of postmodern mass media: they create entertaining simulations of history in the hope of affecting the course of real history.

At its most rudimentary level, the film *JFK* is about the murder of John F. Kennedy, the President of the United States, in Dallas, Texas, on November 22, 1963. It attacks this assassination mainly through the protagonist, Jim Garrison, a New Orleans district attorney who, in 1969, staged the only trial related to the murder of President Kennedy. Even after the Warren Commission had officially concluded that Lee Harvey Oswald was the lone assassin of President Kennedy, Garrison tried a New Orleans businessperson, Clay Shaw, as a conspirator in the assassination. Garrison charged that Shaw was a covert Central Intelligence Agency (CIA) agent who played a role in a government-led conspiracy to assassinate President Kennedy and subsequently frame Oswald for this act. *JFK* could therefore be simply described as a cinemagraphic rendering of Garrison's autobiography, *On the Trail of the Assassins*. But this description merely establishes the film's main subject matter, its point of view, and its aesthetic genre.

Beyond this, the film includes many unusual elements. For example, *JFK* includes the actual footage of Abraham Zapruder's amateur film of the shooting, which Stone has described as the "core" of *JFK*.[36] *JFK* blends Zapruder's actual film with numerous types of film stocks and filming techniques, creating a pastiche, a mix of aesthetic styles and perspectives. Stone has himself noted that *JFK* "is one of the fastest movies ever made."[37]

> It is like splinters to the brain. We had 2,500 cuts, maybe 2,200 set-ups. We were assaulting the senses in a kind of new-wave technique. We wanted to get to the subconsciousness.
>
> So, do these flashes blind or illuminate? In this sense, I like the MTV-style flashes of imagery because they have circumvented conventional narrative in the same way James Joyce in *Ulysses* circumvented Charles Dickens.[38]

Mixing documentary footage with lots of differently staged footage, quickly cutting from one perspective to another, flashing images and then still more images, filled with characters peopled by dozens of major Hollywood stars (including Kevin Costner in the lead role as Garrison, but also Garrison himself playing Chief Justice Earl Warren), Stone's imaginative cinematic form finally coalesces, as he says, to "establish a counter-myth to the official myth of the U.S. Government," that is, the version of these events told in the Warren Commission Report.[39]

So *JFK* is a dramatization of Jim Garrison's autobiography created to establish a countermyth regarding the assassination of President John F. Kennedy. But why? Why establish a countermyth? Oliver Stone's view of the United States is that "we have fascism now. We don't call it that, but that's what you get when corporations own government. The only democracy that American citizens are left with is the choice between Fab or Tide, ABC, CBS, and NBC."[40] This is a strong claim, but Stone even puts this point into the film when, in the last scenes, Jim Garrison (played by Costner) describes the U.S. form of government as fascist. In fact, he hisses "fascism." At about this time in the film, Garrison (Costner) talks at length about returning the United States to its democratic heritage, in particular, by finding the truth behind the assassination of President Kennedy, which the film suggests was a coup d'etat. Garrison (Costner) then looks directly into the camera and says, "it's up to you," meaning it is up to the film's audience to pursue the truth behind the assassination of John F. Kennedy and, in this way, act against our (posited) fascist government on behalf of the project of reestablishing a (posited) lost American democracy. Most Hollywood films do not have such ambitions.

This leaves a number of ambiguities. If Stone thinks that the assassination of President John F. Kennedy was actually a coup d'etat—literally, the removing of the head of state or a violent overthrow of a government via the removal of its leader—then why not simply make a documentary that makes an empirical case for this historical thesis? Why think that this particular murder is significant for our contemporary struggle for democracy? If President Kennedy were the victim of a coup d'etat, why would this be relevant for today's American democracy? If Stone were correct that we live in a fascist state, why would he be allowed to make and distribute his film? Why would "the government" allow this? Finally, since *JFK* did in fact inspire special legislation designed to speed the public release of all government-held documents relating to the assassination of President Kennedy, is this not proof that the thesis of the film is incorrect? Isn't the film's success in spurring a public outcry for more information itself evidence against the film's depiction of American democracy? Here we are closer to the film's ultimate complexities. Let us address each question in turn.

Why not a straightforward documentary? Who needs Kevin Costner? There are at least three answers to this question. First, a straightforward documentary is impossible. There are many, many documents available for rational analysis—from the Warren Report to the Zapruder film—but there is no established and credible "chain of evidence," as crime investigators say, which clearly and cogently establishes the relationship between any bit of this evidence and the crime in question. If the president were killed in a government-directed coup d'etat, then the officials who controlled and who still control "the evidence" cannot be viewed as neutral to the outcome of the investigation. Therefore, from the point of view adopted in the film, all evidence is suspect; not a scrap can be assumed to be authentic. This includes the autopsy performed under the authority of the U.S. military, the fact of the so-called "magic bullet"(which is in nearly pristine condition even though it caused numerous wounds to two men, President Kennedy and Texas Governor John Connally), and even the Zapruder film itself, all of which could have been altered or manipulated. Second, Stone did not have access to the evidence that is available. At the time, most of it was sealed from public access. Third, Stone intended not so much to document a coup d'etat theory of the assassination as to stir-up a public rethinking of the facts surrounding the assassination. For this, Stone needed a film that would be enticing to a mass audience, which is part of the reason he loaded the film with so many Hollywood stars and included so many invented dramatizations. As he says, "What tells you more about what happened that day in Dallas, image or 'historical fact'?"[41] Stone decided to go with what he had access to and control over: images of historical fact. This is the case even though in a later film, *Natural Born Killers,* Stone would launch an attack against "idolizing the image."[42]

But why should anyone care? Why did Stone choose to make a film about this topic? First, Stone intentionally pitched the film toward young viewers, dedicating it "to the young in whose spirit the search for truth marches on." In 1991, "young" viewers of the film would be people for whom the assassination of President Kennedy was a historical event that occurred before they were born. It is an event outside their personal memory. In this sense, Stone's film is meant to instigate an interest in history among the young. As Stone has noted:

> I have been called a revolutionary (apparently a bad thing) and charged with brain-washing the young—even though I have found, in my travels around the country, that the young don't know about history anyway because their teachers haven't taught them anything.[43]

Stone holds that history—even the "history" of one past generation—will be lost without some type of stimulus to mass remembrance. If history teachers are not doing it, then Stone will.

Second, Stone's overarching political theory holds that current political conditions in the United States (an unacknowledged "fascism") are a result of societal forces that emerged during the period immediately before and leading up to the assassination of President Kennedy. The film begins, for example, with President Dwight D. Eisenhower's famous "farewell speech," in which this former five-star general and then-retiring president warned that American democracy was threatened by what he called "the military-industrial complex." Eisenhower was referring to what C. Wright Mills had earlier called "the power elite," mainly the entwinement of military, corporate, and political elites in an undemocratic system of power over the direction of society, particularly in the prosecution of the Cold War. For Stone, it was members of this power elite who organized the coup d'etat in 1963. They supposedly did so because of Kennedy's (posited) opposition to escalating the war in Vietnam but also to forestall Kennedy's (posited) decision to put an end to the Cold War and to dismantle the military-industrial complex as a growing concern.

Stone also suggests that the successful coup plotters later were responsible for the assassinations of Martin Luther King, Jr. and Senator Robert Kennedy, and, the same year, for the return to power of Richard Nixon. Beyond this, Stone also sees connections between these events in the 1960s and the Iran-Contra scandal of the 1980s, which also involved efforts to manipulate national politics in support of anticommunist foreign policy objectives. If Stone is right, then the secret truth behind the assassination of President Kennedy is tied to the emergence of an undemocratic political system in the United States, from Nixon through to Reagan, and is one that still obtains today and that is the structural basis for his posited contemporary fascism. If Stone is correct, then a thorough reconceptualization of American political history since World War II would be necessary. This reconceptualization would also be a revolutionary political act against a state dedicated to the maintenance of an undemocratic society.

But is not Stone's position self-contradictory? Why or how could he make a film that raised these issues and that explicitly appealed to his audience to act against state secrets and a posited fascism? Stone believes he was able to make *JFK* only because of the commercial successes of his earlier films such as *Salvador* and *Platoon*. And because he was also able to attract a star-studded cast, including mostly left-leaning Hollywood actors, the film was assured a substantial box office. According to Stone, the repression of the film came not in any government-led effort to stop its production but in media-led efforts to dismiss its claims and stigmatize its creator.

The film was, indeed, much criticized in nearly every medium of mass culture. Stone had few defenders but hundreds of detractors. Stone and his films were generally discredited as in any way a reliable source of historical knowledge, especially about the assassination of President Kennedy. Once the source of information is discredited, then the information is discredited. In this way, the fact that *JFK* sits on many a video store's shelves means nothing because its point of view cannot be legitimately discussed or advanced without whomever chooses to do so being politically tainted or discredited. If Lee Harvey Oswald is deemed as a lone nut, now so is Oliver Stone and anyone who takes him seriously. As he says of himself, "*JFK* ended my fifteen minutes of being a good guy and placed me forever in the ranks of the damned."[44]

Is Stone overly pessimistic about his own fate? His film did inspire considerable public interest in the facts surrounding the death of John Kennedy and his own career as a filmmaker has not seemed to have been adversely affected, and Congress actually passed a law providing for the release of all "declassifiable" documents concerning the assassination. This process is still ongoing, even though it is no longer funded and even though there are thousands of documents that remain classified and therefore prohibited from public disclosure. Of course, even if all remaining documents were released to the public and even if expert analysts were to study them (a full-time job) and report their findings in an accessible manner to a wide audience, our first point concerning the chain of evidence would still hold. Much evidence was destroyed or has gone missing. Although new and curious facts have been revealed (e.g., that the president's brain is missing from the National Archives, that his original Dallas coffin was dumped into the Atlantic Ocean by a military aircraft), nothing confirming a coup d'etat has come to light as a result of this long process of public disclosure. Perhaps Stone's film was as successful as it could be, at least on its own terms. Perhaps even after all the evidence that can be made public is made public, there will be no need to rethink history. Lee Harvey Oswald killed President Kennedy. Case closed. End of story.

What can we take from this film regarding the forces working against the sociological imagination today? In an address delivered on German radio in 1960, Theodor W. Adorno concluded his remarks "On the Meaning of Working Through the Past" with the following statement: "The past will have been worked through only when the causes of what happened then have been eliminated. Only because the causes continue to exist does the captivating spell of the past remain to this day unbroken." [45]

It would seem that the assassination of President Kennedy continues to cast a captivating spell nearly 40 years after the fact because Americans have not, as it were, worked through this past so as to discern its causes in a manner that satisfies them. The same is true for the Cold War, the Vietnam War, the collapse of the civil rights movement, and the political scandal that capped off this era, Watergate. What forces produced these epochal events? As a result of the absence of a popular consensus about the facts of this history, there remains a perception that the United States is blind to its immediate history and, as a result, blind to its current historical situation as well.

At the same time that Adorno was speaking these thoughts to his German audience, who, of course, were trying to come to terms with their recent history of Nazism, Mills was instigating himself in U.S. Cold War policy against Cuba. Mills thought that this crisis would decisively shape the trajectory of the Cold War, but

Mills did not know—and, although it is documented history, very few even today know—that Kennedy would soon be involved in secret negotiations with Soviet Premier Nikita Khrushchev to end the Cuban Missile Crisis in part because he feared losing control over the U.S. military and soon thereafter would engage Fidel Castro himself in an equally secret dialogue designed to dampen down the conflict between Cuba and the United States that had brought the world to the brink of nuclear war. Mills viewed President Kennedy as Kennedy presented himself to the public, as a staunch and fervent Cold Warrior. In private, however, Kennedy presented himself as a reasonable person. For example, Kennedy told Jean Daniel, the editor of the French socialist periodical *L'Observateur* that "he had approved of Castro's demands for justice while fighting in the Sierra Maestra... [but] he was President of the United States, *'not some sociologist.'* "[46] Mills did not know he was apparently on the president's mind, nor did he live to see the Cuban missile crisis, the limited test ban treaty, Kennedy's American University speech (which J.F.K. called his "peace speech"), J.F.K.'s stated unwillingness to commit to a war in Vietnam, or, of course, the brutal assassination of the president in the city in which Mills went to high school. It is therefore impossible to know what Mills, the author of *The Power Elite, The Causes of World War Three,* and *Listen Yankee,* would have thought of these events or how he would have acted toward them, but it is safe to assume that Mills would have regarded these events as terribly significant because he would have the eventual escalation of the war in Vietnam and the renewal of a bitter period of Cold War competition between the Soviet Union and the United States that lasted into the late 1980s.

Looking back now through the prism of images that dominant postmodern culture, these events easily take on the form of a formless kaleidoscope. Stone says,

In my film, the camera reflected the search for truth. Its various angles captured the simultaneous points of view of an array of witnesses, and their own fragments of apprehension. The camera itself was the critical instrument. It should be self-reflexive. What you see represented over and over again in the film are fractals of consciousness that, altogether, add up to the reality of a moment. They are shards of an event about which the whole truth is perhaps unknowable. *JFK* is a three-hour avalanche of fragments of the truth.

Ultimately, *JFK* is not really a political film. The ultimate questions are philosophical: Who owns reality? Who owns your mind? Isn't history a distorted hall of mirrors that depends on the kind of surface that reflects its essence and its events?[47]

The sociological imagination demands more than just "fractals of consciousness." A sociological account of this subject and this history would want what may in fact be unknowable, "the whole truth." Stone is himself very concerned about the "cynicism" he sees as the standard fare of the mass media dominated by a "constant, re-morseless ridicule of everything and anything."[48] Stone says that he believes in

> unleashing the pure wash of emotion across the mind to let you see the inner myth, the spirit of the thing. Then, when the cold light of reason hits you as you walk out of the theater, the sense of truth will remain lodged beyond reason in the depths of your being, or it will be killed by the superego of the critics.[49]

But Stone's film—his fast movie and its splinters to the brain—is too close to postmodern panic for our purposes. Between "the depths of your being" and the "superego," there ought to be an "ego," which is not "beyond reason" but in fact its very locus. A countermyth, even on behalf of reason and freedom through the recovery of a repressed history, can never mesh easily with a mature sociological imagination. So it is certainly difficult to develop a sociological imagination today. In the face of such a convoluted if also ominous immediate history, the sociological imagination is threatened with dissolution into cynicism and panic and perhaps the alternation of both within a single self-consciousness. Even the careful study of available documents and written histories will probably never be enough to settle with any sort of scientific certainty the nature and meaning of these events. The means of their rational intelligibility do not exist because, if nothing else, the chains of evidence are forever corrupted. Stone's hypotheses cannot be proven, and so a diffuse paranoia is likely to linger. It is as though one of the three necessary legs of the sociological imagination has been amputated, and we are left only to ponder the prosthesis provided by Hollywood films.

Similar in style and purpose to *JFK,* Spike Lee's 1992 *Malcolm X* does little to help restore history and genuine historical understanding. Indeed, because it renders the life and political thought of a revolutionary as Hollywood entertainment, it makes things worse. The film's subject is Malcolm X, the Nation of Islam leader whose significance in the struggle for civil rights in the United States was perhaps exceeded only by Martin Luther King, Jr. Lee uses the famous *Autobiography of Malcolm X* as the basis for much of his script, and the popular and award-winning actor Denzel Washington plays the title role and helps to make the film eminently watchable. For more than three hours, we see Malcolm (played by Washington) go through the three main stages of his life, as he explained them in his autobiography, from a regular guy who was little more than a street hustler (a life that lands him in jail) to the loyal and articulate devotee of Elijah Muhammad and the Nation of Islam (a life that brings him to fame as a dynamic and forceful proponent of black nationalism) and finally to that most important period in Malcolm's life (which lasted less than a year) when Malcolm became disillusioned with the Nation of Islam, broke from its orthodoxy and, most important, began to think for himself. Always an amazingly intelligent man and gifted also by his willingness to learn and to change on the basis of that learning, Malcolm's last days were spent traveling to Africa, Mecca, and elsewhere. This experience spurred in him a fundamental rethinking of the meaning of race and power, and he set about to fashion a new and more expansive political philosophy, one that would be no less radical than his previous "black nationalism" and arguably more so. All of this is represented in Lee's film.

The ultimate point of the film is not to carefully explicate the history of the Nation of Islam nor to analyze the complexities of black nationalism and Malcolm's subsequent critic of black nationalism. The ultimate point is to lionize Malcolm, to render his intelligence, self-discipline, and learning as an objective lesson for today's young people, young black men most of all. Furthermore, the film is a call to arms. It is made to act as a forceful source of political inspiration. Malcolm X is, in short, presented as a masculine role model for today's youth. Given that Malcolm X was a brilliant and dedicated social revolutionary, this seems as odd a choice of role model as would be the promotion of the life and times of Karl Marx, but this is what the film does.

For example, the conclusion of the film represents Malcolm's assassination in 1965 as an act at least partly directed by shadowy agents of the U.S. government, probably the FBI, which had at this time for years been conducting secret and illegal crimes against individuals and groups that its director, J. Edgar Hoover, deemed as threats to the American way of life. As with the murders of President Kennedy, Martin Luther King, Jr., Robert Kennedy, and others, the circumstances surrounding Malcolm's murder have always been suspicious and have always aroused conspiracy theories. The idea presented in Lee's version of this event is that Malcolm's newly found independence and radicalism was simply too threatening to the status quo and that as a result the government, along with the Nation of Islam, participated in his murder. These representations are presented to instigate in the viewer, at a minimum, a sense of frustration at the injustices of the past. Just when Malcolm was really coming into this own, in other words, the government facilitated his murder. This leaves the audience with a sense of unrealized possibilities: what would Malcolm have done had he not been murdered? How might things be different today, especially for black Americans, had he lived?

In a postscript to the film, Lee continues this theme by including footage of a living hero, then-President of South Africa Nelson Mandela, who speaks directly to Lee's audience. If one respects Mandela, then Mandela's immense prestige and credibility is transferred to *Malcolm X*. Lee also uses staged contemporary classroom scenes in which children, chosen apparently to represent the diversity within the Afro-American population, shout "I am Malcolm X." Here, of course, Lee uses a thoroughly unsubtle form of propaganda that seeks to create an identification in the young with the legacy of Malcolm X. Lee's technique is to depict children expressing exactly this identification in the most innocent and direct way possible: "I *am* Malcolm X." Although Lee does not say so in the film, he takes this scene from an actual event that occurred in the wake of the murder of Fred Hampton, the young chairman of the Illinois chapter of the Black Panther Party who was assassinated by Chicago police with the encouragement and assistance of the FBI. After Hampton's murder, a group of children spontaneously shouted, "I am Fred Hampton" as part of a church memorial service in Hampton's community. (This history is told as part of the award-winning documentary series *Eyes on the Prize.*) The role of the FBI in Hampton's death was only revealed after activists illegally broke into an FBI installation and stole secret government documents. Lee makes no mention these historical facts; he uses only the scene that actually occurred with respect to Fred Hampton in order to facilitate an identification with the legacy of Malcolm X.

In his otherwise sympathetic treatment of the film, Michael Eric Dyson criticizes the "unnecessary didacticism" of this aspect of the film (although it is present throughout and in fact defines the film as a whole).[50] Dyson explains,

> This move is Lee's attempt to solve cinematically a perplexing condition: how to get black youth to identify with the redemptive message of Malcolm's racial edification. It comes off needless contrived and facile, but it reveals just how difficult the task of reaching black youth really is.[51]

A respected cultural critic, Dyson, a professor of religious studies at DePaul University, essentially absolves the film of its contrivances and facile uses of propaganda techniques because, in the end, Lee's film "has sent us back into our own memories, or to books and documentaries, in search of the truth for ourselves"; Lee has "set the nation talking about a figure whose life deserves to be discussed, whose achievements deserve critical scrutiny, and whose career merits the widest possible exposure."[52]

Years later, we would have to say that the film has not done these things any more than *JFK* has done them with respect to the murder of President Kennedy. At best, both contribute to skepticism about our immediate history, particularly among the young; but there is no evidence that this skepticism has been fleshed out by the reading of books and the study of documentaries, or that our nation has been engrossed in a collective study of the life and thought of Malcolm X. Spike Lee, however, remains a highly visible celebrity whose advertisement endorsements and popular films remain very much in demand, and Malcolm's image has its place among the pantheon of great American black political leaders.

What lessons, then, does Lee's film contain about the forces working against the sociological imagination? It is worth pointing out that minority groups have an especially strong vested interest in history and in the making of history because they are engaged in a struggle, now latent, now open, for equality and justice. To change conditions of inequality and injustice, members of minority groups are forced to call on their history of struggle to inspire in each new generation the courage needed to engage in social struggles fraught with uncertainty and danger. To the young, it is said: You must risk your own life to redeem your fallen heros who died in the struggle in which you must now participate, lest their deaths be in vain. This is even an explicit message in *JFK,* in which Garrison (played by Costner) says that we should not forget our "dying King."

The possessor of the sociological imagination is today mindful of the role that historical memory plays in the work of social and political change but also, alas, of the trite manner in which this memory is manufactured in a society that lacks a vital public sphere. Imagine yourself saying, "I am C. Wright Mills!" This thought hopefully causes the reader to wince, if not in pain, then at least out of embarrassment for what we have come to. We are not children. We are not big heroic people, either. The sociological imagination is at home somewhere in between these sensibilities, always in between, always mindful of what has been lost, and learning from it. In these examples, lost in the translation of tragic history into docudrama is a sense of tragedy and of history. What we must learn is, again, that the medium is the message, regardless of the intention of the messenger, and that there are no easy short cuts in the development of empirical historical knowledge and politically productive historical sensibilities. Finally, we must realize that we will encounter history that is, even by normal historical methods, irretrievable. Given the means available to falsify history in our time, we will have to live with versions of history that are full of holes. Yet with the proper historical sensibilities, even absent knowledge can be meaningful. We do not know what President Nixon erased from his famous Watergate tapes, nor do we know what was contained in the documents that Lieutenant Colonel Oliver North busily shredded before being arrested for his role in the Iran-Contra Affair, but based on what *is* known about these events, we can reasonably imagine this information as especially scandalous.

After the End of History?

When people first started writing history 5,000 years ago, they could not have imagined that humans would one day build a society that would simultaneously dim the prospects for the continuation of human life and systematically distort people's collective ability to remember and make use of past experience. In both of these senses of the end of history, postmodernity collapses the past and the future into the experience of a timeless present. It would seem that, due to globalization, we are increasingly free to move about the world, but we are not free to move forward or make progress. Our lives seem perilously close to the dystopian vision of Orwell's Oceania, where the great majority of people are prevented from participation in history making because they are without historical sensibilities and denied access to the means intelligibility needed to make history a living force in their lives. Rendered ignorant spectators to history making, the vast majority of Oceania's "citizens" are spoon-fed prole feed and political propaganda in equal doses, their abilities to reason and freely act toward the world as moot as the question of which country Oceania was currently at war with, Eastasia or Eurasia. If Big Brother had been the victim of a *coup d'etat,* it would have been news to them.

But we do not live in Oceania. In this world, at this time, our situation is more paradoxical than what Orwell described in *1984.* It is not that the means to make history do not exist. Indeed, the means to make history are greater now than ever before, but so too are the historical challenges laid out before us. This is not purely coincidental. The structure of postmodern society stands back of our unprecedented powers as well as our unprecedented challenges because it is the institutions of this society that are the source of both our problems and our only means for redressing them. The problem is that postmodern society and culture are also responsible for the promotion of debased historical knowledge and media-scrabbled historical sensibilities. Through ideological distortion and as a result of its inflection through the mass media, "history" is today on life support. Baudrillard has warned us that we may already exist in a posthistoric, not prehistoric, society; it is the task of the possessor of the sociological imagination to act as if his or her exaggeration is not yet true.

Wallerstein's depiction of the modern world system, for example, is the product of an unprecedented expansion in the means of social and historical research, and much of the information presented in Chapter 2 would not be meaningful were we not able to summon natural history as a context in which to measure today's experiences. That we can today speak precisely about the threats that global warming poses to the planet depends on the existence of historical records and our newfound abilities to analyze cores of ice plucked from depths of glaciers. In the ice, the erosion evidenced in the Grand Canyon, meteor craters, and the fossil record, we see the workings of natural history and experience our small place in the universe. Postmodernity demands that we see the relationships between Wallerstein's structural time and the earth's geological space and evolutionary time because our society is set on a course to make human and natural history coincide at a real endpoint of history in which we will produce not a philosophical but a real "last man."

Existing in these long stretches of time are individuals—the "dust" of history. In postmodern culture, individuals are trapped as consumers of a disorienting hyperreality. This is a culture in which an author such as Fukuyama can write a blockbuster whose popularity no doubt hangs on its surreal celebration of the status quo at precisely the moment when the status quo has become evidently untenable and unpraiseworthy. This is a culture in which even the significant events of the immediate past are irretrievable by normal historical means, and in place of history we are given Stone's and Lee's funhouse hall of mirrors. That the mirrors are distorted—and no one denies this, least of all Stone or Lee—makes the task of positioning ourselves "in history" as difficult as the even more pressing need to orient ourselves toward history.

This, then, is the place we find ourselves: living on after the idea of the "end of history" has been popularized (and a bit stale as a result), faced with the prospects for the real actuality of an end to human history in our own lifetime or that of our children and left watching entertaining Hollywood movies about what happened a few years before we were born. What is needed in such a time-space location is access to the means of real historiography (reason) and the means to participate in radical social change (freedom). In this sense, the problem of the degradation of the public sphere intersects with the problem of the end of history because without a space in which to act toward and fundamentally change postmodern social institutions, a democratic history cannot be effected. Unfortunately, neither threat to the sociological imagination we have thus far examined bears obvious or easy solutions.

Notes

1. Jean Baudrillard, *Baudrillard Live: Selected Interviews,* ed. Mike Gane (London: Routledge, 1993), 160, emphasis in original.

2. C. Wright Mills, *The Sociological Imagination* (Oxford, U.K.: Oxford University Press, 1959), 3-4.

3. Ibid., 128.

4. Important sources include David Harvey, *The Condition of Postmodernity: An Enquiry into the Origins of Cultural Change* (Cambridge, U.K.: Basil Blackwell, 1989) and Anthony Giddens, *The Constitution of Society: Outline of the Theory of Structuration* (Berkeley: University of California Press, 1984).

5. Harvey, *The Condition of Postmodernity,* 205.

6. C. Wright Mills, *The Sociological Imagination,* 167.

7. Ibid., page 166, where Mills wrote: "All sociology worthy of the name is 'historical sociology.' It is, in Paul Sweezy's excellent phrase, an attempt to write 'the present as history.' "

8. Francis Fuyukama, *The End of History and the Last Man* (New York: Free Press, 1992).

9. Immanuel Wallerstein, *The End of the World as We Know It: Social Science for the Twenty-First Century* (Minneapolis: University of Minnesota Press, 1999).

10. Fuyukama, *The End of History and the Last Man,* xiv.

11. Ibid.
12. Ibid.
13. Ibid, xiv-xv.
14. Ibid., xv.
15. Ibid., xx.
16. Ibid., xx, emphasis added.
17. Ibid., xi.
18. Wallerstein, *The End of the World as We Know It,* ix.
19. Ibid., 235.
20. Ibid.
21. Ibid., 236.
22. Ibid., especially pages 192-201.
23. Ibid., 124.
24. Ibid., especially pages 7-18.
25. Ibid., 1.
26. Ibid., 130-1.
27. Ibid., 131.
28. Ibid.
29. Ibid.
30. Ibid., 132.
31. Ibid.
32. Ibid., 2.
33. Ibid., 4.
34. Ibid.
35. See Immanuel Wallerstein, *Utopistics: Or, Historical Choices of the Twenty-First Century* (New York: The New Press, 1998), especially pages 35-64.
36. Oliver Stone, "Splinters to the Brain," an interview with the editors of *National Perspectives Quarterly,* in *At Century's End,* ed. Nathan P. Gardels (La Jolla, C.A.: ALTI Publishing, 1995), 224.
37. Ibid., 222.
38. Ibid.
39. Ibid., 224.
40. Oliver Stone, "A Fimmaker's Credo: Some Thoughts on Politics, History, and the Movies," in *Mass Politics: The Politics of Popular Culture,* ed. Daniel M. Shea (New York: Worth, 1999), 140.
41. Stone, "Splinters to the Brain," 224.
42. Ibid., 227.
43. Stone, "A Filmmaker's Credo," 138.
44. Ibid., 139.
45. Theodor W. Adorno, "The Meaning of Working through the Past," in *Critical Models: Interventions and Catchwords,* ed. Henry W. Pickford (New York: Columbia University Press, 1998), 83.
46. Michael R. Beschloss, *The Crisis Years: Kennedy and Khrushchev, 1960-1963* (New York: Edward Burlingame Books, 1991), 658, emphasis added.
47. Stone, "Splinters to the Brain," 223.
48. Ibid., 226.
49. Ibid., 224-5.
50. Michael Eric Dyson, *Making Malcolm: The Myth and Meaning of Malcolm X* (New York: Oxford University Press, 1995), 142.
51. Ibid.
52. Ibid, 143-4.

10

Sociology without Society

A reflection on freedom that concerns itself with the meaning of individual existence and the destiny of the human species must make reference to both collective processes *and subjective experience in everyday life.*

—*Alberto Melucci*[1]

The forces working against the sociological imagination exist not only outside of sociology (as in society's degradation of its public life and in the loss of history) but
also within sociology itself. The sociological imagination is not synonymous with a
generic sociological perspective. It is not a self-consciousness that conceives social
systems as its sole object of study. Instead, sociology that is guided by a sociological
imagination pursues the intricate relationships between changing social structures
and myriad individual experiences within structured social situations. Following
from this, the point of mapping these relationships is not to render a frozen picture of
a thing-like social reality. The point is always to instill within the many potential
mapmakers an accurate sense of their own location and their own potential to work
from within this location to recreate the world.

If sociology fails to integrate analyses of collective life with the self-conscious
actors of everyday life, then we confront the ironic problem the American sociologist Alan Wolfe calls "sociology without society."[2] In his book *Whose Keeper? Social Science and Moral Obligation,* Wolfe contends that sociology's special obligation is to the study of the necessary moral basis of society and to the study of the
active and ongoing process by which people—average people—make the moral di-

mension of society happen day after day, year in and year out. In Wolfe's view, sociology should be a study of people as they interact and relate with other people.

The Problem

As straightforward as this seems, sociologists, Wolfe argues, often fail in this obligation to study people's complex and morally-soaked relationships with others. In Wallerstein, for example, average people are conceived as powerless and fearful victims of large-scale "historical systems." In Fukuyama, they are not much different. To critics such as Norman Denzin, Cornel West, and Michael Schawlbe, even C. Wright Mills lost touch with actual people, their daily lives, their values, and their interactions. Did Mills listen to the voices of the "little people"? Did he offer them a "prophetic pragmatism"? Did he engage those whom he was purportedly serving in a "heartfelt conversation"? In taking it big, Mills lost his focus, or so goes this criticism.

There is truth in this criticism of Mills. Did Mills comment on the early phases of the American civil rights movement? Barely at all.[3] Did Mills actually interview the clerks discussed in his classic book *White Collar*? No. In fact, he more or less plagiarized his central analytical concepts from a student paper![4] Did Mills spend much time in the homes or neighborhoods of the people who formed the basis of his jointly-written book *The Puerto Rican Journey*? No. He merely rode around Spanish Harlem in a jeep (quickly surveying the scene) and relied on others to conduct the interviews that he would later analyze and interpret.[5] Honestly, Mills spent relatively little time systematically engaged *with* people *in* society, and it is therefore not surprising that he rarely included the voices of actual so-called little people in his work.

Nonetheless, Mills spoke for them and wrote as though he intimately understood their lives. For example, in the first paragraph of *The Sociological Imagination*, Mills described what people sense and feel:

> Nowadays men often feel that their private lives are a series of traps. They sense that within their everyday worlds, they cannot overcome their troubles, and in this feeling, they are often quite correct: What ordinary men are directly aware of and what they try to do are bounded by the private orbits in which they live; their visions and their powers are limited to the close-up scenes of job, family, neighborhood; in other milieux, they move vicariously and remain spectators. And the more aware they become, however vaguely, of ambitions and of threats which transcend their immediate locales, the more trapped they seem to feel.[6]

Nowhere does Mills base these claims on research with ordinary people, on interviews with them, or the results of fieldwork among them. But this did not prevent Mills from eventually offering a withering description of ordinary people as potential "Cheerful Robots."

Wolfe maintains that depopulated views of society, such as those produced by Wallerstein, Fukuyama, and even C. Wright Mills, are the outcome of a sociological perspective that attends primarily to the workings of the modern state and the capitalist market or to the integration of both systems working together. Sociologists thus tread on the economist's and political scientist's territory and turn sociology into "political economy," forgetting or merely assuming the existence of such phenomena as "trust, altruism, and empathy,"[7] which are the product of neither states nor markets even though they are essential to the workings of both. Trust, altruism, and empathy do not simply exist in a realm apart from peoples' everyday lives. They are the result of people learning to act, as Wolfe puts it, as "moral agents," moral agents acting in the everyday realm of "civil society."[8] This latter sphere, civil society, or equivalently, society (as distinct from states and markets), should be, Wolfe maintains, the special focus of sociology, but sociologists often fail to realize this. As such, they often practice an ironic "sociology without society."

Can the possessor of the sociological imagination today afford to ignore people as active participants in the making of their society? In particular, can the possessor of the sociological imagination today ignore the processes through which people make moral bonds with one another and therein create the morally-soaked relationships of trust, altruism, empathy, and so much more? As Wolfe observed,

> Even though the market now organizes more activities in civil society, people still agree to serve on committees, run for local office, watch other people's children, contribute lavishly to potluck dinners, clean up their neighborhoods, restrain their wage demands, honor one another, observe traditions, have and raise children, return books to libraries, share facilities, marry for love, serve on juries, refuse bribes, fasten their seat belts, let others pass on the highway, give to charities, donate blood, serve larger portions, tip strangers they never expect to see again, pay back debts, offer refuge, help friends, and volunteer for dirty and difficult jobs.[9]

Furthermore,

> even though the welfare state now organizes many obligations to strangers collectively, some people still pay their taxes willingly, support volunteer efforts, rely on social networks, take care of their parents, and spend as much time with their children as they can. Civil society has certainly been trespassed upon by the market and the state, but it has not disappeared altogether.[10]

It is undeniable that people still do these things that Wolfe describes and that they do them, often and perhaps primarily, *not* because there may be money in it for them and *not* because they are compelled to do so by law or government regulation. People act as moral agents; people make innumerable sacrifices, display faith in others, and take other people's interests to heart because it is, they believe, the right thing to do.

What is more, most people understand themselves as having *learned* the hows and wherefores of moral life—what is right, what is wrong, what is success, what is failure—and they know that they have developed the capacity to act toward these moral rules, sometimes against them, sometimes even making them anew. In postmodern times, in other words, people know that the moral rules they learn to cherish as children exist for them as adults because they recreate them in their daily lives. Realizing their power as moral agents means also, however, realizing the complexity of moral choice and the social settings that constrain and shape these choices. Postmodern people are thus typically their own moral philosophers. The same is true for sociologists, who, in Wolfe's view, are "moral philosophers in disguise."[11]

Can we possess a sociological imagination and simply take all of this for granted? The answer, of course, is no. To do so would be to deny in theory what is evident in practice: people have agency, the power to act toward others, and a morality, which they originally take from others but which they themselves shape in their own self-directed life pursuits. People generally conduct themselves as moral agents within society. Although people must increasingly contend with complex social systems, particularly states and markets that are themselves more globally interconnected, average people are also actively engaged with the making and remaking of the civil society that lies within their reach.

There is an essential tradition in sociology that we have not yet explicitly introduced that focuses on this level of social experience. It is a distinctly American tradition of social theory, which, in many ways, stands apart from the European social theory of Marx, Weber, and Durkheim. This tradition emphasizes exactly the realm of social life identified by Wolfe as sociology's raison d'etre. Here, we encounter the classic teachings of American pragmatist philosophy, particularly the social-psychology of George Herbert Mead (1863-1931). We also find the fruits of community-based and typically qualitative research made famous under the heading of "Chicago School" sociology (because Mead and many of his likeminded sociological brethren worked at the University of Chicago and conducted numerous studies of everyday life in that great American city). It is our contention, then, that the sociological imagination is threatened today by any effort to suppress its roots in this pragmatic background and in this "Chicago" style of sociological practice because to ignore this tradition is tantamount to denying the importance of society itself.

This type of sociology is typically thick in the sense that it is based on an immersion in people's lives and numerous one-on-one conversations, or both. It is thought that these are the best means available for a sociologist to make sense of how other people are making sense of their lives: one has to ask them (and then listen carefully to what is said) and/or one has to live in the same situations that they, the so-called research subjects, live in, but pay special attention to the situation, which they may more or less take for granted. In-depth interviews and participant observation, then, are the primary vehicles for this type of sociological research. The result is often called an "ethnography," which means a rich portrait of an observed way of life. Ethnographies often read like literary works, but the point is not simply to tell people's story but to tell an accurate, reliable, and sociologically meaningful story based on what is really happening in people's lives. The value of this type of sociology is perhaps best revealed by looking closely at an exemplary manifestation.

Sociology with Society

Consider the work of Elijah Anderson, one of America's best known and most respected urban ethnographers. Anderson spends much of his time away from his duties at the University of Pennsylvania hanging out in Laundromats and on street corners in so-called "inner city" neighborhoods and talking with people. He analyzes what Mills would call the "close-up scenes of job, family and neighborhood." Anderson's 1999 book *Code of the Street: Decency, Violence, and the Moral Life of the Inner City* begins, for example, with a stroll down the eight and one-half miles of Germantown Avenue in Philadelphia.[12] This is no leisurely and aimless sojourn. The story Anderson is about to tell is grounded in more than four years—*four years*—of careful, local study, but it is also meshed with many other research experiences and is informed by broader sociological analysis. In other words, this is no drive-by sociology. It is on this basis that Anderson can claim that "the story of Germantown Avenue can . . . serve in many respects as a metaphor for the whole city."[13] Indeed, for Anderson, Philadelphia is just one case in a larger story about urban America at the beginning of a new century.

Anderson takes his reader by the hand. His focus, he explains, is violence. One could look for innumerable other things along Germantown Avenue in Philadelphia, but the nature of violence is what Anderson set outs to depict and analyze.

Our tour of Germantown Avenue will focus both on the role of violence in the social organization of the communities through which the avenue passes and on how violence is revealed in the interactions of people up and down the street. The avenue, as we shall see, is a natural continuum characterized largely by a code of civility at one end and a code of conduct regulated by the threat of violence—the code of the street—at the other.[14]

Germantown Avenue starts in an affluent part of Philadelphia, Chestnut Hill, and passes through Mount Airy, Germantown, Vernon Park, intersects with Chelton, Broad, and then Tioga Street, and further down a predominantly black ghetto and then a Hispanic ghetto, finally ending just north of Philadelphia's downtown. Along the way, Anderson tells the story of each section of the avenue. What is life like on this part of the street? What do people do? How exactly do they interact with one another? What sort of structures (homes, businesses, schools, playgrounds, and so forth) are visible? What can all of this tell us about the social organization of the street at any particular spot and the role that violence plays in this social organization?

In Chestnut Hill, "often called the 'suburb in the city,' " we find mostly "affluent and educated white people" living in mostly large, single-family homes "surrounded by lawns and trees."[15] The business district features a Borders bookstore (indicating a market for people who read) as well as gourmet food shops, jewelry stores, boutiques, a farmer's market, and lots of Range Rovers and Lexuses. Regarding people's interactions in Chestnut Hill, Anderson reports that "a pleasant ambiance prevails—an air of civility."[16]

Of course, Anderson also sees what is not present in Chestnut Hill. He observes few people who are not, by virtue of their cars, clothes, and mannerisms, evidently middle class. He does not see billboards featuring advertisements for cheap liquor or takeout stores that sell beer. He does not observe businesses and homes with windows and doors covered by security bars designed to be noticeable and decorative.[17] He does not observe teenage boys walking around with open beer bottles in their hands or cars stopping in the middle of the street and holding up traffic just so the driver can yell cat-calls at women passersby. These types of scenes would suggest a different type of social organization, one more edgy and dangerous. These types of scenes are not typical in Chestnut Hill, which operates as a "civil" civil society, but these scenes are typical in neighborhoods further down the avenue.

Anderson's is not a picture painted in black and white. Chestnut Hill is the home of many middle-class or wealthier black families as well as white ones, but black families experience this neighborhood differently than do their white, middle-class counterparts. For them, there is extra scrutiny when they enter a store; for them, there is the occasional patronization at the hands of service workers. Few black people are employed in these Chestnut Hill business establishments, but middle-class black shoppers do little more than note and politely accept this fact, even if it also causes them to not feel "completely welcome" in this part of Philadelphia.[18]

Just south of Chestnut Hill is Mount Airy. This is a distinct "social milieu" because Anderson can observe a change in the racial mix of the people (more black people), in the nature of the business establishments (not as upscale), and in behavior on the street (less security, more apprehension). In keeping with his main theme, Anderson notes the following:

> A sign that we are in a different social setting is that exterior bars begin to appear on the store windows and riot gates show up on the doors—at first on businesses such as a state-run liquor store. Pizza parlors, karate shops, takeout stores that sell beer, and store-front organizations such as neighborhood health care centers appear— establishments not present in Chestnut Hill. There are discount stores of various sorts, black barbershops, and other businesses that cater both to the black middle class and to employed working-class and poorer blacks.[19]

The observable street behavior is also different:

> Many of the black middle-class youths use the street as a place to gather and talk with their friends, and they adopt the clothing styles of the poorer people farther down the avenue. So people who are not familiar with black people are sometimes unable to distinguish between who is law-abiding and who is not. The resulting confusion appears to be a standing problem for the police and local store owners, and it may lead to a sense of defensiveness among middle-class residents who fear being violated or robbed. But promising protection on the street, it is a confusion that many youths seem not to mind and at times work to encourage.[20]

Suddenly, in just a few blocks, the threat of violence has apparently and subtly increased. Why else would store fronts feature "riot gates," or why else would young black men want to look potentially threatening (even if they have no intention of threatening anyone) if these were not forms of self-protection from violence? The code of the street, as it were, has changed.

Mount Airy is still a middle-class neighborhood, but economic well-being deteriorates as Anderson continues his movement down Germantown Avenue. He notices everything he can, including the increasing sloppiness of paint jobs on otherwise "beautiful old buildings" and "a prominent billboard" that "warns that those who commit insurance fraud go to jail."[21] Further on, he finds "check-cashing agencies and beeper stores as well as more small takeout stores . . . selling beer, cheesesteaks, and other snack food."[22] He also comes across more boarded-up or gated windows and more riot gates across doorways. On the street, behavior has shifted again: "Here people watch their backs and are more careful how they present themselves."[23] No one wants to appear to be an "easy target."[24] This is Germantown Avenue as it passes through a racially mixed, working-class neighborhood.

Further on, then, the deterioration in both the physical and social landscape continues. There are more vacant lots and more young people loitering on street corners: "a charred McDonald's sign rises above a weed-covered lot."[25] There are police cars in evidence, parked or slowly driving past the young folks standing around. There is also a park, which is cared for by local residents. They plant flowers; but in this same park, during the day, there are "couples 'making time' " and "men drink alcoholic beverages out of paper sacks."[26] At night, the park is a place where drug deals are made. Residents understand this park as a "staging area"; activities that occur here "set the stage for other activities, which may be played out either on the spot . . . or else in less conspicuous locations."[27] For example, "a verbal altercation in Vernon Park may be settled with a fight, with or without gunplay, down a side street."[28] The people in Vernon Park are actors consciously displaying images and playing roles for the benefit of others, images and roles designed, in large part, to thwart violence against them. Anderson summarizes his reading of this neighborhood: "the people of Germantown are overwhelming committed to civil behavior, behavior based on trust and the rule of law, yet there is a sense that violence is just below the surface in some pockets of the community."[29]

How would one behave in a community that was overwhelmingly civil but also where violence is just below the surface? Anderson asks Mr. Don Moses, described as an "old head of the black community." Moses tells Anderson the following:

> Keep your eyes and ears open at all times. Walk two steps and look back. Watch your back. Prepare yourself verbally and physically. Even if you have a cane, carry something. The older people do carry something, guns in sheaths. They can't physically fight no more, so they carry a gun.[30]

For Anderson, this bespeaks a "code," a "form of regulation of social interaction in public."[31] If one lives in this community, one must behave in accordance with its code (i.e., its moral rules) or else invite violence. One would not, for example, stare at the young men conducting business in the park at night. In Chestnut Hill, in contrast, one might refrain from staring simply to be polite, not because staring would invite violence.

Indeed, as Anderson notes, it is far too easy for Chestnut Hill residents to get a faulty impression of the working-class neighborhoods of Germantown Avenue.

> Not venturing to look below the surface, they [Chestnut Hills residents driving by] take in a sea of black faces, the noise, the seeming disorder, and the poverty. When reading about urban violence, they associate it with places like this. In fact, this neighborhood is not as violent as they assume. To be sure, hustlers, prostitutes, and

drug dealers are in evidence, but they coexist with—and are indeed outnumbered by—working people in legitimate jobs who are trying to avoid trouble.[32]

These scenes do not, however, capture the social organization of truly poor city neighborhoods. As Anderson continues down Germantown Avenue, he observes increasing social and physical deterioration, which is related to the increasing impoverishment of the residents.

> As in Chestnut Hill, merchandise is often displayed on the sidewalk, but here it is under the watchful eye of unsmiling security guards. The noise level here is also much louder. Cars drive by with their stereo systems blaring. Farther down, young people walk down the street or gather on someone's stoop with their boom boxes vibrating, the bass turned way up. On adjacent streets, open-air drug deals occur, prostitutes ply their trade, and boys shoot craps, while small children play in trash-strewn abandoned lots. This is the face of persistent urban poverty.[33]

Here also a "women simply stops her car in the middle of the street, waiting for her man to emerge from a barbershop. She waits for ten minutes, holding up traffic."[34] In Chestnut Hill, this would be an outrage. But here, "no one complains, no one honks a car horn; people simply go around her, for they know that to complain is to risk an altercation, or at least heated words," which, everyone knows, could even "escalate into warfare."[35] Since the local police pay little attention to the everyday fears that besiege this community, people know they have to obey the code, defend themselves if necessary, and eke out a life worth living the best way they can. Although they are only eight miles from Chestnut Hill, they are a world apart.

Amid this edgy life at the end of Germantown Avenue, there is still considerable social organization and reminders of social organization now fading. Obeying the code of this street by not honking car horns works to lessen violence, not make it more likely. Moreover, Anderson finds many older people, mostly women, raising children to be law-abiding and to follow mainstream values. He finds vibrant churches and kids who are set on upward social mobility. He finds "a freshly painted 'memorial' for a young victim of street violence" near a hotel "that rents rooms by the hour," a community garden (in a neighborhood where "the idea of a war zone springs to mind"), historical buildings and historical landmarks (such as a site on the Underground Railroad) not far from "a newly built gated community," and giant buildings once home to bustling industrial factories that are now "one by one falling victim to arson."[36] "Finally," writes Anderson,

> we reach the other end of Germantown Avenue in the midst of a leveled area about a block from the river and over-shadowed by the elevated interstate highway that

now allows motorists to driver over North Philadelphia rather than through it—thereby ignoring its street life, its inhabitants, and its problems.[37]

This is an abbreviated account of just the first few pages of a more than 300-page book. Anderson's full analysis expands to the underlying structural causes of the observed moral structure of street life and thus to a broad indictment of prevailing economic arrangements and state policy. Abandoned factories are concrete evidence of economic and political policy. Substandard housing, ill-conceived urban renewal programs with their highways slicing through city neighborhoods, emergency rooms filling up with shooting victims and drug overdoses—these are fragments of life that are all related to broad economic and social trends and to political decisions and nondecisions.

Philadelphia alone, for example, has lost more than 160,000 high-paying, low-skill manufacturing jobs during the past 30 years—more than sixty 60 percent of its industrial job base—due to many complicated political and economic factors, including the U.S. economy's integration in an increasingly postindustrial world economy.[38] Who would think that this fact would not adversely affect the lives of inner-city Philadelphians, who also have to contend with racism and segregation? It is as close as social scientists come to laboratory experimentation: change one variable, say, rapidly remove more than sixty percent of a community's job base and then observe the effects of this change in the lives of the people on whom this experiment is conducted. Would we not hypothesize that there would be a causally related deterioration in the community's physical as well as social fabric? Would we not expect people to respond to this economic crisis by inventing a new, perhaps even oppositional, culture?

This is why Anderson concludes his book by calling for "jobs that pay a living wage" and "political leadership that articulates the problem and presses hard to build coalitions that invest themselves in efforts to secure full inner-city enfranchisement."[39] Anderson notes the tragedy of the current situation in the following:

A vicious cycle has . . . been formed. The hopelessness many young inner-city black men and women feel, largely as a result of endemic joblessness and alienation, fuels the violence they engage in. This violence then serves to confirm the negative feelings many whites and some middle-class blacks harbor toward the ghetto poor, further legitimating the oppositional culture and the code of the street for many alienated young blacks. But when jobs disappear and people are left poor, highly concentrated, and hopeless, the way is paved for the underground economy to become a way of life, an unforgiving way of life organized around a code of violence and predatory activity. Only by reestablishing a viable mainstream economy in the inner city, particularly one that provides access to jobs for young inner-city men and women, can we encourage a positive sense of the future. Unless serious efforts are made to address this problem and the cycle is broken, attitudes on both sides will become increasingly hardened, and alienation and violence, which claim victims black and white, poor and affluent, will likely worsen.[40]

Local and Global

Anderson concentrates on providing a portrait of people in what Mills called the "close-up worlds" of social milieux, but even though he described the interactions among people in specific social settings, he also focused attention on the relationship between these individual lives and the changing structure of American capitalist society—its class system, technological shifts, racial segregation, and the social policies that have affected all of these. To understand Germantown Avenue, Anderson shows, it is necessary to place it in the context of Philadelphia, the United States, and indeed the world system as a whole. This requires an exact and exacting form of imagination, a sociological imagination.

Anderson's intent is to stimulate a quality of mind that relates the very abstract to the very particular, so as to spur in the reading public a sophisticated (because sociologically mediated) understanding of everyday street violence in an American city. Furthermore, if we understand the nature of the social problem, then we stand a chance of restructuring our social systems in such a way as to eliminate the problem as it is experienced in civil society.

Of course, this assumes that we want to eliminate the problem of urban violence, but who is "we" and on what values would we act? Whose interests are at stake? If solutions to the problems of very poor people in America's cities require higher taxes, who will pay them? If the solution requires living wage jobs, who is going to pay these higher wages? Jobs accessible to people with few skills, little formal education, and often without access to practical transportation? Who is going to locate a new factory in a so-called bombed-out section of Philadelphia? What is more, what if the basic structure of the capitalist economy produces inequalities as a normal matter of course—is constructed, in other words, to polarize wealth and income since these are construed as necessary incentives for competition, risk-taking, and self-gain? What if the political system is so constructed so as to suppress the voices of the least powerful and amplify the voices of those who enjoy the fruits of the status quo?

All the people working to be "decent" up and down Germantown Avenue cannot prevail against a political-economic system designed to thwart their efforts and prevent them, as a society, from realizing their cherished values. As Mills noted,

In so far as an economy is so arranged that slumps occur, then the problem of unemployment becomes incapable of personal solution. In so far as war is inherent in the nation-state system and in the uneven industrialization of the world, the ordinary individual in his restricted milieu will be powerless—with or without psychiatric aid—to solve the troubles this system or lack of system imposes upon him. In so far as the family as an institution turns women into darling little slaves and men into their chief providers and unweaned dependents, the problem of a satisfactory marriage remains incapable of purely private solution. In so far as the overdeveloped megalopolis and the overdeveloped automobile are built-in features of the overdeveloped society, the issues of urban living will not be solved by personal ingenuity and private wealth.[41]

If social problems are caused by a "crisis in institutional arrangements," then individual efforts will affect, at best, individuals.[42] Individual people acting as moral agents will be systematically thwarted in their efforts to do the right thing, even if they may positively or negatively affect this or that small-scale fragment of life within the whole of society.

Thus even when we pay attention to civil society, note how people form moral bonds with others and in this way "glue" society together below the realm of politics and economics. Sociologists, at least those possessed of a sociological imagination, cannot ignore the workings of states and markets nor assume that average people can transform their structure. It is, in other words, one thing to show that people still attend meetings, vote, and care for other people's children and quite another to question the importance of these activities from the point of view of our dying world and our dystopian everyday lives.

Recall that the proles in Orwell's *1984* were more or less free to do whatever they wanted. Since they had little political power and plenty of everyday distractions—notably, their workaday experience, but also extras such as beer, prole feed (e.g., pornography), and telescreens keeping an eye on things—there was no need for The Party to actively or openly suppress them. Their petty crimes could be safely overlooked since, for the most part, the proles could only victimize one another. Besides, the more well-to-do and politically pivotal Outer Party looked down on the proles, found them stupid and disgusting, and rarely if ever ventured into the prole quarters of London and thus had little or no personal experience that might disturb their stereotypes of the proles. Likewise, urban street violence does not threaten the overall functioning of the American political-economy. In the absence of a widespread concern for these specific people by the middle and upper classes, there is no systematic compulsion to address this problem in a manner that would in fact get at the roots of the problem. It is as though Anderson is describing the life of America's proles, the surplus and superfluous people and the politically disenfranchised, whose quality of life is not critical for the overall maintenance of social order.

Even if Anderson's relatively radical democratic social policy wish list were somehow enacted tomorrow—living wage, entry level jobs by the hundreds of thousands for inner-city dwellers, equal education, and an equal political voice for all—there would still exist people whose lives have been fundamentally, perhaps irrevocably, damaged either by overt forms of violence or by violence by the self-proscribed violence of drug addiction or educational retardation. Even a sudden and dramatic change in America's social structure could not fully redeem or make right the damage done. Of course, as Anderson notes, this damage is often itself used to justify inaction in the classic mode of using the harms caused by oppression to justify the continuation of oppression: "See, these people are messed up, their lives are not worth saving. Look at how they talk, the way they dress, their menacing manner. Look at them. They are responsible for their own behavior. We owe them nothing." This is a common form of what William Ryan famously called "blaming the victim."[43] It is akin to blaming the Orwell's proles for their enjoyment of Prole Feed and beer, when it is the Party and its total power in an organized society, legitimized in large part by the anti-prole prejudice of the Outer Party, that keeps the proles living as proles.

Even if the structural change Anderson desires were to occur, it would do nothing to affect the larger issues of the dying world. In fact, it could exacerbate them. Millions of new jobs? That is, millions of new workers creating products and services and using their wages to add to America's consumption of resources? Expanding the already most overdeveloped "overdeveloped economy"? Anderson follows a predictable "liberal" pattern of analysis, where the solution to the social problem is pegged on the continued development of existing social institutions. More economic expansion and more political democracy is posited as the solution to the oppositional "code of the street." Simply, if America wants less urban violence, then we should give people steady and well-paying employment and a genuine voice in the public sphere. Cultural changes will follow. Behavior will change. But this ignores the facts of the dying world.

Poverty, racism, and violence in Philadelphia may not be related to the price of tea in China (at least not very directly or meaningfully), but these phenomena are, as Anderson argues, related directly to the structure of the American political-economic system, which is itself tightly integrated with the rest of the world political-economic system, and the structure of the world political-economic system is directly responsible for global ecological crises. In reverse, then, solutions to the global ecological crises demand structural change in the world political-economic system, in particular the U.S. political-economic system (which leads the world) and therefore will affect people living in Philadelphia. Thus it is legitimate to read Anderson's local and national political vision in terms of a larger politics and to ask if his solution is a partial and merely short-term solution or, for that matter, another problem in disguise. Viewed in terms of the current American political scene, his proposals are indeed radical, but are they radical enough? This is a moral and not just a political question.

In charting an individual course of action, however, it is not possible to directly confront "the system" much less the global system, which exists only in vast relations between disparate and distant points of action. In John Steinbeck's *The Grapes of Wrath*, for example, Grandpa Joad wants to shoot someone for the fate befallen his family, who are being evicted from their Oklahoma farm, but one cannot shoot The Great Depression. Given also that social milieux are circumscribed and constrain individual action, it is difficult for most people to rise above the particularities of their immediate circumstances to survey the way that milieux are stitched together to form the fabric of whole societies and whole societies further interconnected across vast spaces and through countless individuals' lives. For these two reasons, attention to the particular cannot become a dogmatic embrace of the merely local much less the merely individual.

The Division of Sociological Labor

Anderson himself did not do the research that produced a picture of inner-city joblessness. Nor does Anderson's book contain any mention of the fact that at a minimum, 100 species of plants and animals are being extinguished each day, and it would be odd if it did, even though Anderson is undoubtedly aware of this and similar facts. Although Anderson's study requires a sociological imagination, not all things that one can and must understand with the sociological imagination will be present in a single book or even a series of books. Sociologists, even those mindful of the importance of civil society, analyze and write at varying levels of abstractions and on many selected aspects of the totality. Some concentrate their energies at a level "above" (to employ a metaphor for "increasingly abstract") ethnography but also learn from the ethnographies that sociologists such as Anderson write, and perhaps they incorporate this learning into their own more abstract studies. In this way, it is possible to retain a strong, empirical connection to actual people and to the moral underpinnings of institutions and social systems. Mills may have not directly interviewed people living in Spanish Harlem for his book *The Puerto Rican Journey*, but he did study what they said to others and on this basis wrote an account that even the actual interviewers felt was perfectly appropriate and well-grounded in their experience.[44] Although *The Sociological Imagination* does not contain a single snippet from an interview subject, Mills had plenty of experience and plenty of sociological data stored up to make his work empirical. As Mills wrote, "the problem of empirical verification is 'how to get down to facts' yet not get overwhelmed by them; how to anchor ideas to facts but not to sink the ideas."[45] The possessor of the sociological imagination is as much concerned with ideas as facts; the trick is to bring them into a meaningful relation to one another and this involves a lot of difficult choices.

It is obviously impossible to have ethnographies about every bit of society. Anderson spent four years on just a few parts of Philadelphia. Lives are short. We must depend on a division of labor in which some people study x and others y, with some at level z and others at level q. We must be willing to generalize from specific studies and read Anderson's work for what it might tell us about Detroit and Baltimore and not just Philadelphia. The possessor of the sociological imagination will inevitably participate in this division of labor, both as a moral actor and as a student or researcher or reader, even though the sociological imagination will always pull its possessor in all directions and require that relative weight be assigned to what is worth knowing, what is urgently in need of knowing, and what one can, in a short lifetime, contribute to these areas. By what scale should these matters be weighed?

According to Mills—and this is very important—one must first risk a sense of the whole, not wait to methodically build this up piecemeal. One must, in other words, quickly capture a working sense of the actual, historical totality of social and cultural experience, make sense of one's historical period within this expanse, and acquire an empirical understanding of the most important features of its social structure. Only then can one pick specific points of reference and fields of inquiry, and then questions about one's starting point must be fed back into the sociological imagination for critical self-examination. Nothing can be left unscrutinized, even the details of one's own biography and values. This is a significant part of what the American sociologist Alvin W. Gouldner meant when he insisted, in his famous 1970 book *The Coming Crisis of Western Sociology,* that all future sociology must be "reflexive sociology."[46] Sociologists must know where they come from, but it is essential to risk a sense of the whole and to project the outlines of the empirically unverifiable total system.

Sociologists must submit to a division of labor: no single sociologist can conduct years of field research in Philadelphia *and* study the intricate details of the crisis in world population, global warming, and species extinction. Perhaps the onus of the sociological imagination falls more heavily on the reader of sociology than on its producers. The reader must be the one who possesses the quality of mind that moves back and forth between empirical details and close-up case studies and the broad trends and structural changes that are the essence of worldwide historical social change. Readers have to fill in the holes that are the inevitable result of myriad and far-flung individual research efforts. Readers need a sociological imagination to accomplish this feat.

Anderson's implicit liberal politics is a case in point. How would his "politics"—his orientation toward social power and social change—play out in a world with many other competing social problems? Those who can judge politics the best are those who can relate proposals to all salient political dilemmas in the world.

Sociology and Society

The sociological imagination, if it is anything, is a form of self-consciousness that mirrors the complexity of the world, reducing that complexity through conceptualization, but never so much so that the problems of milieux or the moral basis of everyday life falls from view or from memory. In the reverse direction, however, no matter how many years of fieldwork one conducts, it is not acceptable to become wholly invested in the local and everyday (what is right in front of our face) because this entails a studied blindness to the truly historical and global and not-as-yet. If the social world is highly complex and mediated, diverse and multilayered, and an ongoing process, so too does our mind require the ever-renewed effort to use our skills to analyze complexity, mediation, diversity, and varying levels of abstraction. On this basis, then, we can aspire to "read" the world.

Speaking of his intended audience, Mills wrote,

> What they need, and what they feel they need, is a quality of mind that will help them to use information and to develop reason in order to achieve lucid summations of what is going on in the world of what may be happening within themselves.[47]

After that, our individuals actions and their moral or political significance are for us to decide for ourselves. Wolfe stated,

> the distinctive contribution of a sociological approach to morality . . .is not to tell people what they ought to do in situations of moral complexity, but rather to help individuals discover and apply for themselves the moral rules they already, as social beings, possess.[48]

In the end, then, Wolfe's empirical claim, like Mills before him, is that civil society—sociology's distinctive field of inquiry, at least in its form as a moral or human science—"has not disappeared altogether." It is threatened from all sides, true, but people must be understood only as "cheerful robots" *in potentia.* In the meantime, people exist as moral agents, as social beings always already have learned moral rules—even if they are street rules as opposed to mainstream, middle-class rules—and sociology cannot afford to lose touch with these/the "people." It would make little sense to write books unless this was still true, and it would make no sense to attempt to "teach" the sociological imagination either, unless this was still the case. Sociology, it could be said, is fated to have faith in people living in civil society.

Notes

1. Alberto Melucci, *The Playing Self: Person and Meaning in the Planetary Society* (Cambridge, U.K.: Cambridge University Press, 1996), 4, emphasis added.

2. Alan Wolfe, *Whose Keeper? Social Science and Moral Obligation* (Berkeley: University of California Press, 1989), 187-211.

3. But see Kathryn Mills with Pamela Mills, eds., *C. Wright Mills: Letters and Autobiographical Writings* (Berkeley: University of California Press, 2000), 313-4 for Mills's own reflection on this point.

4. See Guy Oakes and Arthur J. Vidich, *Collaboration, Reputation, and Ethics in American Academic Life: Hans H. Gerth and C. Wright Mills* (Urbana: University of Illinois Press, 1999), especially 106-11.

5. See Rose K. Goldsen, "Mills and the Profession of Sociology," in *The New Sociology*, ed. Irving Louis Horowitz (New York: Oxford University Press, 1964), 88-93.

6. C. Wright Mills, *The Sociological Imagination* (Oxford, U.K.: Oxford University Press, 1959), 3.

7. Wolfe, *Whose Keeper?* 188.

8. Ibid., 19.

9. Ibid., 189.

10. Ibid.

11. Ibid., 23.

12. Elijah Anderson, *Code of the Street: Decency, Violence, and the Moral Life of the Inner City* (New York: Norton, 1999).

13. Ibid., 9 and 15.

14. Ibid., 15-6.

15. Ibid., 16.

16. Ibid.

17. Ibid., 18.

18. Ibid., 19.

19. Ibid.

20. Ibid., 20.

21. Ibid., 20-1.

22. Ibid., 21.

23. Ibid.

24. Ibid.

25. Ibid., 22.

26. Ibid.

27. Ibid.

28. Ibid.

29. Ibid., 23.

30. Ibid.

31. Ibid.

32. Ibid., 24.

33. Ibid., 26.

34. Ibid., 27.

35. Ibid., 26-7.

36. Ibid., 31-2.

37. Ibid., 32.

38. See William Julius Wilson, *When Work Disappears: The World of the New Urban Poor* (New York: Vintage, 1996), especially 29-30. Wilson states the following: "The manufacturing losses in some northern cities have been staggering. In the twenty-year period from 1967 to 1987, Philadelphia lost 64 percent of its manufacturing jobs; Chicago lost 60 percent; New York City, 58 percent; Detroit, 51 percent. In absolute numbers, these percentages represent the loss of 160,000 jobs in Philadelphia, 326,000 in Chicago, 520,000—over half a million—in New York, and 108,000 in Detroit."

39. Anderson, *Code of the Street,* 323-4.

40. Ibid., 325.

41. Mills, *The Sociological Imagination,* 10.

42. Ibid., 9.

43. William Ryan, *Blaming the Victim,* rev. ed. (New York: Vintage, 1976).

44. Goldsen, "Mills and the Profession of Sociology."

45. Mills, *The Sociological Imagination,* 125.

46. Alvin W. Gouldner, *The Coming Crisis of Western Sociology* (New York: Basic Books, 1970), especially 481-512.

47. Mills, *The Sociological Imagination,* 5.

48. Wolfe, *Whose Keeper?* 211.

IV

LOOKING BACK, LOOKING AHEAD

Epilogue

Sociology as Critical Theory of Society

Know that the problems of social science, when adequately formulated, must include both troubles and issues, both biography and history, and the range of their intricate relations. Within that range the life of the individual and the making of societies occur; and within that range the sociological imagination has its chance to make a difference in the quality of human life in our time.

—*C. Wright Mills*[1]

C. Wright Mills was a sociologist who imagined himself as a political writer. This is one way of expressing what it means to be a sociologist-as-critical theorist. Sociologists who are critical theorists are those whose self-defining purpose is to critically engage their world in the hope of changing it for the better. Their individual work as sociologists is always therefore conceived as a means for participating in the larger struggle of achieving individual liberation and social emancipation. They never separate their life or their work from this purpose. They never merely *do* sociology—engage in research, discuss theories, attend scholarly conferences, teach or write books—for its own sake. While they may conduct a variety of research projects, study numerous topics at varying levels via disparate methods of research, and teach, write books, and attend scholarly conferences, the overriding aim of their work and their lives is always emancipation. At least in Mills's reading of sociology's "classic tradition," this was always the way that the classic sociologists—Marx, Weber, Durkheim, and Mead among them—viewed themselves and conducted themselves in their work. For Mills, then, sociology originated as critical theory. It began with this pragmatic and emancipatory raison d'etre.

Sociologists who see themselves as critical theorists in this classic tradition are, like their predecessors, inevitably intellectuals. There is no need to blush when saying this because all it really means is that the primary and defining medium for their lives and their work is the realm of ideas. Intellectuals are people who care about ideas: the ways in which ideas are created, criticized, and put to use in social, cultural, and political life. Sociologists who are critical theorists thus generally set themselves the task of criticizing sets of ideas, in particular those that legitimize social oppression and confuse individuals about their own experience with social oppression. Such ideas or sets of ideas have traditionally been called "ideologies."

In effect, then, sociologists as critical theorists are critics of ideology. The hope is that, once stripped of its veneer of respectability and once shown as false or limiting, ideology will loose its power over individuals and groups of individuals. Thus freed to use their own minds, their own reason, and their own experience, people will also be able to better act toward oppressive social institutions and the oppressive conditions systematically created by these social institutions. In so doing, people can and will revolutionize society and recreate themselves for the better. In the parlance of common language, the point of sociology as critical theory is to "empower" people to act for themselves. This is just another way of talking about enlightenment and self-enlightenment vis-à-vis what Mills liked to call the "issues" and the "troubles" of the age.

It should be clear at this point that, while we have discussed a number of varying topics, the central and defining theme of this book is the importance of critical thinking itself. How do we conceive, conceptualize, analyze, in a phrase, *critically think about* the social world today? The topics are in and of themselves important, but here we have used them to illustrate the significance of critical sociological thinking.

The sociological imagination is a form of mind that leads to a very particular type of critical thinking. If we conceive of the interplay between individual biographies, social structures, and history making; if we often shift perspectives and attend to extreme experiences; and if we are as mindful of the totality of human experience as we are our own particular experience, we stand a chance of cognitively mapping the world, of representing it to ourselves in a way that can open our eyes and ears to the sight and sound of its unraveling. We awake in the midst of calamities, calamities involving billions of people as well as those living on the wrong end of Philadelphia's Germantown Avenue—preventable, unnecessary, and thus tragic calamities.

For that is the overriding point, after all. One does not work to acquire a sociological imagination for academic or leisurely fun. It may well be that there is pleasure and joy in the sheer fact of seeing and hearing the world anew, in the sheer fact of liberating one's mind from ignorance or socially imposed banality. Mills conceded that acquiring a sociological imagination can be exhilarating, that it portended "magnificent" lessons, and that it could also serve its possessor in at least a somewhat therapeutic manner, transforming sheer panic, for example, into a less damaging and more productive sensibility. But the possessor of the sociological imagination who did not, *in this world, at this time,* also accept responsibility for its critical uses would be a cynical person indeed. Given what is socially and historically given to us, the chief responsibility for those who come to possess the sociological imagination is to criticize the dominant ideologies that forestall, hold in check, suppress, and distort liberatory and emancipatory thinking. The sociological imagination tears down ideological barriers and thus creates a free space in the mind for new and better thinking about the world, which creates openings for inherently unpredictable forms of emancipatiory action. That is what freedom in human life is all about, that is what history making is all about, and that is what it means to possess reason and to use it in the making and remaking of society; this is what is meant by a life worth living, this is what the promise of enlightenment once entailed, this is where sociology originated, and this is what is meant by real-live utopian thinking.

The Challenges Ahead

What are the challenges that confront sociology as critical theory today? In his famous 1944 essay, "Theses on the Philosophy of History," Walter Benjamin wrote the following:

> This is how one pictures the angel of history. His face is turned toward the past. Where we perceive a chain of events, he sees one single catastrophe which heeps wreckage and hurls it in front of his feet. The angel would like to stay, awaken the dead, and make whole what has been smashed. But a storm is blowing from Paradise, it has got caught in his wings with such violence that the angel can no longer close them. This storm irresistibly propels him into the future to which his back is turned, while the pile of debris before him grows skyward. This storm is what we call progress.[2]

In his 1993 book *Postmodern Ethics,* Zygmunt Bauman commented on this passage:

> The dead will not be awakened, the smashed will not be made whole. The pile of debris will go on growing. Those who suffered, did. Those who got killed, will stay dead. It is the escaping from (or, rather, being blown away by) the horror of the irreversible and the irredeemable that seems to us—us who have been repelled—to be a "chain of events."[3]

Along these same lines, but at the level of natural (as opposed to human) history, Fredric Jameson observed the following in Theodor W. Adorno's work:

> For there is the nightmare of natural history that is even grislier than that of the human one; and it is this that the postmodern mind has been able to repress fairly successfully (save for biological death itself) for reasons that are scarcely mysterious: what better way to avoid being reminded of the nightmare of nature than to abolish nature altogether?
>
> Yet a glimpse into the interstices that not merely open to view the pecking order of all living species, a hideous eternity of domination and hierarchy designed at least to leave its subjects alive but also and finally the violence of nature itself, organisms obligated to eat their whole waking life long and to eat each other (in Adorno's most frequent characterization of it); this dizzying perspective brings with it a nausea more fundamental than the sight of malice with which humans attempt to culturalize their own internecine slaughter.[4]

Jameson wrote the following in his 1994 book, *The Seeds of Time*:

> Even after the "end of history," there has seemed to persist some historical curiosity of a generally systemic kind—rather than a merely anecdotal—kind: not merely to know what will happen next, but as a more general anxiety about the larger fate or destiny of our system or mode of production as such—about which individual experience (of a postmodern kind) tells us that it must be eternal, while our intelligence suggests this feeling to be most improbable indeed, without coming up with plausible scenarios as to its disintegration or replacement. It seems to be easier for us today to imagine the thoroughgoing deterioration of the earth and of nature than the breakdown of late capitalism; perhaps this is due to some weakness in our imaginations. I have come to think that the word *postmodern* ought to be reserved for thoughts of this kind.[5]

Certainly these are difficult passages to read—the reader is encouraged to read them more than once—but this is not surprising since Benjamin, Bauman, and Jameson are among the most challenging social thinkers of modern and postmodern times. But they are intelligible. Each strikes a blow at the notion of the end of history, and each seeks to open history making to us today.

In Benjamin, we find a criticism of our backward look at progress, whose victims are forgotten—killed a second time—when we think of history as merely an impersonal chain of events that leads, of all places, to us in the here and now. In Bauman, we are reminded that remembering is an ethical act, as he remembers Benjamin. We are thus positioned in history, not in an empty or linear or egocentric history but, rather, in a history filled with lost human beings in need of recovery and the only sort of redemption that, at this late date, can be offered to them. In Jameson, at first we remember Adorno's insight that nature is not just forgotten but is repressed and destroyed for our own short-sighted and ultimately self-destructive benefit. Then we see ourselves inexorably alienated from nature, for it does not (and never did) provide a model for a human life worth living. We are thus fated to take responsibility for ourselves, to stand on our own feet (if a landmine, real or metaphorical, has not removed them). Finally, Jameson notes that it is easier for us today to imagine a future ecological holocaust than the relatively mundane need to revolutionize our way of life, something that has happened many times in human history. Perhaps, he says, this is due to our lack of imagination.

The first challenge for the sociologist as critical theorist today is to develop the ability to understand the entwinement of human and natural history, to develop the ability to morally connect with those no longer present and those who are not-yet, and to develop the ability to imagine social change of an undramatic (relative to natural history), revolutionary sort. These are postmodern times; such systemic curiosity is very much needed. Remember James Lyon Bérubé and those like him that there is no such thing as Generation X and that this is a good thing and that religion is an eminently social, social institution. Remember also that history is and is not at its end, propaganda is ubiquitous and invades even the book in your hands, and sociology without society is as lifeless as what a cheerful robot would be if we ever were to mass produce one.

Yet we must also, as the American sociologist Ben Agger has argued, "prefigure a good society by our treating ourselves, each other, and nature well in the here and now."[6] Neither panic nor cynicism—understandable and common responses to our situation—are advisable, productive, or pleasant inner states to bear. We are necessarily bounded by our place in civil society, which is a moral order, and it is incumbent on us to act toward specific others in the here and now as we hope general human relationships will be when life is through with us. As students of social structure, we cannot assume that merely individual action in local milieux will spur change in society. We understand that the postmodern situation is, as Bauman described it, filled with "endemic ambivalence" that is "excruciatingly painful to live with." So we develop in ourselves the ability to successfully cope with this liminal space for, as Bauman also stressed, "postmodernity is the moral person's bane and chance at the same time"; it is "modernity without illusions."[7] What choice do we have as individuals?

The second challenge facing the sociologist as critical theory, then, is to care for our own minds and our own lives. Jackie Orr is a model; Jose Borain, perhaps, is not. The sociological imagination need not acquiesce before the postemotional world. Further critical and dispassionate reading and rereading of the works and authors referred to in this introductory text is needed, but one cannot forget to be alarmed by

Time magazine. Quiet and impersonal reflection on cold and impersonal statistics is needed, but so are warm feelings about wrong children and hot feelings about global warming. Passive listening to R.E.M. or other popular poets is good, but so is actively hearing what they say and always bearing in mind what the culture and the authenticity industry demand. It is possible to live with endemic ambivalence. It is possible to go about in this world with one's mind and one's feelings intact and in touch with each other. It is possible to act in this world as a human being and not as a cheerful robot. So it is our task to do so the best we can, or so it is our faith that, in actually existing civil society, this is still possible.

Finally, there is the matter of social structure itself. As an exact form of thinking, the sociological imagination needs precise and accurate moorings in social reality. This is essential and basic; the entire house of cards will crumble without it. One has to become intimately familiar with the fruits of careful research. One also has to develop the ability to assess what makes for reliable and care-filled research and what makes for unreliable, careless research. How much, exactly, is the earth's average temperature expected to rise during the next 100 years? How many species, exactly, are extinguished each and every day? How many more earths would be needed to create a social life for everyone in the world by London's standards? What is the distribution of income and wealth in the United States or in other countries or in the world as a whole? How many people have ingested Prozac? What is the United States's leading cash crop? How many Americans tan indoors every year? How many manufacturing jobs have been lost in Philadelphia in recent decades? How many people worldwide are defined as disabled? It is vitally important to know these facts and many more, lest our imaginations get the best of us and lest our mind's eye close to the world as it is constantly changing around us. It is also vital to learn how such facts are produced and communicated. Ross Gelbspan reminded us of the importance of this point.

The third and final challenge for the would-be sociologist as critical theory is to remain in close contact with empirical research. The complexity of the world always exceeds our ability to conceptualize it. The actions of people always make society different before the ink is dry on the latest study. Our understandings of what is actually happening in the world and in ourselves will become no better than myths, perhaps self-serving or even harmful myths, if we are not always ready to learn, even to learn something that might radically destabilize prior conceptualizations, assumptions, and moral commitments, indeed, radically destabilize our lives. The sociological imagination is a radical form of self-consciousness, but one must understand that its radicalism implies the possibility of its own radical reconfiguration and demise. Recall that it is not possible to logically deduce what will result from its widespread adoption any more than it is possible to know what young people today will do once oriented to the urgent issues and troubles of our time.

If one met the challenges of sociology as critical theory and thus attained a working sociological imagination, then one would be in a position to decide for one-self if, in fact, we live in a dying world where yesterday's dystopian visions are to-day's everyday life. Then one would be in a position to frame a sense of the totality, and from this initial projection, decide for oneself whether it is a context of delusion. One would then be in a position to act toward the world and toward oneself as a par-ticipant in the most important human science—perhaps the most important and ur-gent human endeavor of any kind—as a sociologically mindful and self-empowered individual. That this form of critical thinking about the social world should emerge among the young members of today's politically pivotal American middle class is a profoundly pressing matter, as there has never been a time in human history when so much is riding on the actions (or as it may be, inactions) of so few facing such great problems. The thought that there is little time to decide these matters, little room for maneuver, is what has all along framed this discussion.

Notes

1. C. Wright Mills, *The Sociological Imagination* (Oxford, U.K.: Oxford University Press, 1959), 226.

2. Walter Benjamin, "Theses on the Philosophy of History," in *Illuminations,* ed. Hannah Arendt (1944; reprint, New York: Shocken, 1969), 257-8.

3. Zygmunt Bauman, *Postmodern Ethics* (Cambridge, M.A.: Blackwell, 1993), 224.

4. Fredric Jameson, *Late Marxism: Adorno, or, The Persistence of the Dialectic* (London: Verso, 1990), 95-7.

5. Fredric Jameson, *The Seeds of Time* (New York: Columbia University Press, 1994), xi-xii, emphasis in original.

6. Ben Agger, *The Discourse of Domination* (Evanston, I.L.: Northwestern University Press, 1992), 13.

7. Zygmunt Bauman, *Life in Fragments* (Cambridge, M.A.: Blackwell, 1995), 3 and 8, and also *Postmodern Ethics,* 32.

A Personal Note

Writing this book spurred me to autobiographical reflection, in particular, to remember how it was that I came to be a sociologist writing a book that encourages readers to acquire and act on a sociological imagination. Some things are clear. While I never took a course in sociology as an undergraduate student, I was fortunate to have a few extraordinary educational experiences that pushed me to think in the ways that I do now. For example, in 1984, when I was a second-year student and 19 years old, I spent a semester in London, England. I had never previously traveled abroad, and so London and the rest of the United Kingdom was a revelation to me.

I was, for example, exposed to a wide variety of political ideas. In one course, we met with representatives from Britian's Conservative Party, Labour Party, and Social-Democratic Party. We also met with the leader of the British Communist Party. We read a variety of books authored by leading political thinkers in British society, from the conservative sociologist Ralf Darhendorf, who was the director of the London School of Economics and Political Science (L.S.E.), to the radical sociologist Ralph Miliband, a Marxist famous for his criticism of capitalist society and himself once a fixture at the L.S.E. Outside of the classroom, Britain was racked by a nationwide coal miners' strike. This was a bitter labor struggle that seemed to pit average workers against the stern and unsympathetic Conservative Party Prime Minister, Margaret Thatcher. Indeed, within days of arriving in London, I found myself sitting in the front row of a major demonstration when the city's transportation workers, who were also striking, gathered in Parliament Square to hear Labour Party Leader Neil Kinnock. Kinnock and his trade union allies made mention of me and my classmates in their speeches—"these young American students," "our cousins here in the front row." The atmosphere was electric. I do not recall if others felt as I did, but I was transformed. I believe that I acquired then and there an unshakeable feeling that, in this world, people were engaged in social struggles and that, therefore, politics truly mattered. I was in Orwell's *Oceania* in 1984, and contrary to his expectation, there seemed to be a good deal of freedom and a good bit of political ferment afoot.

It took me almost two years to find a way to get back to Britain, but when I did arrive again in the spring of 1986, the coal miners' strike was still continuing! Now, I was located a bit north of London, in the privileged enclave of Cambridge. I went to a coal miners' meeting one evening and listened to mostly very despondent if also proud workers describe their lives without jobs and without success in what would be for them a losing battle. From a table in the back of room, I bought a book by Ralph Miliband, while at the front a young American woman sang what she described as an old West Virginia coal mining song. (I've wondered if that singer was not Michele Shocked.) This version of Britain was much more depressing than the first. Social change, alas, had *not* occurred.

Yet during my very brief stint at Cambridge, I attended the inaugural lecture of the very first Cambridge University honorary professor of sociology, Anthony Giddens, who is now, like Darhendorf was earlier, the director of Britain's prestigious L.S.E. I also read Giddens's *A Brief But Critical Introduction to Sociology.* The entire book fascinated me, but his last chapter (titled "Sociology as Critical Theory") grabbed me the most. Giddens argued that sociology must "outflank Marx from the left." He discussed the importance of ecological problems but also sociology's long-standing inattention to matters such as male domination and ecological crisis. The day before I left for home, I met Professor Giddens in his Cavendish Laboratory office. Since I was utterly frightened of him and therefore terribly awkward and inarticulate, I usually try to repress this memory.

It was clear to me that I wanted very much to be, so to speak, a critical sociologist. My only other viable option was to see if General Motors would have me as a well-paid, white-collar supervisor. Once defined in my mind as "success," this career path had lost its appeal. I loved the workers I knew at General Motors, but the thought of assuming the role of a manager in a large corporate bureaucracy was hopelessly beyond me. I recalled one boss of my boss saying to me once, "So, you're going out to work with the orangutans?" meaning the hourly workers. So it was on to graduate school—actually, graduate schools—and to writing a book roughly 15 years later in the hope that, as Giddens's book did for me, mine could do for others.

Of course, this is not the whole story. It was, after all, right here in these United States that I first encountered C. Wright Mills in a general education course in political science. My ears perked up, as I recall, when the professor discussed this guy who thought that power in the United States was more or less monopolized by a "power elite." Other than in literature classes, I do not think I had ever heard before of a person who adopted that sort of uncompromisingly critical perspective on society. That is, in part, why I sat up in my seat. It was just such a shock.

But, presumably, I *wanted* to hear such a critical perspective. I was primed to listen, to care. Why? I think, for me, anyway, the answer goes back to childhood when I had the experience of moving from a pretty rough-and-tumble, inner-city neighborhood to a pretty affluent, at least very middle-class and virtually all white suburb, where I was essentially thrown into a new world. That kind of abrupt change in circumstances made me feel terribly anxious, but it also caused me to think differently and to have an outsider's perspective on social life, mine included. Many other things somewhat unusual for middle-class life were part of my growing up. One of my older brothers, for example, spent a long stint in prison. In junior and senior high school, I threw myself into sports, primarily football. This, too, was unusual since we were subjected to extraordinary discipline and training, our work as football players treated as the most important thing in the world. This win-at-all-costs mentality came to dominant my adolescence. And we did win, a lot.

By the time I graduated high school in 1982, the city in which I lived was experiencing an economic depression. Many factories had been closed or would soon be closed. My own family's economic standing, never truly middle-class, began to worsen as a result. Somehow, perhaps because of the extreme nature of the economic downturn, I seemed to understand the relationship between this issue and the family stresses I witnessed and experienced (my "troubles"). My adopted parents, for example, could not in any way afford to send me to college, although they very much wanted me to go. I would be, for all intents and purposes, the first member of my family to attend a major, four-year institution of higher learning. This was thought a very good thing, but I had to pay for it on my own. I majored in business, materials logistics management in particular (whatever that is), and I worked for General Motors during summer breaks. Only after London did I switch to economics, and there really to Marxian economics. After living through a depression in my hometown and watching coal miners struggle and lose in Britain, this seemed the right thing for me to do. Besides, I was thoroughly fascinated by what I was learning.

By time I actually read C. Wright Mills's *The Sociological Imagination* at the age of 22 during the first semester of graduate school, I had already been pretty well prepared to hear what he was saying. I identified immediately with the sense of "trap" that opens this book and also with the idea that we can think ourselves out of traps. While I have learned a great deal since, nothing has ever caused me to reject or fundamentally question the value of what I learned then. Quite obviously, I suppose, this book in your hands speaks to my continued sense that the world needs the sociological imagination as much as I did at this point in my life.

The vast majority of introductory books in sociology do not challenge beginning students with the task of developing a sociological imagination. Typically, it is mentioned, although not always, and then passed over. Why is it that sociology withholds from its introductory students the very thing that is most valuable about sociology? The reasons for sociology's apparent hesitancy to put its self-consciousness at the forefront of its teaching are probably complicated. Most sociologists do not practice sociology in Mills's style. Another reason might be that the sociological imagination is an inherently political form of self-consciousness, and this in itself can make for a number of sticky situations. Why this politics and not another? Also, sociology is an extremely broad and multifaceted discipline, and there are a great many possible ways to introduce the field and many important topics to survey. I am a bit chagrined when I think of all the important topics, important sociologists, and important issues that I have not mentioned in this book. But in the end, all reflexive self-criticism notwithstanding, I am still convinced that the sociological imagination is the most needed form of self-consciousness in the world today.

Index